Plea

Plea Bargaining

The Experiences of
Prosecutors, Judges, and Defense Attorneys

Milton Heumann

The University of Chicago Press
Chicago and London

For my mother and father

The University of Chicago Press, Chicago 60637
The University of Chicago Press, Ltd., London

 Published 1978
Paperback edition 1981
Printed in the United States of America

88 87 86 85　　　　3 4 5 6

Library of Congress Cataloging in Publication Data

Heumann, Milton.
Plea bargaining.

Bibliography: p.
Includes index.
1. Plea Bargaining—United States. 2. Criminal statistics—Connecticut. I. Title.
KF9654.H4　　345'.73'072　　77–9970
ISBN 0–226–33187–3 (cloth)
0-226-33188-1 (paper)

Contents

Acknowledgments

I am indebted to many institutions and individuals for assistance at various stages of this research project. Yale University's Institution for Social and Policy Studies, the University of Michigan's Horace H. Rackham School of Graduate Studies, and the American Motors Corporation Fund provided the financial support necessary to transcribe the interviews and to type the manuscript. The Department of Political Science of the University of Michigan surrounded me with colleagues and students whose advice and encouragement were of great aid in revising draft upon draft. I am especially appreciative of the assistance of Norman Ankers, Ron Burda, Al Cover, Wayne Hillyard, and Dan Levine.

The prosecutors, defense attorneys, judges, court clerks, bailiffs, secretaries, bondsmen, and defendants whose comments are reported in this study must remain anonymous. But their contributions were invaluable, and without their cooperation, this study would still be a proposal for future research. I am particularly grateful to the public defenders of one of the circuit and superior courts included in my sample, and to one very distinguished circuit court judge. In addition to their thoughts, these individuals offered me friendship, office space, and enthusiasm. I hope the end product justifies their efforts.

I had the benefit of working closely with two individuals on this project: Professor Jonathan Casper of Stanford University and Professor David Mayhew of Yale University. Their assistance extended above and beyond any formal academic relationship. They read, criticized, and evaluated my draft chapters in an extraordinarily brief period of time, and with great insight. Their friendship and encouragement, as well as their academic advice, were crucial to the completion of this book.

My wife, Elaine, has lived with this study for more years than we care to contemplate. She has endured the anguish and frustration when chapters have gone awry, when ideas have faltered, when confidence has waned, and has done so with a reservoir of cheer, confidence, and advice. Only others who have experienced the total absorption that a study such as this requires can fully appreciate the contribution of one's spouse. No words can adequately describe the contributions that Elaine has made. I know, though, that without her, I would have neither a manuscript nor happiness. With her, I have both.

1 Introduction

Plea bargaining is the process by which the defendant in a criminal case relinquishes his right to go to trial in exchange for a reduction in charge and/or sentence.[1] Most cases in most criminal courts in this country are plea bargained; notwithstanding the nomenclature, the "trial court" is really a "plea bargaining court."[2]

In this book I am concerned with one aspect of these "plea bargaining courts." Specifically, I will explore the postrecruitment adaptation of new prosecutors, defense attorneys, and judges to the "plea bargaining court."[3] How do newcomers adjust to plea bargaining? What is the adaptation process and what are its substantive outcomes?

Three factors influenced my decision to choose this research problem. First, there is a curious gap in the local court literature between the material on recruitment of personnel to the courts and the discussion of the internal plea bargaining dynamics of the court.[4] The recruitment studies end at the point where individuals are chosen for a court job; the internal dynamics literature begins with a cross-sectional view of the court and discusses the way experienced personnel process cases. Very little work has been done on what happens to the newcomer after he is recruited and before he becomes a seasoned plea bargainer. And there are simply no systematic studies of why (or if) a novice to the criminal court is transformed into the "eager-beaver" plea bargainer portrayed in studies that concentrate on the internal dynamics of plea bargaining .

The second factor that influenced the choice of this problem was my disenchantment with the internal dynamics of plea bargaining literature itself. As will be demonstrated in chapter 3, the literature strongly suggests that plea bargaining is a function of case pressure—that court personnel plea bargain because of the pressure of "onerously large case loads."[5] Preliminary research in the local criminal court, and quantitative case disposition data for Connecticut's courts dating back to 1880, raise serious doubts about this "case-pressure hypothesis."[6] I felt that by studying newcomer adaptation to the plea bargaining system, I could test the efficacy of the case-pressure explanation.

Finally, a policy concern directed my interest toward plea bargaining. Within a span of six years, two national commissions have considered the merits and justifications for plea bargaining, one concluding that plea bargaining is the vital force that keeps criminal cases moving through the courts,[7] the other rejecting this argument, and calling for the abolition of plea bargaining by 1978.[8] Again, I hope that my detailed inquiry into newcomer adaptation and my exploration of the efficacy of the case-pressure hypothesis will yield some insights useful for evaluating these divergent conclusions, and more generally be of import for generating realistic policy recommendations about plea bargaining.

Adaptation and the "Organizational Context"

As used here, *adaptation* refers to the process in which a newcomer learns and is taught about his role obligations, and the related process in which he translates these obligations into a perspective on plea bargaining. Included in the inquiry into adaptation are both attitudinal and behavioral changes. Thus, I will trace the evolution of the newcomer's attitudes toward his role and toward plea bargaining and will detail changes in his actual role and plea bargaining behavior.

This description of *adaptation* parallels many definitions of *socialization* found in the literature, but I am more comfortable working with the former term.[9] The socialization literature did not yield any frameworks particularly useful to my approach, and I think the term *socialization* extracts certain costs because of the connotations attached to it.[10] For example, *socialization* suggests that there are agents of socialization "teaching" newcomers something.[11] I will argue below that a significant portion of the newcomer's adaptation can be explained without reference to the efforts of any such agents, that newcomers simply learn about an environment that differs from what they expected. Though *socialization* need not necessarily exclude this sort of "learning," I think *adaptation* better captures the process which I am trying to describe, and I think it is less likely to evoke false connotative implications.

Newcomer adaptation will be discussed as being shaped by a "learning" and "teaching" component. The learning component refers to the newcomer's discovery that the reality of the local criminal court differs from what he expected. The teaching component refers to the use of rewards and sanctions by others in the court system to direct newcomer behavior down a particular path. He learns that features of his environment—that is, the characteristics of the cases he must process—are different from what he anticipated, and these differences then "cause" changes in his attitudes and behavior.[12] Alternatively, he may be taught that rewards and penalties are attached to certain actions, and after experiencing these rewards and penalties, his attitudes and behavior may also change.[13]

As will become clear when we discuss adaptation to the defense attorney's role, as well as to prosecutorial and judicial roles (chapters 4 through 6), failure to consider the "learning" component of newcomer adaptation has led some observers to conclude falsely that the transformation of idealistic newcomers into seasoned plea bargainers reflects the "success" of the court's reward and sanction mechanism.[14] I will argue that much of the variance in newcomer adaptation is a function of the newcomer's learning about his role and about the associated constraints that the "realities" of the case characteristics impose upon him. Though he is also "taught" some lessons about plea bargaining,and though failure to consider these would lead to an oversimplified perspective on newcomer adaptation, I will show that "learning" is at the heart of newcomer adaptation.

The dichotomy between learning and teaching also suggests the importance of understanding the "organizational character" of the local criminal court, the "organizational context" in which newcomers adapt. If we are to examine what newcomers learn and what is taught to them, we must have a good grasp of the essential features and "flavor" of the organization within which adaptation takes place. As Stanton Wheeler observed in his discussion of adult socialization: "The emphasis . . . is on features of the social context within which the more immediate processes occur. The justification for the emphasis is simply that these features are an important but little-studied part of the socialization experience . . . Much can . . . be learned about the process of socialization by taking a close look at the structure and situations within which it occurs."[15]

Chapter 3 is devoted exclusively to clarifying the "organizational character" of the local criminal court. Therein I will try to "capture" the essence of the context in which newcomer adaptation unfolds.

Adaptation in Trial Courts

Despite the recent outpouring of literature on local criminal courts, there has been very little systematic research concerned with the adaptation of newcomers in the criminal courts. Instead, one is confronted with a potpourri of prerecruitment socialization studies,[16] biographical and autobiographical accounts,[17] impressionistic forays into the criminal courts that occasionally—and usually pejoratively— discuss the travails of a newcomer to the court,[18] and only two studies whose main emphasis is on adaptation.[19] And these two studies, though encouraging in their emphasis on the importance of the problem, fall short of providing a theoretical framework for further research and/or a set of substantive findings or hypotheses of applicability to the criminal justice process.[20] Thus, it is fair to conclude that the study of adaptation in the criminal court is largely unexplored terrain.[21]

This gap in the literature appears all the more curious and disconcerting when we find a substantial research tradition dealing with the adaptation of the freshman congressman[22] or the rookie policeman,[23] contrasted with little research on local court actors on one hand, and frequent, and sometimes harsh, testimonials to the effect that a newcomer to the court is ill-prepared for actual practice by his law school education, on the other. Witness, for example, Paul Savoy's graphic description of the inadequacy of law school training for work in the criminal court.

> There is not a single lawyer I know with whom I went to law school who feels that his legal education adequately prepared him for the practice of law . . . My experience in one of the larger postgraduate educational institutions in America—the New York District Attorney's Office—was sobering. Trying to reconstruct an incident from interviews with witnesses; awakening to the ritualistic performance of police officers on the witness stand; plumbing the subtleties of the plea-bargaining process; learning the nuances of communication between judges and attorneys, I became suddenly aware of the unforgiveable irrelevance of my legal education to what was happening in my head, in the courtroom, and in the streets of our cities. The first case I tried was a numbing experience. My only consolation was that the legal aid lawyer who represented the defendant was as hopelessly untutored as I.[24]

Of late, even the chief justice of the United States Supreme Court has been wont to complain about the shallowness of preparation of attorneys for courtroom practice. "We are more casual about qualifying the people we allow to act as advocates in the courtroom than we are about licensing electricians. No other profession is as casual or heedless of reality as ours."[25]

The limited scope of prior adaptation studies, the testimonials on the lack of preparation of newcomers for practice in the local criminal court, and the research that has been conducted on adaptation to other roles (congressman, police officer) combine to suggest the need for more research on local criminal court actors. In the next section, the theoretical approach employed in this study to fill at least part of the gap in the postrecruitment literature will be discussed.

Adaptation in the Criminal Court: A Theoretical Springboard

The decision to study postrecruitment adaptation within local criminal courts immediately requires some difficult choices of research priorities. Where should one begin, when the literature, rather than foreclosing the examination of broad questions, mandates precisely such a strategy? To what extent should realistic research constraints such as time, money, and access influence one's theoretical design?

There are neither hard-and-fast, nor totally satisfactory, solutions to these queries. Neither the choices in theory outlined below, nor the choices in research methodology discussed in chapter 2 are ideal; they are, however, my estimates of where the balance ought to be struck, given conflicting claims (and problems) of the theoretical and descriptive literature—certainly not optimal choices, but I hope at least adequate ones.

A major decision entailed limiting the scope of the inquiry into adaptation. Instead of trying to obtain a catalog of problems faced by the newcomers, I thought it more valuable to assess the adaptation process from the perspective of one major aspect of the local criminal court that the newcomer would have to come to terms with. The plea bargaining process, which accounts for the disposition of the overwhelming majority of cases, seemed to be of sufficient interest and significance to warrant examination in this light. In other words, when I speak of adaptation to the local criminal court, I mean adaptation to the plea bargaining process of that court. This focus delimits my interest to job-related norms, system norms, and to the characteristics of the organizational context that are apposite to plea bargaining.

If one is to study adaptation vis-à-vis "something," that something must be fully understood. In Asher's study of the learning of legislative norms, for example, he was able to "borrow" the relevant norms from prior research and ask freshmen about them.[26] Similarly, I initially expected to rely on the plea bargaining literature for my descriptions of the "something," and to structure my questions about adaptation on the foundation established by this literature. To both my chagrin and fascination, I found that the plea bargaining literature seriously misconstrued the reality of the process in operation in the local criminal court.

I have already noted that the burden of my disagreement rests with the proposition that plea bargaining is a by-product of high case pressure. In chapter 3, I will present data supporting my objections to the case-pressure hypothesis, and I will detail the salient features of the organizational context in a manner not dependent upon this hypothesis. For the moment, it is sufficient to note that since plea bargaining is the "something" to which newcomers are adapting, it must be correctly understood before dealing with the more specific adaptation questions. I want to emphasize that although this conceptualization about plea bargaining is a necessary prior consideration, it is not neatly separable from the study of adaptation. Some of the arguments that I will make about the plea bargaining process emerged only because the focus of my study was on adaptation.[27]

The emphasis that is to be given to explaining the plea bargaining process led to my decision to examine the adaptation of prosecutors and defense attorneys, as well as judges. Each of these actors participates in the plea bargaining process, and the synthesis of their interactions helps define the plea bargain system of the court under scrutiny. Furthermore, a cross-checking of propositions put forth by any one group of role incumbents is made possible by this trifurcated approach, thus reducing the chances of a bias in viewing the system writ large.

The primacy given to explaining plea bargaining dynamics, however, extracts some costs for the study of adaptation. By including judges, prosecutors, and defense attorneys—the major participants in plea bargaining—the overall number of newcomers, and the number of newcomers to particular roles, is correspondingly decreased. Without enormous resources, it simply is not possible to include enough veterans and enough newcomers to obtain a large sample for each group and each role, and thus, the analysis of newcomer adaptation is necessarily "exploratory" in quality.

In light of the arguments already advanced, I believe opting for the more systematic study of the "something" to be learned, and a more "exploratory" approach to adaptation to plea bargaining makes good sense. The organizational context and the plea bargaining process can be thoroughly scrutinized. Tentative descriptive hypotheses about adaptation can then be more realistically generated. This is not an uncommon research strategy to follow when one is confronted with only minimal prior research on a problem.[28]

The exploratory quality of the analysis of adaptation is also reflected in the range of issues that will be considered.[29] These extend from the newcomer's expectations about the plea bargaining aspects of his role, to a review of his actual early experiences in the criminal justice system, through his eventual adaptation of a particular plea bargaining style. Attitudinal and behavioral changes over time will be examined in the context of the learning/teaching approach discussed earlier.

2 Research Design

The Court System of Connecticut

The research for this study was conducted in Connecticut. Connecticut was selected partly because it seemed a practical choice, but, more importantly because the structure of the court system in that state provided an excellent arena for research on adaptation within plea bargaining systems.

There is a tripartite division of trial courts in Connecticut: circuit courts, courts of common pleas, and superior courts. The court of common pleas only has trial jurisdiction over civil matters and thus is largely inconsequential for the research.[1] On the other hand, both the circuit courts and the superior courts are intimately involved in the disposition of criminal cases and have direct import for my study.

The circuit court system was established in 1961, replacing the hodgepodge of town courts, police courts, city courts, and justices-of-the-peace with a modernized statewide system of local trial courts of original jurisdiction.[2] There is a total of eighteen circuit courts in Connecticut, staffed by forty-four judges who rotate among circuits every three months. The judges are nominated by the governor and are appointed to four-year terms if they are confirmed by Connecticut's general assembly. The judges, in turn, are formally given the power to collectively appoint (generally upon recommendation of the resident judges of the circuit) the prosecutor and/or assistant prosecutors and public defender and/or assistant public defenders for each circuit. Though the judges are full-time employees, the prosecutors and public defenders may be full-time or part-time; the number of prosecutors and public defenders varies across districts, as does the proportion of part-timers and full-timers (see table 1).[3]

Table 1 Connecticut Circuit Court Prosecutors and Public Defenders

	Prosecutors			Public Defenders		
Circuit	Full-Time	Part-Time	Total	Full-Time	Part-Time	Total
1	3	6	9	2	3	5
2	4	3	7	2	2	4
3	1	3	4	1	1	2
4	2	2	4	1	1	2
5	0	4	4	0	2	2
6	4	4	8	5	0	5
7	2	1	3	1	0	1
8	2	0	2	1	0	1
9	0	3	3	1	0	1
10	0	5	5	0	2	2
11	2	0	2	0	1	1
12	1	3	4	1	0	1
13	1	1	2	1	0	1
14	4	2	6	2	2	4
15	1	3	4	1	0	1
16	0	3	3	0	1	1
17	1	2	3	1	0	1
18	0	3	3	1	0	1
Central Office	4	0	4	3	0	3
Total	32	48	80	24	15	39

Source: Judicial Department, State of Connecticut

Prior to 1972, the circuit court had jurisdiction over traffic offenses, misdemeanors, and felonies punishable by a maximum imprisonment of one year. In 1972, its felony jurisdiction was increased to include crimes punishable by up to a maximum of five years in prison and/or a five thousand–dollar fine.[4] Additionally, the circuit court may conduct hearings of probable cause on cases that are initially brought to circuit court but that must be bound over to the superior court because they involve crimes whose potential sentences place them outside the circuit court's jurisdiction. About three-quarters of the superior court's cases are bindovers from the circuit court.[5]

The superior court's origin dates back to the Connecticut constitution. Established in 1818 on a county basis, it was reorganized in 1855 into a totally state-financed system, in which the bulk of judicial personnel are concentrated in the three most populous counties, but with a requirement that criminal cases be heard at least four times a year in the less populous counties.[6] Judicial assignments to a county change every four months.

The thirty-five judges of the superior court are chosen in the same way as circuit court judges, but for terms of eight years instead of four. As in the circuit court, they in turn appoint the state's attorney (title of a prosecutor in superior court) and/or assistant state's attorneys and the public defender and/or assistant public defenders. Each of the eight counties in Connecticut has at least one state's attorney and one public defender (see table 2).[7] Though there are still some part-time state's attorneys remaining in the system, their replacements will have to accept full-time appointments. No such requirement exists for assistant state's attorneys, or for the public defenders and their assistants.

Table 2 Connecticut Superior Court State's Attorneys and Public Defenders

	State's Attorneys			Public Defenders		
	Full-Time	Part-Time	Total	Full-Time	Part-Time	Total
Fairfield	2	4	6	0	3	3
Hartford	3	4	7	3	1	4
New Haven	5	2	7	0	3	3
Litchfield	1	0	1	0	1	1
Middlesex	0	1	1	0	1	1
New London	0	2	2	0	2	2
Tolland	1	1	2	1	0	1
Windham	1	0	1	0	1	1
Waterbury	3	0	3	1	0	1
Total	16	14	30	5	12	17

Source: Judicial Department, State of Connecticut

The jurisdiction of the superior court, as indicated above, covers felonies with potential sentences of more than five years. The 25 percent of the cases not coming to it from circuit court bindovers are obtained directly through the issuance of a bench warrant, requested by the state's attorney and approved by the superior court judge.

Brief mention should also be made of the appellate structures within Connecticut. Basically, circuit court cases are appealed to a division of the court of common pleas, while superior court cases are appealed directly to the Supreme Court of Connecticut. The latter has six justices, five of whom hear appeals, while the sixth serves as chief court administrator. In addition to these standard forums for appeal, Connecticut provides a mechanism for review of any prison sentence greater than one year. A special panel consisting of three regular superior court judges is formed to hear the request. This panel can increase as well as decrease the sentence.

Several major points emerge from this sketch of the formal organizational structure of the Connecticut court system. It is in some ways an atypical system. In most states, trial judges do not rotate among circuits; it is even rarer to have the judges appoint prosecutors and public defenders.[8] These features militate against any broad-sweeping claims to generalizability.

It is my feeling that the disadvantages posed by these somewhat aberrant features are more than offset by other aspects of the Connecticut court system that make it a prime area for inquiry. The abandonment of the old city court–justice-of-the-peace system and its replacement by the circuit court reflects a step toward structural modernization.[9] The trend in court reorganization is toward consolidation of local city courts into a single trial court, which is then itself incorporated into a larger state system. Legal reformers have often maintained that this structural change will eliminate any "anomalous" behavior found in the politically permeated town courts. Without speaking directly to the merits of this contention, what is clear is that examining a "reformed" or "modernized" court offers the opportunity to deal with a "purer" specimen. Attributing a particular court style or practice (for example, plea bargaining) solely to the continued existence of an unmodernized city court system is not possible.

Additionally, the circuit courts and the superior courts are located in towns and cities of differing size, and with markedly different crime rates. This presents the researcher with an opportunity to compare criminal court disposition patterns for similarly structured organizations under varying degrees of case pressure. The rotation of judicial personnel, when viewed in this light, provides a further "control," for the same judges will serve in high and low case volume areas.

A related factor also weighed in my decision to work in Connecticut. Though several Connecticut cities are properly classified as urban centers, with the concomitant problems of urban courts, none of these is so large that detailed studies of one would foreclose, because of time constraints, examination of another. Furthermore, inquiry into the cities with populations of 150,000 to 200,000 within one state can at a later point be expanded to comparable cities in other states. I do not mean to imply that areas such as New York City or Chicago are not proper sites for research; I am simply suggesting that they are perhaps better treated as unique cases, rather than as subsets of a larger universe.

The Research Sample

Six courts were included in this study: three circuit courts and three superior courts. These courts are located in three different cities, that is, each city has a circuit court and a superior court. Two of these cities are urban centers in Connecticut; both have a high incidence of crime and relatively high case pressure in court—at least at the circuit court level. The third is a smaller city, typical of the many low case volume–low crime jurisdictions in Connecticut.

I felt it necessary to promise anonymity to all participating respondents. In the closed community of criminal justice—even in the larger cities—it would not be very difficult to guess the identity of a particular actor being discussed. Therefore, I cannot identify by name these three cities. The two large cities will be called Arborville and Ortaville, and the smaller town Centerville. Furthermore, I will alter a few minor characteristics of the respondents to provide further protection against any violation of my promise of anonymity.

Most studies of plea bargaining have been limited to the disposition of felonies[10] and have either concentrated systematically on a single court system[11] or have been impressionistic, sketchy forays into a great number of courts.[12] The three-city design for circuit courts and superior courts is directed at providing a comparative perspective of plea bargaining processes. Though this task could have been accomplished by following the usual "felonies only" tract, for several reasons I felt it imperative to include systematic analyses of circuit court processes. First, we have already seen that the circuit court is intimately tied to the superior court by the bind-over machinery. Second, I suspected that I would find more new, inexperienced personnel in the circuit courts; relatedly, I also expected that some of those working in the superior court had their initial contact with the criminal justice system in the circuit court. Third, I wanted to determine whether plea bargaining in courts dealing largely with misdemeanors was similar to plea bargaining in felony courts. I did not want to assume that what is, or has to be, learned about plea bargaining in felony courts is necessarily applicable to the circuit court.

Within each court an effort was made to interview *all* the prosecutors and the public defenders working in the system.[13] No sampling decisions for these actors were necessary. Judges were interviewed if they were assigned to the court under investigation and if I had actually observed them presiding.[14] The defense attorney sample was obtained from a perusal of court calendars and from my inquiries to prosecutors and public defenders about which private attorneys played major roles in their courts. Finally, in one city I interviewed the four legal aid attorneys (LAA) who practiced criminal law. The remainder of the LAA's in the city, as well as in the rest of Connecticut, were prohibited from practicing criminal law.[15] In all, seventy-one interviews were conducted.

Table 3 shows the distribution by job in the court of those interviewed. Though I was successful in interviewing almost all the prosecutors and public defenders of each court, comparisons of this table to tables 1 and 2 will not reveal the names of the cities studied. Occasionally, a prosecutor or a public defender was not sampled; also, the personnel figures of tables 1 and 2 sometimes under- or overrepresented the number of prosecutors and public defenders present at any one time. For example, during a personnel changeover period, both the departing and incoming officials could be available for an interview.

Table 3 Distribution by City and Job of Interviewed Court Personnel

	Circuit Court			Superior Court			Circuit and Superior Court	
	Prose-cutors	Public Defenders	Judges*	State's Attorneys	Public Defenders	Judges*	Private Criminal Attorneys	Legal Aid Attorneys
Arborville	5	6	—	7	4	—	7	4
Centerville	2	1	—	1	1	—	2	0
Ortaville	4	2	—	4	4	—	4	0
Total	11	9	8	12	9	5	13	4

* Judges rotate among circuits, so only totals will be entered.

Research Problems

Jerome Skolnick has observed that "in attempting to understand a social or political process such as democracy, oligarchy, bureaucracy, or justice, the process itself must be learned in intricate detail."[16] The initial task, then, when studying any aspect of local court operations, is to "penetrate this haze" surrounding the bureaucracy and determine the essentials of the plea bargaining process.[17]

Two immediate problems arise in this connection. The first relates to the setting of plea bargaining. Unlike appellate court hearings or trials in the local courts, no formally designated area is set aside for plea bargaining, nor is any formal record kept of most plea bargaining negotiations. Plea bargaining can take place in innumerable locations, at no specified time. Patterns of plea bargaining—as we shall see later—vary significantly across courts and actors. How does one go about "cutting paths into the wilderness of non-hearing procedures?"[18]

Compounding this problem is the oft-noted unwillingness of local court actors to discuss these plea bargaining practices with "outsiders." "Members of the various occupational roles, if only in terms of their own work experience, are deeply suspicious of—almost hostile to—any effort to unearth embarrassing material . . . This virtually hostile attitude toward outsiders is in large measure a psychological defense against the inherent deficiencies of assembly-line justice."[19] This problem is more severe than the one posed by nonstructured plea bargaining settings. If cooperation is obtained, it seems to me, the "wilderness" could be manageably explored; absent cooperation, it is likely that the highways and byways of plea bargaining will remain untraveled by the researcher.

But even assuming for the moment access and cooperation in the study of plea bargaining, how would this assistance aid the inquiry into adaptation?

Obviously, there is somewhat of a methodological tension inherent in my research design. In emphasizing the importance of outlining the realities of plea bargaining, some tradeoffs in the sample size of new personnel were made. Though I did try to include as many newcomers as possible, I did not run up and down the state interviewing each and every individual who recently obtained a job in the local court; even if I had thought this to be worthwhile, it would *not* have increased the newcomer sample greatly, simply because there is not a great turnover from year to year. A method had to be designed to obtain data about adaptation in plea bargaining systems without the benefit of a large panel study.

Furthermore, some "clues" about the adaptation process culled from Cook's, and Wheeler and Carp's research, as well as from the review of the socialization literature, suggested that learning takes place in a number of settings (some formal, some informal), in a number of ways (reward/sanction, simply learning about the reality of the local criminal court), about a number of things (norms, folkways, and so on). Simply gaining access to, piecing together, and parsimoniously accounting for this complex mélange pose substantial difficulties in their own right; when viewed together with the imputed reluctance of court personnel to discuss plea bargaining, the devising of an adequate research design presents a most intractable problem.

The situation is not actually as bleak as this parade of problems might suggest. I have reviewed the argument—held almost as a matter of faith—that local court actors will resist scrutiny of their plea bargaining. No doubt this was true in the early 1960s, when Blumberg and others first began examining the plea bargaining process. Plea bargaining seemed then—and to an extent still seems—to have an air of questionable legality surrounding it. Conducted *sub rosa*, with occasional and sometimes frequent wheeling and dealing, it often led to charades in court, wherein all would deny that they had engaged in any bargaining whatsoever.[20] Little wonder that Blumberg predicts that local court officials will resist inquiries from outsiders.

What Blumberg et al did not foresee was the United States Supreme Court intervention in plea bargaining. Before 1970, the Court had literally ignored plea bargaining. For example, all the great Warren Court decisions of the 1960s—*Mapp, Gideon, Miranda*—[21]were predicated on an assumption (or a wish) that trials characterize the disposition of cases in "trial" courts.[22] The Court chose to close its eyes to the realities of plea bargaining, thus adding to the sense that plea bargaining was somehow illegal at worst, and distasteful at best. However, indirectly in *Brady* v. *United States*[23] and in *North Carolina* v. *Alford*,[24] both decided in 1970, and directly in *Santobello* v. *New York*,[25] decided on December 20, 1971, the Court not only dealt with plea bargaining issues, but appeared to sanction the process. In short, *Santobello* mandated that a prosecutor must fulfill his end of a bargain with a defendant vis-à-vis sentence recommendation. If a particular sentence recommendation is promised in exchange for a guilty plea, the prosecutor must make this recommendation known in open court, though the judge does not necessarily have to follow it.

The substantive issues of *Santobello* are of less import for this section than is the interpretation given the decision by court personnel. The latter interpreted—justifiably—this decision as providing a Supreme Court imprimatur to plea bargaining. No longer did they necessarily have to feel that plea bargaining was a tainted process. I suspected that this changed perspective—coupled with the general public clamor about criminal justice—could be capitalized on in my research. Unlike most of the prior plea bargaining studies, my research was conducted after the Supreme Court recognized plea bargaining, and it seemed reasonable to anticipate that local court personnel would be willing to speak more openly and frankly about negotiated dispositions.[26]

This suspicion was confirmed in my research. Many of the seventy-one subjects interviewed pointed out—without mentioning *Santobello* by name—that the "Supreme Court said plea bargaining is OK . . . ." It seems that a threshold was established by the Supreme Court case. Whereas court participants were formerly reluctant even to admit the existence of plea bargaining, now one can at least move past the gibberish denials. This is not to say that frankness is insured, not that anyone can simply walk into court, grab hold of the nearest prosecutor, judge, or defense attorney, and obtain a detailed accounting of plea bargaining. But the potential to obtain cooperation and frank responses is now greater.

Research Strategies

I have already indicated that seventy-one interviews were conducted with judges, prosecutors, and defense attorneys in six courts in Connecticut. Though these interviews are at the heart of my research, they must be viewed as part and parcel of the larger research design that included observation/participant-observation, and analysis of various court records.

I followed the same research strategy in each of the six courts. I would spend a day or two inconspicuously observing courtroom operations— pleas, hearings, motions, and so on. After obtaining some sense of the flow of business in the court, I would approach either the assistant prosecutor I had observed in court or an assistant prosecutor that I had heard mentioned while sitting in court.[27] Introducing myself as a Yale graduate student interested in criminal court practices, I would then ask the prosecutor if he had any objections to my observing him in action and to eventually discussing with me his views of the criminal justice system.

This method proved to be quite efficacious. Nary a prosecutor so approached refused cooperation. Note, though, that I toned down the interview requests with the proper air of humbleness, coming across, no doubt, as a kind of Uriah Heep/befuddled academic hybrid—I was simply expressing an interest in the operations of the criminal justice system as seen through his job. Since most of these assistant prosecutors or assistant state's attorneys were only a little older than I, I would guess they felt somewhat flattered by my request. In fact, I actively sought out the names of the younger employees to begin my interviews with.

I should also call attention to what I did *not* do in this first contact. I rejected the idea of writing to the head prosecutor or state's attorney for permission to interview the staff. It seemed to me that such a step would have several major risks attached to it. The head prosecutor might simply refuse permission to conduct the interviews at that time—case load considerations, overworked staff, and so on, always provide convenient rationalizations—or, he might have asked for a copy of my questionnaire and the right to edit it. I felt that if the less formal approach worked—as it did—it was preferable to this higher-risk option.[28]

In any event, once I made my first contact, I quickly found that the prosecutors were allowing me to follow them around. For example, soon after I introduced myself to an assistant prosecutor in Arborville's circuit court, we moved into a little room behind the court proper, the room in which plea bargaining took place. Though the assistant prosecutor may have, in passing, checked with the head prosecutor to make sure the latter had no objections to his speaking with me, I am certain that the head prosecutor never explicitly gave permission for my presence in plea bargaining discussions. I just tagged along; the assistant prosecutor never objected, and there I was. Again, I suspect that if I had explicitly asked to be allowed into these discussions, my request would have elicited extensive hemming and hawing. The non-decision route, the muddle-around method, seemed to me to be more effective.

Once I gained access to plea bargaining negotiations, I knew I had overcome the major observational hurdles. It became a simple matter to parlay this access to include other plea bargaining settings (for example, the prosecutor's office) and other prosecutors. I acted as if it were natural for me to be present, and because I had already been seen by other prosecutors and public defenders in plea bargaining sessions, no questions about my presence were raised. I had made it to the team.

Similarly, in the superior courts, where plea bargaining takes place in less structured settings, once I had established a rapport with a particular assistant state's attorney, I was rarely asked to leave the office when a deal was in the works. Indeed, I often was introduced to the defense attorneys, told the facts of the case, and even asked for my opinion.

The point to be emphasized here is that my role extended beyond that of a simple observer. In many ways, I was treated as an insider—becoming a sort of participant-observer.The interview experiences generally served to reinforce this perception of me, for in all the interviews, I would use examples from cases in which I had observed the respondent. In this fashion, we almost became colleagues discussing problems forthrightly and exhaustively. My semi-insider status provided the assurance the respondents needed; I would and could interpret their problems realistically.

The insider status was, then, the key to building on the potential willingness of court personnel to discuss plea bargaining. The United States Supreme Court had paved the way, but the confidence of those working in the local courts still had to be won. Once I achieved this trust, I found the amount of cooperation from court personnel startling—particularly in light of the "resistance to outsiders" argument. I stress this point not only because it runs counter to the prevailing pessimism about researching local court operations, but also because it bears the seeds for the development of court assessment measures and for the institution of reform in the local courts. I will return to this argument in later chapters; here, I only will repeat that court personnel were willing to be critically evaluated, were open to suggestions for reform, and were quite curious about my findings in other courts and about the implications of those findings for their own jobs. Again, I think this openness was a function of their perception that I understood the constraints under which they operated.[29]

My observations, and insider status, extended beyond the prosecutor's office to include the public defenders, and to a lesser extent, judges and private attorneys. To understand how contacts with these individuals were made, I must detail the logistics involved in interviewing prosecutors. As I have indicated, I would follow a prosecutor around, be it in court, or in closed-door plea bargaining sessions. After building up a store of actual dispositions rendered by the prosecutor, I would interview him. Then I would move on to another prosecutor, repeat the observations, and eventually conduct the interviews. Generally, I tried to complete my interviews with one group of role incumbents before shifting my "loyalties" to another. In the large courts of Arborville and Ortaville this took approximately three to four weeks.

Interviews were usually conducted at the end of the court session, and occasionally during recesses. I would spend the time before the interviews sitting in court observing formal case dispositions. Whenever possible I introduced myself to the public defenders, private attorneys, and judges who were in court that day. Thus, at the same time that I was working my way through the prosecutorial staff, I also was establishing contacts among the other groups that I wanted to interview. For example, when I called up a private attorney for an interview, I was able to remind him of our prior court encounter. Similarly, judges saw me sitting in court day after day, and if I was not introduced to the judge by the prosecutor, the judge frequently would tell me when I finally got around to interviewing him that he had been wondering who I was. Finally, a most interesting pattern emerged vis-à-vis the public defenders. They were quite easy to meet in court, since they shared with me the prime seats in the court—the jury box. Additionally, they seemed to sense a natural affinity between my interests—qua liberal academic—and their jobs. In any event, after a week or two of interviewing prosecutors had elapsed, the public defenders would begin to ask me about when I was going to reach them. Thus, they were almost arranging their interviews for me.

During the time spent in court, I also established a rapport with many of the "low visibility actors" typically found in local criminal courts. These include clerks, bailiffs, secretaries, bondsmen, summer law student interns, family relations officers, and probation officers. It is hard to pinpoint precisely all of the advantages that accrued from being "on their good side," but perhaps some examples can serve to make the point. Secretaries and clerks frequently provided me with data about the disposition of a case that had been of interest to me. Bailiffs allowed me to sit in the jury box—one of the few places in many of the courts from which one could hear what was going on during nontrial proceedings. Bondsmen would fill me in on the "inside stuff" about defendants, police, judges, and so on. A probation officer I met in Arborville superior court was subsequently transferred to Centerville. There she gave me an extensive tour of the facilities, introduced me to several judges, and greatly simplified matters for me. In another court, the public defender had given me permission to go through his files and also provided me with an office. His secretary proved to be a gold mine of information regarding the dispositions of cases. I could go on and on, but I think the point is plain—in many little ways the research path was smoothed by the collective "cultivation" of these figures.[30] Contrastingly, had I alienated them in some fashion, I am certain they could have hindered my research substantially.[31]

Research Instruments: The Interview

As indicated above, interviews were conducted after observing a particular role incumbent. Though originally I had planned to be armed with ten complete case histories in which the respondent participated, I quickly learned that the ebb and flow of business in the court, the ever-present postponements, delays, motions, and so on, made this impossible. Indeed, the volume in circuit court is so high that it is likely that the respondents would have had to refer to their file to refresh their memories about the details of any particular case. Additionally, logistical considerations made it impossible for me to witness this number of cases for each respondent. Instead of attempting to reach the ten-case goal for each respondent, I gathered my rather copious notes on those cases in which I had seen the respondent participate, supplemented these with my notes on cases handled by his colleagues, and formed a "package of real cases" that I could and did refer to in the course of the interview. I hoped that my ability to cite the disposition of specific cases would increase the respondent's sense that I was an insider, privy to actual practices, and decrease any propensity on his/her part to offer flippant generalizations or civics book answers.

Prior to beginning the formal interview schedule, I asked the respondents a series of factual background questions. Included in this preliminary questionnaire were the standard socioeconomic and educational background questions, a probe on party affiliation and political liberalism-conservatism, and a series of questions on professional organizational participation.[32]

There were four major sections within the interview schedule. The first dealt specifically with adaptation to the job. Here I asked about recruitment, expectations, and vivid recollections of early experiences. Additionally, I asked the respondent to indicate who helped him "learn the ropes," and whether he was ever subject to pressure to act in a specific fashion. If the respondent had held a number of jobs in the local criminal court, I repeated these questions (as non-monotonously as possible) for each of his jobs.

In the second section, I moved directly into court operations. Here I began with questions about the cases I had observed; these were followed up with some general questions about plea bargaining. Sometimes, the major "adaptation to plea bargaining" questions were asked in part one; if not, I would raise them in this second section. In other words, I would constantly probe and push with questions like: "How did you learn what sentences were okay in X case?" Frequently, because the respondent had been sensitized to my interest in his adaptation, he would return to part one issues during part two. He might recall some "critical lesson" he had learned, or some "deviant" pattern that he had eschewed. The point, most simply, is that no neat separation was maintained; my inquiries emphasized his adaptation to the current plea bargaining practices.

The third set of questions covered the respondent's career goals and variables related to these goals. I wanted to examine how ambition for jobs within the system affected compliance to local court norms and folkways. In asking the respondents to define what they thought constituted effective performance in their roles, I sought further indicators of the reward/sanction system. Of course, other insights into reward and sanction were garnered in parts one and two.

Finally, in part four, I extended the inquiry into rewards and sanctions to include factors (public opinion, appellate decisions, and so on) outside the local court organization. Additionally, I tested the feasibility of several reform proposals, including the currently fashionable idea of abolishing plea bargaining.[33]

In sum, the seemingly broad scope of the interview schedule ought not to obscure the primary motivation behind the design of this instrument: to understand newcomer adaptation within plea bargaining systems. The constant probing on plea bargaining, the juxtaposition of actually observed cases with the respondents' contentions, the positing of alternatives to plea bargaining, collectively yielded a wealth of data on folkways and norms associated with this process of case disposition. When combined with several other sources of plea bargaining data (to be discussed below) and with my observations, I think a fairly realistic appraisal of plea bargaining becomes possible.

The interview schedule also contained an extensive series of questions on adaptation. Newcomers were asked to discuss their adjustment as they were going through it, that is, at the time of the interview; experienced court personnel were asked to recall their adaptation to the court and to the role(s) they had held. This amalgam of newcomers' reports and veterans' recollections seemed to be the most fruitful means of generating substantive adaptation data. I rejected the idea of interviewing prospective court employees (for example, just-graduated law students) because it was unlikely that they could answer with any specificity the questions about actual plea bargaining practices of the local criminal court.[34] Thus, it became necessary to rely on questions of old-timers to supplement the limited number of newcomer reports.[35] Notwithstanding the problems of selective and faulty recall, the former still are an important data source; in addition to clarifying the respondent's own adaptation experiences, they provide some clues about his expectations of how the newcomer will/ought to adapt.[36]

The theoretical questions discussed in chapter 1 necessitated research instruments, then, that extensively and intensively examined adaptation and plea bargaining from the perspective of newcomers and veterans. However, I harbored a fear that court personnel would be unwilling to sit through so lengthy an interview schedule. Fortunately, this fear proved to be unfounded.

The modal time for completion of the interviews was approximately two-and-a-half hours; some interviews were conducted in an hour and a half, while a few lasted as long as four hours. Not one respondent—even among those who expressed initial skepticism, or who claimed they could only give me forty-five minutes—terminated the interview before completion.

While this research was still in the planning stage, I weighed the costs and benefits of utilizing a tape recorder during the interviews. The negative arguments centered around frankness—would court personnel be as forthright and truthful if they knew their remarks were being recorded? On the benefit side, in addition to obtaining a more complete and accurate record of responses, I felt that I could do a better job of interviewing if I was unencumbered by having to take notes, or by having to remember key points to jot down frantically after the interview. This assessment led to my decision at least to try the tape recorder. If court personnel refused to be taped, or if I felt that frankness was being jeopardized, I could always go the pencil and paper route.

As things turned out, I did not regret my decision.[37] Seventy-five percent of the respondents (53 of 71) consented to the taping.[38] Though there is no absolute check on whether frankness was sacrificed, several indicators suggest that no severe antiseptic bias was introduced. For one, I have on tape many very personal, and sometimes sensitive, bits of information. I think it reasonable to conclude that these would not have been proffered if the respondents had questioned the sincerity of my promise of anonymity. Also, some respondents felt that it was preferable to have their comments completely recorded rather than to have me take selective notes.

A final indicator of the efficacy of the interviews (both those on and off tape) in eliciting detailed and thoughtful responses is found in the postinterview comments and actions of the subjects. Frequently, after the interview, respondents would thank me for affording them an opportunity to think systematically about their jobs. Apparently, in the clamorous atmosphere of the local court, such semi-theoretical discussions are a rarity.[39] Their interest, furthermore, did not wane once the interview was completed. It was not uncommon for them to approach me and tell me that they had given further thought to an issue raised in the interview; or to call me in to witness a particular deal being negotiated, a deal illustrative of a point made in the interview. When this feedback came from newcomers, it proved to be particularly significant. Their reports about rewards/sanctions, surprises, and more general adaptation experiences subsequent to the interview provided a veritable gold mine of observations about the adaptation process. Not only could I tease out the details of the incident from them, but I could also pursue it further when I interviewed or ''bumped into'' the significant others involved. In this fashion, the receptivity accorded the formal interview, as manifested in subsequent interaction with the respondents, had the effect of improving and structuring the direction of my observations and interviews.

Additional Data Sources

To complete this inventory of data sources, mention should be made of the several additional channels of information that I pursued. General case disposition data were available in public records.[40] However, for more specific case-by-case data, I needed the cooperation of court personnel. Again, I was very fortunate in this regard.[41]

The public defenders in one of the circuit courts allowed me to copy their individualized records of case dispositions. Unlike the published data, these sheets show the original charge as well as the final disposition, thus enabling one to discern the patterns of charge reductions employed. Similarly, a second set of public defenders—this time in a superior court—gave me complete access to their case files. I drew a sample of eighty-seven of these cases and coded them along a number of dimensions. Data contained in these files included (a) comments by public defenders about the state's attorney's offer in the case, (b) copies of the police reports, and (c) copies of the confidential presentence reports (summaries of the defendant's history prepared by the probation department). At a minimum, the review of these superior court cases provided additional insight into the range of factors that have to be considered when attempting to explain the plea bargaining process.

Finally, with the cooperation of a criminal court administrator, I was allowed to peruse some of the internal organizational correspondence and memos of one superior court. Though much of the material was peripheral to my study, a few of the memos dealing with "moving the business" in court proved to be useful.

The Research Experience: Some Recollections and Reflections

The field research for this project was begun in July 1972, and took eight months to complete. I have already discussed the general approach followed in each court, and the receptivity accorded me by court personnel. In the next chapter I will offer my impressions of the court facilities visited and attempt to capture the ambience of the plea bargaining settings. But, between the accounts of the research instruments and strategies of this chapter, and of the plea bargaining settings of the next, many of the incidents and observations that breathe life into a research project of eight months duration are lost. It is of course impossible, unnecessary, and perhaps occasionally unethical to be completely comprehensive. Yet, I think it worthwhile to describe very briefly a few of these research-related incidents, if only to convey to the reader the character of the research experience (leaving out plea bargaining considerations) and some of the difficulties experienced. These will be summarized under three headings.

Biographer Syndrome

Several of the respondents perceived my interest in them as biographical. Despite my protestations, they chose to believe that I was most interested in their careers, attitudes, and so on. A circuit court judge flooded me with biographical data, and frequently called me into his chambers long after I had completed the interview to tell me about recent changes in his life. In one of the superior courts, the state's attorneys were calling me "O'Hara's Boswell," because O'Hara was the first state's attorney I interviewed, and I had spent a long period of time with him. The chief state's attorney of yet another superior court interpreted my persistence in interviewing his staff as indicative of my desire to obtain an interview with him. He was impressed, he told me, with my diligence, and therefore he would grant me the "important" interview.

On its face, there appears to be no problem with this somewhat narrow perception of my role. But in practice, it caused difficulties. When the circuit court judge insisted on speaking to me during recesses, the clerks and prosecutors of the circuit court became incensed at the resultant delay. I could not afford to incur their wrath, but neither did I want to offend this very kindly and learned judge. Eventually, I settled on a "disappearing strategy," absenting myself from court during recess.

The more general problem posed by this biographer perception is the expectation raised in these individuals about the product that will emerge from my research. Despite my protestations that this was a large-scale study, with anonymity guaranteed, I simply could not shake the notion several of the respondents held that "they would be in the book." Fortunately, this was not common, and most preferred anonymity, but I fear that the handful that felt otherwise will be very disappointed.

Ethical Dilemmas

A wide variety of ethical problems came to the fore during my eight months in court. A few of the respondents who had been harshly criticized for their activities as public defenders told me that they felt the interview could be therapeutic. Not being trained as a psychologist—and particularly concerned about one individual who suffered a job-related nervous breakdown—I had to opt between treading very lightly and sympathetically or pursuing my inquiries to the fullest and risk reviving serious unpleasantness. I tried to strike a middle course, but nonetheless, at times these interviews became very uncomfortable.

Relatedly, in several of the interviews I had to countenance attitudes that were personally repugnant to me. There was no point in becoming embroiled in debates with the respondents, but I feared that my silence (was) would be interpreted as agreement. I relied on my assessment of the individual to decide whether speaking out would be a source of alienation, thereby jeopardizing subsequent access.

I doubt very much that my presence in court during sentencing affected actual dispositions. But one incident gave me cause to wonder. The day after an interview with a circuit court prosecutor, an interview in which he had stressed his compassion, a case came up for sentencing. The defendant had a horrendous prior record and was charged with a series of burglaries (maximum sentence: five years). The presentence report, however, contained a recommendation for probation. The prosecutor stood up and told the judge that though he rarely disagreed with the presentence report, he had to take exception in this case. He felt that the defendant should receive a year in prison, a sentence subsequently handed down by the judge. Given the fellow's record and the facts of the case, I thought personally that, if anything, the sentence was an excellent bargain for the defendant. But the prosecutor came over to me and said: "You must have thought I was a real prick asking for a year. But there's something you don't know.'' He showed me an outstanding warrant for another series of crimes charged to the defendant, and said that because the defendant received the year he would not prosecute these. I wondered then, and still wonder, whether or not my presence led to a disposition lower than the prosecutor might have desired, and perhaps lower than what was really called for in that case.

The Lighter Side

In contrast to the seriousness of the issues raised in the biographical and ethical sections, the field research also held its share of rather amusing and interesting occurrences. One private attorney, after being questioned about his views of his clients, suddenly turned to me and said: ''They're not all such nice people ... That's why I keep this with me.'' He pulled out a large pistol and pointed it directly at me. Another private attorney lectured—with visual aids—on the use of his spittoon.

Sometimes things got to be a bit embarrassing. I had been interviewing a judge during the morning recess, when the clerk came in to tell the judge it was time to resume the hearing. I packed up my papers and tape recorder, asked the judge if I could see him for lunch, and walked out. But instead of using the exit, I left by the way of the door leading to the courtroom. The clerk routinely shouted, ''All rise,'' and there I stood in front of a hundred people. I beat a hasty retreat, but unfortunately the embarrassment did not fade as quickly.

In another court, I was sitting in the jury box listening to the day's proceedings. I knew the prosecutor well, but the judge was new to the circuit. It had been a busy morning and there was a delay at the moment caused by the absence of any public defenders in the courtroom. The judge, becoming increasingly upset, asked the prosecutor: ''Aren't there any public defenders here? What about that fellow over there?'' The prosecutor looked in the direction of the judge's gaze, saw the judge meant me, and assured, ''No, Your Honor, he's ... uh ... nothing.''

3 The Context of Adaptation

Plea Bargaining and Case Pressure: The Prevailing Explanation

A number of explanations of the dynamics of the plea bargaining process have been advanced in the literature; for the most part, these rest on the assumption that case pressure best (though not necessarily exclusively) explains plea bargaining. Several illustrations of this assumption follow.

> Only the guilty plea system has enabled the courts to process their caseloads with seriously inadequate resources. The invisible hand of Adam Smith is at work. Growing concessions to guilty plea defendants have almost matched the growing need to avoid the burdensome business of trying cases.[1]

> So long as it remains impossible for our criminal system to permit every defendant to claim his right to a jury trial, some inducements for the surrender of that right will be necessary. At the moment, plea bargaining is our only vehicle for granting such inducements. Moreover, absent a dramatic increase in legal resources or the appearance of some other strategy which compensates for our shortage of these resources, plea bargaining is likely to endure.[2]

> The guilty plea concept is a relatively recent phenomenon. The ever-increasing crime rate over the past 30 years has led the American criminal justice system to the point where 85 to 90 percent of all criminal convictions are obtained by guilty pleas.[3]

> Because the contemporary American criminal justice system suffers from a critical lack of resources, it has come to rely on the continual sacrifice of the trial rights of the individual. To dis-

pose of the maximum number of cases at minimum cost, prosecutors often attempt to induce a defendant to plead guilty by offering him a bargain—a sentence or charge reduction in exchange for a guilty plea.[4]

Realizing the need to relieve its congested dockets, the courts have resorted to various methods to expedite the legal process. One of these methods, plea bargaining, is not designed to accelerate the trial level but instead eliminate it.[5]

Properly administerd, it [plea bargaining] is to be encouraged. If every criminal charge were subjected to a full-scale trial, the States and the Federal Government would need to multiply by many times the number of judges and court facilities.[6]

They [negotiated dispositions] serve an important role in the disposition of today's heavy calendars.[7]

These comments are illustrative of the purported case pressure–plea bargaining linkage. Heavy case loads in the criminal courts coupled with the prevalence of plea bargaining suggest to many that plea bargaining is the expedient developed to manage these case loads. The impression conveyed by this theory is that plea bargaining results from increases in case pressure, although quantitative analysis of the relationship has not been undertaken. The literature does not posit direct variation between plea bargaining and case pressure; for the most part, it is silent on the precise nature of the relationship and is content to observe that case pressure and plea bargaining appear to "go together."

Further evidence of the reliance on the case-pressure argument can be discerned in the prevailing explanations of the incentives which ostensibly motivate each of the actors in the criminal justice system to negotiate cases. The prosecutor's willingness to plea bargain is described in terms of his need to "move the business" and to "dispose of cases." Faced with an unmanageably large backlog of cases, he has to bend to cope. He agrees to dismiss some of the charges or to recommend a more lenient sentence if the defendant pleads guilty. In this fashion, his "batting average" (that is, his conviction rate) remains high, and he avoids a buildup of cases awaiting jury trial.

Defense attorneys are more than willing to cooperate with the prosecutor. A public defender suffers from the same twin problems as the prosecutor: shortage in staff and heavy case load. Plea bargaining provides a means of arriving at a satisfactory disposition; time and resource constraints militate against a more adversary posture. Private attorneys also have heavy case loads; they need a fairly large number of clients to survive economically. The plea bargain enables the private attorney to "turn over" cases rapidly and expeditiously; he can earn substantially more money than if he tried each case.

The judge is not inclined to put a damper on the plea bargain. Sharing with the prosecutor a sense of responsibility for "moving the business," or alternatively, for insuring that "justice is not delayed," he views plea bargaining as a means of rapidly clearing the docket. As a result of the plea bargain, he can marshal evidence to show that he is working diligently (number of cases processed) and efficiently (conviction rates). The risk of black marks intruding on these claims of success is minimized as well. Without a trial, the risks of reversal on appeal are next to nil.

Admittedly, I have somewhat oversimplified the arguments advanced in the plea bargaining literature. Certainly, factors other than case pressure are noted and discussed in the literature, and we will have cause to return to these later. But when one strips away these peripheral "after-thought" explanations, one still finds a central argument that rests on an assumption that case pressure is the single most important explanation for plea bargaining.

Abraham Blumberg's *Criminal Justice*, one of the more influential books concerned with plea bargaining, typifies the case-pressure approach and suggests the implications of this approach for the question of adaptation of new court personnel.[8] Blumberg discusses "the emergence of 'bureaucratic due process,' a non-adversary system of justice by negotiation. It consists of secret bargaining sessions, employing subtle, bureaucratically ordained modes of coercion and influence to dispose of *onerously large case loads* in an efficacious and 'rational' manner."[9] (Emphasis mine.) Particular note should be taken of the almost conspiratorial tone of the Blumberg quotation. Though this perspective and tone are not inevitable by-products of the case-pressure explanation, they are frequently part of it. The need to dispose of large numbers of cases requires mutual accommodation of the different role incumbents. "Deals" have to be consummated, and cases have to be moved quickly through the system. An individual not willing to "go along" can upset the workings of the plea bargaining system. Thus, he will be subject (or so the argument runs) to the collective wrath of the court personnel, regardless of the role he occupies.

Obviously, this view of the treatment accorded an outsider is of direct import to the problem of adaptation of the newcomer. It suggests that the newcomer will be coerced into cooperating in the semi-secretive move-the-business plea bargaining system. Blumberg's view is quite straightforward on this issue: "The deviant or even maverick individual who predicates his official conduct solely on accepted notions of due process, or chooses possibilities of action which run counter to normatively established routines, is quickly isolated, neutralized, or re-socialized."[10]

To recapitulate, the case-pressure position is the prevailing explanation of plea bargaining dynamics. It fosters an image of a court attempting to cope in an almost conspiratorial fashion with more cases than it can reasonably handle. The implication for the adaptation of the newcomer is clear: he must be taught to cooperate and share in the pleasures of negotiated dispositions.

Plea Bargaining and Case Pressure: A Reconsideration

Despite the centrality and importance of the case-pressure explanation of plea bargaining, the proposition that case-pressure best explains plea bargaining and low trial rates is largely untested. Only a handful of scholars have explicitly questioned what is in fact the case-pressure *assumption*.[11] Their comments underscore the need for a more thorough and systematic consideration of the matter. Malcolm Feeley, one of the few who has actually questioned the reliance placed on case pressure, reports his suspicion that "Blumberg has somewhat overstated the importance of heavy case loads" and calls for "systematically gathered and presented evidence" to test alternative hypotheses.[12]

Fortunately, disposition data for Connecticut's superior courts were available, and I was able to use these data in a test of the case-pressure hypothesis. The figure most frequently bandied about as indicative of the pervasiveness of plea bargaining is that roughly only 10 percent of all criminal cases go to trial.[13] Table 4 confirms the fact that in recent years, recourse to trial has been the exception rather than the rule in Connecticut's superior courts. In not one of the seven years included in this time frame does the ratio of trials to total cases disposed exceed 9 percent.[14] The trial, perceived by many as the touchstone of our legal system, accounted for the final outcome of only 114 of the 3004 cases resolved in one fashion or another by the superior courts in 1972–73.

Table 4 Disposition of Criminal Cases by Defendants in Connecticut Superior Courts, 1966–73

Method of Disposition	1966–67	1967–68	1968–69	1969–70	1970–71	1971–72	1972–73
Guilty Plea	1635	2107	2696	3186	3680	3332	2244
Nolle or Dismissal	267	419	686	1110	1302	1302	646
Trial	164	241	301	191	231	156	114
Total Dispositions	2066	2767	3683	4487	5213	4790	3004
% Trial/ Total Disposition	7.9	8.7	8.2	4.3	4.4	3.3	3.8

Sources: For 1966–67 through 1970–71, Connecticut Planning Committee on Criminal Administration, *The Criminal Justice System in Connecticut—1972*, p. 111. For 1971–72, *Twenty-third Report of the Judicial Council of Connecticut* (Dec., 1972), p. 41. For 1972–73, personal written communication with Joseph Shortall, Assistant Executive Secretary, Judicial Department, State of Connecticut.

Setting aside consideration of the complexities involved in interpreting year-to-year fluctuations, the inescapable conclusion is that during these years the probability of trial in a given case was very low. If the case was not filtered out by means of a nolle or a dismissal, it was at least eight times more likely that the defendant would waive his right to trial and plead guilty.[15] In the "trial court," the guilty plea reigns.

We have not yet encountered any novel ground—as indicated above, the 10 percent trial figure is quite well advertised. But what is not commonly realized, though critical for an appreciation of the reality of plea bargaining, is that the relative lack of trials versus alternate modes of disposition is *not* a recent phenomenon. Figure 1 plots the percentage of trials to total dispositions for the superior courts from 1880 to 1954.[16] The mean percentage of trial to total disposition ratio over this seventy-five year period is 8.7 percent. From 1880 to 1910, the ratio was slightly above 10 percent; from 1910 to 1954, it reached the 10 percent plateau only three times. Overall, the trial ratio for these years does not differ to any great extent from the current figures. Historically, it appears that the trial, as far back as 1880, did not serve as a particularly popular means of case disposition.

Figure 1. Ratio of Trials to Total Dispositions for Connecticut Superior Courts, 1880–1954.

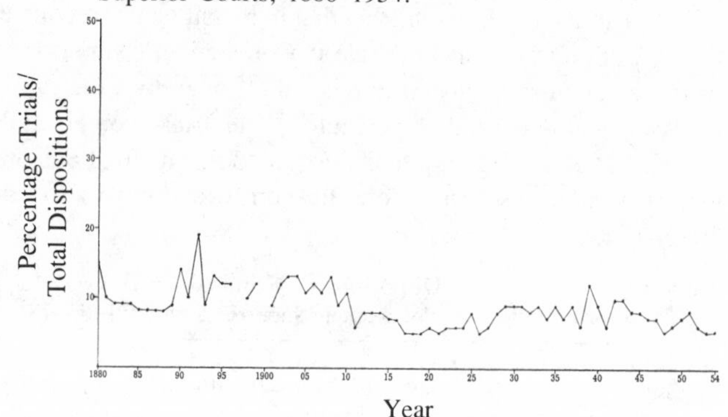

Sources: For 1880–1900, "Annual Report of the Comptroller of Public Accounts . . . ," *Connecticut Public Documents*. For 1901–1925, "Annual Reports in Relation to the Criminal Business . . . ," *Public Documents of the State of Connecticut*. For 1926–1954, Judicial Council of Connecticut, *Connecticut Judicial Statistics* (March, 1956). See note 16 for detailed citation. Data for 1897 and 1900 were unavailable.

These data speak indirectly to the nature of the relationship between plea bargaining[17] and case pressure.[18] However, if we break down the data presented in figure 1 by individual courts and compare trial rates in the low and high volume superior courts, a direct test of the relationship is possible. This test is at best "rough" because without data on the number of prosecutors and judges working in the court, we cannot be sure that volume reflects pressure. Nevertheless, these data should yield some clues concerning the ability and desire of local court officials to try cases.

Table 5 Rank Ordering of Connecticut Superior Courts by Mean Number Cases Disposed Annually, 1880–1954

Superior Courts	Total Cases	Mean	Standard Deviation
Tolland	2468	34	21
Middlesex	4143	56	20
Windham	5362	73	25
Litchfield	6235	85	51
Waterbury*	5220	87	37
New London	8553	117	43
Fairfield	19,043	261	71
New Haven	20,326	278	104
Hartford	24,212	332	158

Source: Same as for figure 1.
* Data missing for 1897 and 1900. The Waterbury Superior Court was established in 1893, thus the *N* is 60 for Waterbury and 73 for the others.

For purposes of analysis, case volume was used as a surrogate for case pressure.[19] Connecticut's nine superior courts were arranged on the basis of the mean number of total cases disposed of annually between 1880 and 1954. Table 5 shows the rank order based on these means.

The three courts with the lowest mean number of cases per year (34, 56, and 73) were called "low volume courts"; Fairfield, New Haven, and Hartford were labeled "high volume courts." The ratio of trials to total dispositions for each of these six courts was calculated, and the mean of these ratios for the low and high volume groupings for each year was determined. The summary statistics over the seventy-five year period for each court are presented in table 6; the means of the high and low volume groupings for each year are plotted in figure 2.

Table 6 Means of Annual Trial to Total Cases Ratio for Low and High Volume Superior Courts, 1880–1954

	Low Volume Courts			High Volume Courts		
	Tolland	Middlesex	Windham	Fairfield	New Haven	Hartford
Mean Trials/Cases	.16	.14	.11	.07	.12	.07
Standard deviation	.12	.07	.07	.05	.06	.04

Source: Same as for figure 1.

Figure 2 and table 6 indicate that over this seventy-five year period, the low volume courts did not try a substantial percentage of their cases, and did not try substantially more cases than the high volume courts. Though in certain years and certain time periods (particularly from 1894 to 1904) the predicted greater rate is found and is pronounced, I think it fair to conclude, especially from 1910 and on, that despite the large difference in actual case pressure

Figure 2. Mean Annual Trial to Total Cases Ratio of High and Low Volume Connecticut Superior Courts, 1880–1954.*

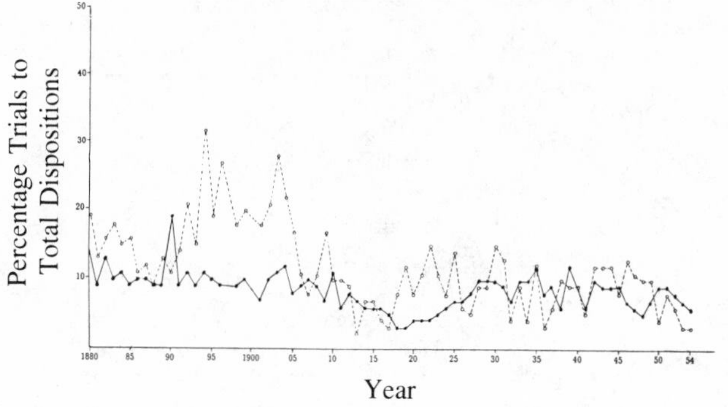

Source: Same as for figure 1.

*----- Low Volume Courts (Tolland, Middlesex, Windham)
—— High Volume Courts (Fairfield, New Haven, Hartford)

which was used to dichotomize the groupings, trial rates between them varied minimally, and indeed, often the low volume courts tried proportionately fewer cases.

A second test of the relationship between the case-pressure and trials argument is afforded by the data presented in table 7. As of September 1971, the circuit court's criminal jurisdiction was extended to include crimes punishable by up to five years imprisonment. Previously, it had bound over to the superior court all cases with potential sentences of more than one year. One of the effects of this increased circuit court jurisdiction, then, was to lighten the superior court case load. However, during this same period, no decrease in superior court personnel levels took place; the same number of state's attorneys and judges that disposed of 5213 cases between July 1970 and June 1971, disposed of 3004 cases between June 1972 and June 1973.[20] The fact that personnel levels remained constant allows us to examine the impact of the relative decrease in case pressure on specific superior courts.[21]

In the three busiest courts, case pressure was roughly halved and personnel levels remained constant, but the rate of trials stayed the same; it did not increase appreciably as the decreased case pressure–increased trials relationship would have predicted. In the lower volume courts, the pattern was mixed. Litchfield shows substantial decrease in trial rates, while Middletown and Tolland show slight increases. Overall, though, one is struck more by the relative constancy of the trial rates in the face of dramatic changes in case pressure, than by the slight, and not always consistent, changes in these rates.

Collectively, these data cast doubt upon the efficacy of the case pressure assumption as an adequate base upon which to build an explanation of plea bargaining dynamics. We have seen that trials are not now, nor have they been since 1880, the predominant method of case resolution in the local

Table 7 Trial Rate Pre- and Post-Change in Circuit Court Jurisdiction for Connecticut Superior Courts, 1970–71and 1972–73.

	Pre-Changed Jurisdiction: 1970–71			Post-Changed Jurisdiction: 1972–73		
Superior Court	Total Cases	Trials	Percent Trials Total Cases	Total Cases	Trials	Percent Trials Total Cases
Tolland	196	11	5.6	117	8	6.8
Middlesex	203	7	3.4	134	4	3.0
Windham	160	6	3.8	101	3	3.0
Litchfield	164	30	18.3	108	6	5.6
Waterbury	536	18	3.4	345	6	1.7
New London	286	19	6.6	349	13	3.7
Fairfield	889	42	4.7	441	21	4.8
New Haven	955	43	4.5	482	23	4.8
Hartford	1822	55	3.0	927	30	3.2

Sources: For 1970–71, Connecticut Planning Committee on Criminal Administration, *The Criminal Justice System in Connecticut—1972*, p. 114. For 1972–73, personal written communication with Joseph Shortall, Assistant Executive Secretary, Judicial Department, State of Connecticut.

criminal court. This fact is clear both from the annual aggregate statistics for all the superior courts, and from the breakdown of these statistics by court. Furthermore, we have seen that variations in case pressure do not directly and appreciably affect trial rates—historically, low volume courts have not tried significantly more cases, and recent decreases in volume have not led to markedly greater rates of trial.

The guilty plea is, and has been, the best-traveled route to case disposition in high *and* low volume courts. Today we know that the plea is a result of plea bargaining negotiations, a fact well documented by my court observations and interviews. Additionally, some of the evidence I have collected suggests that there is nothing new about this reliance on the negotiated settlement.

I spoke with "old-timers"—court personnel and private attorneys active in criminal courts since the 1930s—who scoffed at the current clamor about plea bargaining. Though they agreed that some of the steps followed in negotiating dispositions have changed, these "old-timers" maintained that the core notion of arranging a deal with the state's attorney in return for a guilty plea has always been central to the practice of criminal law.[22] The following exchanges with an Ortaville prosecutor and defense attorney illustrate the "old-timer"view.

> *A*. I'll tell you something about that, I mean everyone comes into this court and finds that . . . plea bargaining is universal. It's always been there, and these law school kids, I mean, I am aghast sometimes when I meet some of the kids from the University of Connecticut Law Clinic . . . the phrase is new, but there was always plea bargaining.

Q. You mean you have always plea bargained?
A. Right. It has always been, and it's had to be, in the lower courts because we could never operate without it. I mean ... well, I understand the problems of the defense lawyer which the brand new kid today doesn't understand. He had to earn a living, he had to get a result for his client, and sometimes the results were foolish ... like a shoplifting charge changed to a breach of peace. But there's the same fine anyway. Then he could tell his client, "See, you're not a thief, you just made a little peccadillo, and I did a great piece of work for you." That's always the way of the lower courts and always the way of the police court lawyer.
Q. I think there has been this tendency to treat plea bargaining as something new.
A. Well, of course, that's been straightened out with the ABA standards anyway. But it's amazing for me to find kids from law school coming in, and they're like children: "Oh, now we're going to plea bargain?" Tell me what you want, and if it is close enough, you can have it. [52]

Q. Has there always been plea bargaining in the courts?
A. Yeah ...
Q. They called it a different thing?
A. Well, I've been in practice twenty-seven years, and its always been there. You get a drunk driving case, a first offender on a drunk driving case, and suppose the guy has got a wife and six kids and he is working forty miles out of [Ortaville]. Frequently, even in the old days, you get a guy to say, "Hell, how am I going to cost this guy his job, getting him a divorce, blow his family, put his kids on welfare for six months ..." [34]

In sum, plea bargaining is not new to the criminal court, nor is it a direct function of case pressure. Recourse to the trial as a mode of case disposition is the exception, not the rule, and this proposition holds even when case volume is controlled. This is true of our courts today and appears to have been true historically. To develop an explanation of plea bargaining and of the incentives of each of the participants to engage in it, and to base that explanation on case-pressure considerations, is to ignore these findings. The guilty plea and the plea bargain are far more central to the local criminal court than the plea bargaining literature suggests. Rather than being simply an expedient dictated by unmanageably large case loads, plea bargaining is integrally and inextricably bound to the "trial" court.

I will not attempt here to develop systematically the explanation of *why* plea bargaining is so inextricably tied to the court. This task is better undertaken after we view the plea bargaining system through the eyes of the newcomer. Suffice it to say now that a simple dichotomization of plea bargaining and trials founded on case pressure misrepresents the plea bargaining reality. The decision to plea bargain is not fundamentally a function of case pressure; other factors and incentives account for the decision to go to trial or to plea bargain.

It is important to emphasize that rejecting the case-pressure hypothesis and positing an explanation of plea bargaining that rests on alternative considerations casts the organizational context which the newcomer must confront into a very different mold. Recall that Blumberg-type arguments rest on the notion that the need to dispose of ''onerously large case loads'' dictates a collective ''socialization'' effort to insure newcomer participation in plea bargaining. If case load is removed as the dominant factor, how are socialization efforts and/or the lack of these to be explained? What other plea bargaining-related norms are inculcated? If the newcomer plea bargains, can we infer the ''success'' of coercive ''socialization'' efforts? Is it not plausible that he may simply have learned that for certain cases and under certain circumstances, the plea bargaining alternative (regardless of case pressure) is preferable to the trial? These and other questions move to the fore when the simplistic—though dominant—case-pressure perspective is questioned, and again, we will consider these matters systematically in later chapters. I raise them now only to illustrate how our reconsideration of the explanatory power of case pressure restructures questions about the adaptation of the newcomer to the local criminal court.

Plea Bargaining Settings and Processes: The Circuit and Superior Courts

In developing the argument that plea bargaining is inextricably bound to the court, that it is the lowest common denominator crosscutting criminal courts regardless of case-pressure loads, I have ignored distinctions among plea bargaining systems. But once we move beyond this position—that is, once we accept the centrality of plea bargaining—differences among systems become a more important concern. After all, plea bargaining is not a homogeneous process with identical connotations and denotations for all criminal systems. Indeed, I think one explanation for the confusion that surrounds plea bargaining is directly attributable to the failure to note these distinctions.

This section will be devoted to a preliminary delineation of plea bargaining system differences. An exhaustive classification is precluded by the limited data available and by my sense that our relative lack of sophistication militates against premature carving of hard-and-fast boundaries. Nonetheless, this descriptive undertaking is important, insofar as it sheds more light on the organizational context(s) which the newcomer to Connecticut's courts faces and provides dimensions that subsequent research can focus on for the development of a more satisfactory classificatory scheme.

The obvious way to search for plea bargaining differences is to compare data from the circuit and the superior courts. Though the circuit court had felony jurisdiction of up to five years, during the period this study was conducted,[23] the overwhelming majority of its cases stemmed from misdemeanor offenses,[24] such as breach of the peace, intoxication, violations of town ordinances, and disorderly conduct.[25] As would be expected, the circuit court's case volume was substantially higher than that of the superior court.

Table 8 presents the disposition figures for non-motor vehicle criminal cases in Connecticut's eighteen circuit courts in 1972. Unfortunately, these data are not as useful as the superior court data we have examined, insofar as they are broken down by offenses rather than by defendants; also, they fail to distinguish among guilty pleas and court trial verdicts of guilty.[26] Nevertheless, the data do reflect the almost complete absence of recourse to the jury trial in both the high and low volume courts and indicate the extensive use of the nolle to dispose of charges against the defendant.[27] Beyond these basic observations, the shortcomings in the reporting method of the circuit court data, and in some of the superior court data as well, caution against pushing solely statistical comparisons too far.

Table 8 Disposition of Non–Motor Vehicle Criminal Cases by Offenses in Connecticut Circuit Courts, Calendar Year 1972

Circuit Court	Total Offenses	Jury Trial	Guilty Pleas and Verdict	Not Guilty Court Trial	Nolled	Bindover	Other*
1 Stamford	12,184		5,790	391	4,606	129	1,268
2 Bridgeport	8,713	2	4,073	271	3,747	202	428
3 Danbury	2,704		1,292	70	1,058	60	234
4 Waterbury	5,005		2,378	247	2,083	191	106
5 Ansonia	3,579		1,789	111	1,462	39	178
6 New Haven	10,955		5,211	310	5,126	211	97
7 Meriden	4,630		2,518	100	1,826	82	104
8 Branford	3,132		1,381	185	1,119	65	382
9 Middletown	2,962	2	1,306	125	1,267	60	202
10 New London	7,307	1	3,895	209	2,788	194	220
11 Danielson	2,439		997	33	1,253	55	101
12 Manchester	4,428		1,879	170	2,152	63	164
13 Thompsonville	2,466		1,416	56	747	109	138
14 Hartford	14,135		6,710	383	6,526	431	85
15 New Britain	3,715		1,715	317	1,519	80	84
16 West Hartford	1,948		853	69	836	58	132
17 Bristol	2,601		1,254	81	1,065	89	112
18 Winsted	1,869		1,002	84	625	62	96
Total	94,772	5	45,449	3,212	39,795	2,180	4,125

Source: Personal written communication with Joseph Shortall, Assistant Executive Secretary, Judicial Department, State of Connecticut.

* Six cases referred to Juvenile Court; the rest referred to Violation Bureau.

There are many aspects of the plea bargaining process in both the circuit and superior courts that could not be quantified in any event. Circuit court plea bargaining takes place in a very different atmosphere and is concerned with very different matters than superior court plea bargaining. There is a prevailing and predominant ''flavor'' to each of these plea bargaining settings, and though we can only distinguish between the two in a fashion which is, admittedly, imprecise, the differences are important enough to warrant our attention.

The Circuit Court

Typically, in the circuit court, a line forms outside the prosecutor's office the morning before court is convened.[28] Defense attorneys shuffle into the prosecutor's office and, in a matter of two or three minutes, dispose of the one or more cases ''set down'' that day. Generally, only a few words have to be exchanged before agreement is reached. The defense attorney mutters something about the defendant, the prosecutor reads the police report, and concurrence on ''what to do'' generally, but not always, emerges.

The Ortaville prosecutors and public defenders have pushed the process to its extreme. The public defenders literally take home the prosecutor's file the day before the case is scheduled, and return the file in the courtroom the next day. The prosecutor calls the case, opens the file, and finds a note placed there by the public defender, indicating the disposition desired. A few words are exchanged in front of the bench, and the deal is consummated.

After agreement is reached in the prosecutor's office or by way of the note in the file, the case is ''called'' in the courtroom. A prosecutor shouts the defendant's name and corresponding file number. The defendant and his attorney approach the bench and stand beside the prosecutor. The prosecutor makes a few remarks about the facts of the case and then discusses his preliminary decisions. He may nolle some or all of the charges against the defendant; he also may have a sentence recommendation to offer the judge.[29] The prosecutor's contribution to the disposition of the case ceases here. His subsequent interest is not directed to the remarks of the defense attorney, defendant, or judge, but instead is given to the stack of files on the table in front of him. These are the cases that remain on the docket for that day; thus, while the formal decision is being made on the defendant, the prosecutor is already reviewing his presentation for the next case.

The judge now replaces the prosecutor as the actor in this little ceremony. He may, after the prosecutor's presentation is completed, ask the defendant a series of questions concerning the voluntariness of the plea. ''Do you realize that you are waiving your right to a trial by jury by entering this guilty plea? Are you making this plea voluntarily and without coercion or promises of a more lenient disposition? Do you realize that I am responsible for sentencing and that no one can guarantee you any specific sentence? Do you realize that by pleading to [charge] you could receive up to ——years in prison?'' More likely, the judge dispenses with these questions, particularly if the case is relatively minor.[30] Instead, he simply asks the defendant if he wants to plead guilty. Invariably the defendant nods, or murmurs, "Yes, Your Honor." The judge notes the defendant's response and asks him if he has anything to say. Generally, the defendant's attorney, not the defendant himself, responds.

The attorney embellishes the defendant's perfunctory plea of guilty with a brief statement about how repentant the defendant is, and/or how trivial an offense this actually was, and/or what a wonderful person the defendant really is. As the defense attorney drones on, the judge joins the prosecutor in directing his attention to matters other than the words being spoken in the court. With at best half an ear on the defense attorney's "pitch," his focus of attention turns to some forms on his desk. These are not, as one might suspect, the police reports of the offense or the defendant's file. Instead, they are the judge's copy of the penal code (which lists the possible range of penalties for an offense), and his copy of the court docket for the day. The judge more than likely is entering his disposition for the case on the docket form as the defense attorney speaks. Thus, like the prosecutor, he will be ready to move quickly to the next case without any paperwork delay. When the defense attorney's "pitch" is completed, the judge announces the disposition, and, as the defendant and his attorney walk away, the prosecutor calls the next case. The process starts again.

While this brief drama is enacted, the spectators in the courtroom engage in a number of activities which create an atmosphere of bustle, as well as an often intolerable noise level. Defendants confer with attorneys; bail bondsmen discuss rates and collateral with defendants; defendants greet old acquaintances; prosecutors and defense attorneys negotiate cases; clerks and bailiffs wander about, bringing files, various forms, incarcerated defendants, and coffee. Occasionally a prosecutor from another courtroom pops in and reads off a list of defendants' names. These defendants are instructed to move to another courtroom for their cases. In one of the circuit courts, the public defender also reads off lists of names while court is in session. These are the names of his clients, defendants who failed to consult with him that morning about their cases. The public defender corners them (quite literally) in the courtroom and discusses disposition for the first, and probably only, time.

The turmoil in the courtroom is matched only by the confusion in the adjoining corridor. Prosecutors, bondsmen, defense attorneys, defendants, police officers, family members, victims, witnesses, and clerks meander about passing the time, arranging deals, looking for someone—or simply because they are confused.[31] No neat boundary separates courtroom and corridor; activities flow back and forth between the two.

The physical structure of the courthouse contributes to the atmosphere of "almost anything goes on, almost any time." Two of the three circuit courts included in this study were housed in old, run-down buildings. In one of them, plaster was falling from walls, restrooms were filthy, garbage was strewn in corridors, fans were kept running constantly (in summer months), making it almost impossible to hear anything said in court. In the other run-down court, the courtroom was so large, and the distance between the judge's bench and the rest of the courtroom so great, that it was nearly impossible to follow what was going on. The physical design of the courtroom itself was an open invitation to engage in conversation while court was in session.

Similarly, the office arrangements in these older courts left much to be desired. Prosecutors and public defenders had, at best, cubicles separated by paper-thin walls. Private discussions between defendants and public defenders, or between public defenders and prosecutors, were precluded by this arrangement. In one of the circuit courts, the office layout of the public defender and the prosecutor can only be described as Kafkaesque. The public defenders were assigned a suite of rooms, but one of the rooms was reserved for a prosecutor. In the morning before court sessions began, lines of defendants waiting to see public defenders formed parallel to lines of attorneys waiting to see prosecutors. Additionally, police officers scheduled to testify that day ''hung around'' this suite of rooms. Thus, defendants desiring to speak with their public defenders found themselves in a room filled with other defendants, prosecutors, private defense attorneys, and police officers. A public defender described the resultant pandemonium.

> *Q*. You have a prosecutor's office within the public defender's office?
> *A*. Yeah . . . image wise . . . the prosecutor sends his witnesses over here to wait in the morning. My clients are waiting for me at the same time . . . some of them . . . call us prosecutors.
> *Q*. You mean . . .
> *A*. The physical thing . . . in addition to sending their witnesses over, they'll send over the police officer who was present on the scene to make the arrest. They'll end up in our office. Some days we'll end up with private attorneys in here looking for their client's file, which the prosecutor gave to us [public defenders] by mistake, with police officers asking: ''Well, when are we going to do the case, I want to go home, I've been on the twelve to eight shift, I want to get out of here,'' and with a couple of the state's witnesses . . . and then we also have a Spanish-speaking woman that I've got to get in because my secretary doesn't speak Spanish, and then some kid and his mother in the room . . . fifteen people in here and there will be ninety-five conversations going on . . . The sanctity of the whole thing and confidentiality is completely lost. [49]

These structural arrangements and the resultant confusion they foster no doubt contribute to the ''anything goes'' atmosphere of the circuit court. It should be emphasized, however (and we will return to this point in chapter 5), that poor facilities do not explain the prevalence of plea bargaining. In the one modern circuit court included in this study, the courtrooms were carpeted; judges, attorneys and prosecutors spoke through microphones in court; court personnel had their own modern offices; yet plea bargaining took place in essentially the same fashion as in the older courts. Just as we stripped away case pressures earlier and found that plea bargaining remained, so, too, it seems that we can strip away the poor facilities as a key explanatory factor and still find the same plea bargaining dynamic operative. Lines form in court; judges give scant attention to defense attorneys' pitches; cases are processed quickly in both old and modern courts.[32]

Thus far we have seen that cases are handled in almost assembly-line fashion in the circuit court. A minimum of haggling is involved. There seems to be agreement among circuit court personnel that the charges leveled against the defendant are not of particular import and are not worth extensive time in trial or even in plea negotiations. The actors share a sense that it is "just the circuit court," and that matters ought to be resolved quickly. "Nickel-dime" cases are not seen as being worthy of extensive negotiations. This feeling is illustrated in the following remarks by a circuit court prosecutor, judge, and public defender, respectively.

> Most of the stuff that comes through the court is garbage. You wonder if they should even be arrested in many instances, why the police even bother . . . a husband gets into an argument with his wife, they call a cop . . . that kind of thing. Two neighbors get into a sort of back-fence type thing . . . There have to be criminal laws to take care of this kind of thing, but so much of this is routine, small petty crime. Motor vehicle violations, you have a speeding case and another speeding case, and then you have a case where somebody got into a minor accident, and so he gets arrested, that's what I mean by all this minor garbage, and most of it is just minor stuff. [42]

> Well, we're dealing with cases primarily which are not that important, you understand that. Most of the cases . . . I hate to use the word, we use it all the time . . . we call them junk. It means of such minor . . . it was such a minor matter that the most you can say for it is that technically it happens, and so almost all of our business is in that category, and I could ponder on that for four hours, and it's just not worth it. [32]

> Usually in one of these Mickey Mouse cases . . . I use Mickey Mouse a lot because the whole place seems Mickey Mouse sometimes . . . [49]

"Garbage," "junk," "Mickey Mouse," "nickel-dime" cases furnish the grist for the circuit court plea bargaining mill. Dispositions are handed out quickly in the prosecutor's office or in front of the bench. For most of the cases in the circuit court, "plea bargaining" simply means the rapid determination by consensual agreement that the facts of a case dictate a certain disposition—be it a reduced charge, a nolle, a nolle of a few counts for a plea to one charge, and so on. The slot-machine theory of justice advanced by the mechanical jurisprudential school supposedly received its death blow at the hands of the legal realists. It appears, though, that the slot machine is alive and thriving in the circuit court.

Not all circuit cases—minor or serious—are resolved in this rapid slot-machine fashion. Some cases require more maneuvering, "shuffling," or as one attorney put it, "hustling."

> I'm a master of the circuit court. If I think a case should be ... oh I'm not a master ... but if I think a case can be beat, I'll hustle it through every judge, every prosecutor, every courtroom till I think it should fall. If it can't be beat, then it ... if it's going to be beat, it'll be beat by getting on the jury [jury trial list] and if they come down ... or ... put it on the court side [court trial list] or get the right prosecutor ... Yeah, ... I know what a case is worth, so I'll just play it until I get what I think it's worth. I'm so busy I can't even ... I don't even think of, you know, these things in their own whole terms anymore. [10]

Another private attorney with a very active circuit court practice echoed this view.

> *A*. You look [after an initial attempt at a deal failed] who's in there [prosecutor's office]. If it's ——, you got to sell him a legal answer ... you can't tell him his mother's a hell of a girl, he won't buy it. But now, if another prosecutor's in there, like ——, you know him? I mean, you know ——, he was in the building and I'd see him every day, we'd have cases together and I know how to sell ——. Or if it was ——, I'd always tell him about his father [a deceased prosecutor]. Jeez, he looks just like him. It's not that I'm picking on the kid, because I like him. He's a very capable kid, chomping at the bit over there. And there's this other guy, ——. He went to Wake Forest. I went to Carolina, and he's always giving me the Wake Forest shit, and I give him old North Carolina stuff. I talk to him about a case for a while and he still won't do anything. I tell him: "Hey, ——, I'm going over I'm going to file a motion and I'm going to work you to death." They don't care, really, in the —— Circuit, because they're [part-time prosecutors] not on the following week, and they don't see the case. What you eventually do, if you can't work it out, you put it on jury [list], then like it goes to bed. Sooner or later they'll call you and say come over and try it, and you go over and you might try it, or they'll settle ...
> *Q*. How about nolles that you can't get right off the bat?
> *A*. A husband-wife breach of peace, they're only too glad to nolle that, and sometimes you can come in with a good point of law, a bad search and seizure, or a bad arrest, and they'll nolle it. But they're not prone to nolle everything, you know, you've got to sell them a bill of goods. You've got to ... sometimes I'll say: "Hey look I've been ... for

> Christ's sakes, I've been in all week, you haven't given me one nolle." Or sometimes I'll go in and say: "Hey, I'm getting five hundred dollars for this one, I want a nolle." . . . They can work it out if they want to. They can twist that report around, and all arrests aren't that good either; the cops exaggerate. [36]

A circuit court prosecutor recounted the following incident as illustrative of the extent of hustling that takes place in the court.

> How about this one? When one of these private counsels will make up a case, right? To support his point, he'll say to the prosecutor: "I see you haven't heard of so and so versus so and so, 138 Conn 252?", and no case really exists . . . so, the prosecutor makes up one that overrules it. That's happened. [25]

Finally, the comments of one of Arborville's elite private practitioners suggest the ease with which a minor fine for a possession of marijuana charge can be obtained in the circuit court, and the more vigorous advocacy he relies on to secure a nolle or dismissal.

> *A*. Now I'm not talking about the sales to agents in superior court, there is damn little you can do with most of those. But I'm talking about possession [of marijuana] where they come in without a warrant, or with a warrant, and you're talking about all of the nit-picking crap, the Fourth Amendment. I can usually win it on the law somewhere or make it so unpalatable for the other side that they'll do something for me or because they want to do something for me . . . here's a nice kid, what the hell, he's a college kid.
> *Q*. But it's not in terms of a moderate disposition? It's a matter of not getting a record?
> *A*. A moderate disposition I can have at any time. The first thing I'll tell the fellow when he comes in is "Look, if you want to walk away from this for a fifty-dollar fine, you can hire any one of two dozen lawyers around here much cheaper than . . . you could probably go in there yourself and talk to the prosecutor without a lawyer and walk away with a fifty-dollar fine. If you want someone to take a real run at getting you off completely, that's the only thing you want to hire me for." On these I hang in there, and they know they're going to have grief with me, and sooner or later, one way or another, we walk away from those. Almost always, not always, but almost always . . . [37]

The complete range of options and resources (rewards/sanctions) available to the defense attorney—and to the prosecutor—in the mutual hustling, wheeling and dealing, and testing of commitments is extensive, and need not be considered here. The point is simply that if rapid disposition is not satisfactory, there remains much room in the circuit court for additional strategies aimed at achieving a desired result.

The Superior Court

Plea bargaining in the superior court is a less hurried and less sloppy process than in the circuit court. Lengthier discussions take place in the office of one of the assistant state's attorneys. The facts of the case as well as the defendant's background and prior record (if any) are more thoroughly reviewed. Less room for postplea-discussion "hustling" is available. Witness the remarks of the following attorneys, who practiced in both the circuit and superior courts.

> *Q*. In the superior court you plea bargain just like you do in the circuit court?
> *A*. No, no, all your cards are out on the table, it's not very much of a hustle, not a hustle at all . . . you don't prosecutor shop, there's a lot more at stake, it's totally different. It's like night and day. [10]

> I guess in the superior court you see the guy in his office, and you're alone, and there isn't a line out there, and I guess you're a bit more prepared for what you're doing, and it's more serious, so I guess there is a difference . . . In the circuit court, if you don't work something out, you just continue the case a number of times until you hit each prosecutor at least once in an effort to work something out. [33]

> In the superior court . . . when I get in to see a circuit court prosecutor . . . "How are you? When did you get laid last?" You know, talk about everything . . . "What have you got here?" You have the numbers of the files, he's reading them, you're reading them over his shoulder, right? And he'll say: "What do you want?" And you've made up your mind that you want . . . This one this, that one a nolle . . . You know, you're trying to confuse him, you're bullshitting him. In the superior court you don't do that. It's more at the upper level . . . and when you are in court you can't push a superior court judge as far as you can push a circuit court judge. They'll fine you, hold you you in contempt if you step out of line too far. [36]

The seriousness of the charges in the superior court case weigh against too heavy a reliance on pure gamesmanship. Delay and prosecutor shopping will only get you so far; the facts of the case will not disappear, and ultimately they will have to be confronted. Unlike the circuit court, in which "time," that is, a jail or prison sentence, is a rarity, "time" is what it is all about in the superior court.[33] This distinction is highlighted in the following comments by a prosecutor who worked in both the circuit and superior courts of Arborville, and by a defense attorney in the same community.

> In the circuit court we didn't get as involved in plea bargaining as heavily as

> we do in this court [superior court] because the offenses were of a minor nature and most people could go in, enter a plea of guilty without having discussed it with the prosecutor, knowing that the penalty in full would not be too heavy. [15]

> They expect you [in superior court] to be a forceful advocate in plea bargaining because they know for the most part if your client is convicted [in a trial] he's going to State's Prison. And there's no bullshit. In circuit court, they figure you're either playing with a suspended sentence or fine, and therefore, you know, you don't make a big deal out of it, and in many cases they may be right. But maybe that's why I like the superior court better. [25]

The single most important question, then, that state's attorneys and defense attorneys in the superior court confront in plea bargaining discussions is whether or not the defendant will have to "do time." If the answer is a mutual "no," but agreement exists on the defendant's guilt, the disposition of the case is a relatively simple matter; some combination of a suspended sentence and probation can be worked out with little difficulty. But "if you are talking time," negotiations become strained.[34]

To appreciate fully the importance of these negotiations concerning "doing time," one must be cognizant of the pattern of charging defendants in the superior court. I examined the files of 88 defendants in one superior court public defender's office and found that only 12 of these defendants were charged with a single count of a single offense. The remaining 76 defendants had a total of 288 charges leveled against them. This piling on of charges, when combined with mandatory five-year minimum sentences for offenses such as sale of heroin, and robbery with violence, and with repeated offender statutes, which double the exposure for the second offender in particular crimes, provide ample years for the state's attorney to "play with" in negotiations. In the superior court, then, "charge bargaining" becomes far less important than "sentence bargaining." Charges can be dropped without reducing the realistic range of years within which the defendant will be sentenced. For the most part, charge bargaining retains its significance only when a mandatory minimum sentence would be necessitated by a plea to a particular charge, or when the charge can be reduced from a felony to a misdemeanor. In almost all other situations, the state's attorney can appear to yield much in the way of charges without really giving much in the way of "time."[35] As one state's attorney noted:

> Look, if a guy is charged with robbery but will plead to assault what the hell difference does it make? It was in the same attempt, and it carried the same penalty. Quite often you can get three or four different offenses for the same facts. As long as the record has a description that fits factually with what happened ... Theft from person can be used in place of robbery as

> long as five years later someone can tell what the guy did, what do we care what we put him to plea on? Indecent assault can become risk of injury. There are a number of offenses that you put the facts into, and still have an appropriate record. Okay, we say, maybe it's not robbery, but assault. A lot of defendants don't want to plead to particular types of offenses—that's part of plea bargaining. [62]

With the exceptions already noted, sentence bargaining is the key to superior court plea bargaining. Unlike the circuit court, no atmosphere of bustle, turmoil, and of the assembly line permeates the discussion. Instead, discussions take place in the leisurely confines of the state's attorney's office (which, in contrast to its counterpart in the circuit courts, has thick, insulated walls). Pure hustling, slaps on the back, and so on, do not lead to an appreciably different result in sentencing. Certainly, a good rapport with the state's attorney does not inhibit the resolution process, but the facts of the case and the legal questions outstanding cannot be treated lightly, no matter how close the personal relationship.[36]

The agreement that emerges from the sentence bargaining can take several forms, all of which relate to what will, or will not, be said to the judge on sentencing day. The defense attorney and state's attorney may agree that the state's attorney will simply present the charges and read the facts but will not make any sentence "rec" (recommendation). This leaves the defense attorney free to make his "pitch" to the judge, and leaves the final sentencing decision up to the judge. A second pattern allows the state's attorney to make any "rec" he desires, and the defense attorney can again respond with his pitch. This is commonly employed when the state's attorney "gives a lot" on charge but refuses to budge on sentence. The third form of agreement on sentence is the "agreed rec." This is by far the most controversial form of sentence bargaining, and the one that best distinguishes among superior courts. In two of the superior courts, the "agreed rec" means that the state's attorney will not ask for more than a number of years specified in advance; the defense attorney remains free to "pitch" to the judge for less. The expectation is that the judge will almost never go above the state's attorney's recommendation, that he will most likely follow it, but that he may occasionally be swayed by the "pitch" and go below it. The "agreed rec" in the third superior court, however, has a somewhat different meaning. The state's attorney requires the defense attorney to agree to the "rec" he will make. Thus, the defense attorney simply "urges Your Honor to accept the state's recommendation"; and the judge, in the face of this mutual concurrence by the state and defense attorney, almost always rubber-stamps the agreement, despite the perfunctory though mandatory warnings he gives that he is not bound by any recommendation.[37] The difference in these two forms of the "agreed rec" are illustrated by the following comments by a superior court judge.

Q. How do defense attorneys feel about having the option to make a pitch?
A. Oh, they love it. They know they have an upper limit of three to five, let's say, so they can tell their client: "Well, the worst that can happen is three to five, but, I'm going to work on them, and by the time sentencing day comes I'll put on a big show for you and maybe get you down to one and a half or two to five." So sentencing in these counties is much more exciting than it is here . . . They bring in ministers and doctors and employers and they all testify . . . which I think is better because down here, as I told —— [the state's attorney] the other day: "You're just trying to make the judge a figurehead because they have nothing left to do but to go along with you like a lap dog."[38] [29]

On sentencing day (usually one day a week is set aside for sentencing), these various sentence agreements are presented in open court. In contrast to the circuit court, the courtroom is nearly empty, and the proceedings have a dignified aura about them. The courtrooms themselves correspond to the layman's notion of what halls of justice should look like, and the quiet and seemingly serious atmosphere surrounding the presentations of the central actors reinforces the idea that these are "real" courtrooms, rather than "sausage factories."[39]

The state's attorney speaks first, reviews the facts surrounding the offense, the charge (s), and, in the case of a sentence agreement, offers his sentence recommendation. With the defendant at his side, the defense attorney responds. His pitch varies, depending upon the facts of the case, the amount of time the defendant might receive, the defendant's prior record, the judge on the bench, and a host of other factors. [40] Generally, though, he stresses the futility of punishment per se, and emphasizes the need for rehabilitation of one sort or another. Addicts need drug programs; alcoholics, treatment at Connecticut Valley Hospital; youths, assignment to Cheshire Academy; other offenders, probation and close supervision. Occasionally, the defense attorney recognizes that the judge will give the defendant time, and to anticipate the judge's decision, he himself argues that some period in a "structured environment" might benefit his client. He stresses that this ought to be a short experience in which his client—already repentant—learns through reinforcement that crime does not pay.

The judge is the final actor to participate in this ceremony. He has heard the state's attorney and the defense attorney and has received the presentence report. The latter is a detailed account of the facts of the case, of the defendant's prior record, of his family situation, and so on. The presentence report is prepared by the probation department for felony cases, and is submitted in advance of sentencing day.[41] It provides the superior court judge with a wealth of data not available to the circuit court judge.

The judge's questions to the defendant concerning the voluntariness of the plea are also more detailed than in the circuit court.[42] Though judges vary in the manner in which they give "the warnings," for the most part, few judges omit any of the requisite questions. The extent to which the judge tries to insure that the defendant understands what the questions mean varies. Some will simply read the questions and nod in the defendant's direction when a "yes or "no" is required. Others go beyond the formal questions, adding explanations and clarifications. Regardless of the type of "warnings," the defendant invariably responds correctly; he was either coached in advance by his attorney or is coached as the questions are read.[43]

With the "record protected" through the issuance of these warnings, the judge is ready to pronounce sentence. He summarily reads his sentence aloud;[44] explanation of the rationale underlying the sentence is either absent from his remarks or is kept to a minimum.[45] The defendant is led away by one of the court officers, the defense attorney leaves the courtroom, and the state's attorney readies himself for the next case. Not infrequently, a recess is called after one or two sentencings have been completed.

A visitor to the superior court on sentencing day would probably be impressed with the proceedings, particulary if he had also observed circuit court sentencing. The leisurely proceedings, the well-maintained courtrooms, the legalistic aura, the detailed judicial questioning—all combine to create an impression of justice being dispensed equitably and with great care and consideration. This may or may not be true, and this is a question that we will have to address later. What ought to be made plain, though, is that there is more than a bit of charade to superior court sentencing day activities. State's attorneys indicated in their interviews that they have heard just about every imaginable "pitch" by a defense attorney, and predicted (correctly) that as my period of superior court observation increased, I, too, would be able to predict the attorney's presentation after hearing only a few of his words. Defense attorneys have a set number of sentencing appeals and they draw on these on sentencing day, embellishing them a bit, depending on the circumstances of the case. Essentially, however, they are the same old cloth pieced together into a slightly different final product. For the most part, the state's attorney can, and does, "turn off" the defense attorney's presentation; he is just less obvious about it than are his circuit court counterparts.

Similarly, the defense attorney, regardless of the amount of flourish and rhetoric employed in the "pitch," knows that often the sentence has already been agreed upon in negotiations with the state's attorney, or that the judge has already made up his mind, and, therefore, that these courtroom histrionics are for naught. The defendant and/or his relatives in court may be impressed, the visitor to the superior court may be impressed, but the judge and the state's attorney realize that the defense attorney is just playing his role in the courtroom drama. In the same fashion, the judge inquires whether any promises were made to the defendant (''correct'' response: ''no''), when he knows full well that the defendant probably received a promise in return for his plea.

Our hypothetical visitor probably comes away impressed by the drama and seriousness of superior court sentencing day. The court actors, though, know better; they know that this is merely a formal routine required by legal strictures, but one which has little bearing on case resolution. They know that the key decisions were made during the closed-door plea bargaining sessions and that on sentencing day these decisions are simply ratified. The pandemonium of the circuit court suggests that justice is meted out whimsically; the calm of the superior court does not necessarily mean that the process is different there.

4 Adapting to Plea Bargaining: Defense Attorneys

The adaptation of new defense attorneys is initially conditioned by the poor fit between reality and their expectations about the local criminal court. But these expectations are not unique to the defense attorney. All newcomers share certain basic assumptions. Let us begin by examining these newcomers and the shared beliefs they bring to their jobs.

The Newcomer Sample

Newcomers are defined as individuals with less than one year's experience in the criminal justice system. I chose one year as the cut-off point because it seemed that those with less than one year's experience saw themselves as still in the process of adjusting to the criminal justice system; those with more time seemed to feel that their period of adjustment was over.[1]

Table 9 lists by job the number of respondents fitting this newcomer definition. In all, fifteen subjects were new to their jobs and to the court.[2] Additionally, four individuals were new to their jobs but had more than a year's experience in the criminal justice system. The interviews with these "experienced" newcomers are important in providing data on adjustment to specific roles; the newcomer interviews provide data on both adaptation to the specific role and to the court in general. Finally, as discussed in chapter 2, data on adaptation were obtained by my asking court veterans to recall their experiences and from my own observations of newcomer behavior.

Law School Preparation

The newcomers have in common their professional status. They have all graduated from an accredited three-year law school and have passed the state bar examination. They are—in short—all lawyers. But what, if anything, does this tell us about their preparedness for practice in criminal courts?

Table 9 Distribution of Newcomers by Role in Court

Role	New to Job and to Criminal Court	New to Job but Prior Experience in Criminal Court
Circuit court prosecutor	3	1
Circuit court public defender	6	—
Circuit court judge	1	1
Superior court state's attorney	—	2
Superior court public defender	2	—
Superior court judge	2	—
Private defense attorney	1	—

Discussing the impact of law school education in general, Packer and Ehrlich note: "Law schools teach very little substance and offer perhaps even less 'how-to-do it' training; instead, they focus on various more general 'skills,' such as legal bibliographical research, legal reasoning, and 'thinking like a lawyer.' Moreover, today's law student is in no position during his years in law school to decide what area he would like to specialize in. Specialization begins only when the young attorney enters practice."[3] In the same vein, they sum up their assessment of the preparation provided by law school by stating: "The nature of legal education has been to train students in some basic fundamentals . . . only and . . . as a result the law school graduate generally is not competent to do *anything* very well. Experience is the real teacher of specific tasks . . ." [Packer and Ehrlich's italics][4] The failure of law schools, in general, to prepare their graduates adequately for specific jobs becomes a particularly acute problem when we turn to preparation for careers in the criminal court. Edward Levi has singled out preparation for criminal law as one area in which the law school has been notoriously remiss. "It has long been recognized that the criminal law and its operations have been insulated away from a large part of the bar. The insulation operates not only for the greater part of the bar, but for the law school as well."[5] These remarks suggest that the newcomer to the criminal court bears twin burdens. He suffers from the problems associated with an education qua generalist and, furthermore, enters a field given short shrift, at best, in law school. These contentions are overwhelmingly supported by my findings. Almost without exception, the respondents indicated that they were ill-prepared for their jobs by their law school education. Several illustrative comments follow.

> Any resemblance to law school is truly coincidental. There is no resemblance between the actual practice of law and what you learn in law school. [47]

> All law school taught me was how to think in a legal manner and how to research something to defend my argument. I never really learned the realities until I got here. [53]

What I consider to be the classic fault in our legal education is that we go through law school reading appellate cases. We really don't know the first fucking thing about a guy coming in and saying, "Look, I did this" and having to go over and negotiate for him, try a case for him, select a jury for him. We never got into this. [25]

I took one course in criminal law and . . . I had ——, who was a former editor of the Yale Law Review, and he didn't teach criminal law. He taught his version of Judy in the Sky with Glasses.[6] [51]

Well, first let me say this. The practice of the law is so completely different than what they teach you in law school, or what you see as a clerk for a judge.[7] It's astounding . . . it's really astounding. [55]

Newcomer Expectations

Newcomers shared several general expectations about what working in the criminal justice system would be like. They assumed that most cases would be treated with great care, would be thoroughly researched, and would be given lengthy and detailed consideration. In law school, they had been trained to dissect appellate cases; their briefs on legal cases were finely honed pieces undertaken only after extensive research and deliberation. As one judge put it, they had learned to have a "romance with each case."

> You have a romance with each case. You're interested in the legal aspects, you go up to the stacks, you go to this book, that book, the index of legal periodicals. You do this because you have a romance with each case. You rewrite, and each one means something. And as you write, you change your style, and you find that there is a phrase here, or a phrase there, it's creativity that you are in love with. Each appellate case, each line, each finding, each paragraph would mean something. [4]

Because of both substantive and procedural concerns, newcomers expected that their criminal court cases would require comparable time and effort. They assumed that disputable legal questions would characterize many of those cases.

> *Q*. Did you think that legal issues would be more important in terms of the criminal cases you would be handling?
> *A*. Well, I suppose, coming out of law school, you thought that justice . . . you know, we had some really good teachers; they talked about justice and the great principles of the Constitution to be upheld, and the great Fourth Amendment, and the Fifth, and the Sixth, and such. [13]

> On an abstract level, I thought, and this was a mistake, there would be a lot more constitutional law, and I anticipated that I would be working on

constitutional cases much more than has been the case . . . I guess I had this expectation from my appellate work. [56]

Probably, yeah, there are so few legal issues that actually come into play. You really would expect more, no matter how low your expectations were. [12]

Procedurally, newcomers assumed that they would be working in an adversary system. They were taught in law school that a Bill of Particulars and a Motion of Discovery were to be filed in every case. Essentially, these motions ask the prosecutor to disclose some of the evidence he has collected about the defendant and the offense. The motions are argued in a formal court hearing. New defense attorneys expected to file these motions; new prosecutors expected that the outstanding legal questions would be resolved in adversary hearings in which the appropriate motion was argued.[8] Again, they expected that filing and responding to these motions would take considerable time and effort. Finally, newcomers expected that a sizable percentage of their time in the trial court would be spent in trial. The following comments typify the newcomers' expectations that the system would be adversary in nature.

I think that you come out of law school filled with all kinds of ideas and notions of, you know, the lawyer being the gallant knight on the white horse and all this . . . [55]

In law school, of course, you're seeing Perry Mason. *The Defenders* were on when I was in law school . . . I suppose you have this feeling [as a defense attorney] that you are going to have the jury say not guilty, and walk your client out . . . [24]

A. I expected a great deal of competition from prosecutors on motions, and so on, and to say the least, I've been heartily disappointed.
Q. What do you mean by that? Let's focus on what you expected and what you found.
A. Right. Well, when I came in I was expected to really go in knowing the law. You either know the law or you don't go in . . . [45]

Q. Did you expect to find more trials?
A. Yes, I expected to practice law here.
Q. What did you expect the process to be like?
A. I expected it to look like what you see in television. I expected trials. I expected investigation of cases, presentation of cases, judges expounding brilliant jewels of wisdom. [3]

At first blush, it is difficult to fathom the degree of naiveté suggested in these remarks. The newcomers drew on television attorneys for their data about the practice of criminal law. Law school's contribution was technical (they learned the proper motions to file) and supportive of their television expectations (they read appellate cases dealing with legal issues raised at a trial). Newcomers remained largely ignorant about plea bargaining, despite its prevalence in the local criminal court. Some noted that they had "heard of plea bargaining" and that they had read a few cases about it. But for the most part, they tended to know very little about plea bargaining and to consider it either reflective of poorly motivated court personnel, or a necessary expedient of somewhat questionable propriety in crowded urban courts. The "real" practice of criminal law involved research on cases, motions, and trials.

The short shrift accorded criminal law in law school accounts for this lack of sophistication. Newcomers simply were not exposed in any systematic fashion to criminal trial courts. They were not forced to think rigorously about plea bargaining. Thus, when they came to the court, they held certain vague expectations about the criminal justice system, most of which comported quite closely with the ideal "fighting" model.[9]

These views can be clarified by reference to figure 3. The guilty/not guilty axis indicates newcomers' empirical expectations about the culpability of defendants in criminal courts. The disputable/nondisputable axis represents their assessment of whether or not a disputable question exists in a case. Finally, the trial/plea bargaining option is their evaluative judgment of how to proceed for each of the four options.

Figure 3. Theoretical Matrix of Newcomer Expectations

Expectations about Defendants' Guilt		Expectation of Disputable Issues: Disputable	Expectation of Disputable Issues: Nondisputable
	Guilty	1 Trial: Expects many cases in this cell	2 Plea Bargaining: Expects few cases in this cell
	Not Guilty	3 Trial: Expects many cases in this cell	4 Plea Bargaining Trial: Expects few cases in this cell

Newcomers assumed that a sizable percentage of criminal court cases fell in cells 1 and 3. They expected many disputable cases independent of their assessment of the defendant's guilt. New defense attorneys and new prosecutors differed in their expectations about the actual guilt of the defendant, but both agreed that many of the cases would be disputable. Furthermore, they felt that the trial was the appropriate means for resolving cell 1 and cell 3 conflicts.

The newcomer expected nondisputable cases to be the exception. For these cases, however, he felt that plea bargaining might be appropriate. The obviously guilty defendant could negotiate his case; the obviously innocent person could have his case dismissed or nolled. Plea bargaining could enter the system in these special circumstances.

If pressed, the newcomers also admitted that for a few exceptional cells 1 and 3 cases, plea bargaining could also be undertaken, particularly if the court's volume was high. But, generally, they felt that plea bargaining would be inappropriate in these two cells, and overall, they expected to engage only occasionally in plea bargaining.

Let me stress that newcomers did not formalize their expectations in this fashion; instead, they shared the rather simplistic formulations already presented. But it seems to me that newcomers implicitly assumed that most cases fell in cells 1 and 3. They expected disputable cases, and they felt that these ought to be resolved through adversary proceedings in the preliminary stages and by trials at the final stage. The following discussion of the adaptation of newcomers to the criminal justice system will indicate the extent to which these general expectations comport with the reality that the newcomers encounter.

The Adaptation Process: Introductory Comments

There are two ways we can now proceed. We can study the adaptation of all newcomers to the criminal justice system, lumping together prosecutors, defense attorneys, and judges; or, alternatively, we can discuss the adaptation of newcomers to specific roles in the criminal court. Costs and benefits can be assigned to each of these options. The former is more parsimonious, since there are a number of similarities in the adaptation process of each of the role incumbents. Also, this approach highlights the shared norms and folkways that are learned. However, by lumping together these role incumbents, continuity is sacrificed. We would be forced to qualify continually generalizations for different roles. I will therefore opt for the second approach; that is, I will discuss separately the adaptation of defense attorneys, prosecutors, and judges. Though some repetition will be unavoidable because of similarities in adaptation experiences, I think we will be able to get a better "handle" on the flavor and content of the adaptation process by discussing each role separately.

This is not to say that mention of prosecutors and judges will be anathema when discussing defense attorneys; indeed, the contrary is the case. One cannot realistically deal with one role without treating the others. As Skolnick observed: " . . . one of the pitfalls of studying the administration of criminal law from the point of view of only one of the institutional participants is that the analyst may fail to see the possibilities of reconceptualization."[10] We will, then, treat the role incumbents other than the ones under study as veterans and focus on how the newcomer deals with them. Then when we move to another role, we will simply reverse our analytical framework.

Defense Attorney Adaptation: Early Experiences

The new defense attorney brings to the court expectations of doing battle with prosecutors. He ends up plea bargaining most of his cases. Why? What is it about working as a defense attorney in the criminal court that leads the idealistic newcomer to end up a seasoned plea bargainer?

The answers are as complex as the adaptation process itself. The newcomer learns that the raw material he works with—that is, the defendants and their cases—differs from what he expected. He is also taught that certain penalties are attached to being an adversary in the criminal court. He learns how to evaluate a case; he is taught that certain practices which he expected to be routine are verboten, except in the most unusual of circumstances. He learns, and is taught, to plea bargain.

The distinction between learning and teaching is an important one. Newcomer adaptation must be understood as a mix between the newcomer's learning about a previously misconceptualized environment (or an environment which he had not thought about) and his being taught through rewards and sanctions the way to proceed in this environment. It is true, as we will shortly see, that the system encourages plea bargaining and that it backs up its encouragement with some powerful rewards. But even without these rewards and sanctions, it is likely that the new attorney would eventually opt for plea bargaining in at least some of his cases.

The newcomer rarely conceives of his adaptation in this fashion. He enters the court, anxious about his own inexperience and expecting that most cases will go to trial. His anxiety is increased by the absence of any formal socialization program. Indeed, not even a printed handout on the basics of court procedure is available. The private attorney attempting to establish his own practice relies on observation of the court (he has the time, since clients are not flooding his office) and on grabbing bits and pieces of information from any and all court personnel who will speak with him. The following exchanges illustrate the private attorney's initial problems.

> *Q*. Let's talk a little about your earlier years. When you started getting cases, how did you know what to do with them?
> *A*. I didn't. I didn't, and I found when I first started practice . . . I didn't know how to handle it. I'd go over and watch, or I'd go over and ask some other lawyer and say: "What do you do with this? It's a breach of peace." And you go up and talk to a prosecutor. You didn't know how to handle it, but what I used to do—I had time—I used to go in and sit and watch the other lawyers practicing . . . and how they worked it. You'd watch their results. [36]

> *Q*. You mentioned earlier that it's kind of hard when you don't have other attorneys in the office?
> *A*. Right, I had to learn everything from scratch. I had to sit down and get into the rules of practice and everything, and I didn't have anyone to rely on. And in things such as . . . court procedure that you don't find in the books, not the judge's procedures but the clerk's office, things like that drive you crazy. They have certain ways of doing things, and if you don't have it all together, say well . . . Trial and error, believe me. [45]

> *Q*. I am very interested in that early period. You learn by . . .
> *A*. Well, you learn by, you've got a lot of time to sit down and learn, but you don't know, you know nothing, for example, about plea bargaining. You don't know anything about it, and you have to speak to the prosecutor before a case. This is all new, speak to what prosecutor? What do you speak about? I don't know, this is what someone told me. Why don't you go see the prosecutor in this one, and discuss the case. So you go, but you're unaware of this. This is totally new. [47]

Public defenders may have an advantage over the private practitioners in this regard. They can, in principle, discuss cases with their experienced colleagues. One public defender, new to the court at the time of my interview, outlined his plans.

> Well, what I've talked over doing with the other fellows is at least for the first few weeks or so, is sit down with one of them probably——[the chief public defender] as much as I can and show him what I have on a case, what I may think about it, what the defendant says about it, what the police report says about it, and get his ideas about what options he feels are viable, and then discuss the way I have been thinking about it, and see what his thoughts are on the way I've been thinking about it. It's the only way you can do it, I think. [2]

However, another public defender in the same office suggested that this newcomer's expectation of institutionalized assistance would not be met.

Q. Has the office told you to do things in a certain way?
A. No, quite the contrary. My instructions were: "We're all attorneys and you handle the case any way you want to handle it, at your complete discretion." Just right on, brother, and good luck.
Q. Would you perhaps have liked more assistance?
A. Sure, I'd love it. Every time I see a book on search and seizure or anybody that's knowledgeable in the field, I sit right down and talk to them or read it.
Q. You kind of had to grab for bits and pieces?
A. Right. Well, not so much the law . . . But any time I can meet anybody with any knowledge of dealing, or the system, I just sit them down, you know, if I have the opportunity, and talk to them. [53]

The veteran public defender more accurately gauged the assistance (or lack of planned assistance) that the newcomer receives. Public defenders are quickly given full responsibility for cases, and the experience, especially in the circuit court, is often quite overwhelming.

Q. Could you describe what happened the first few days on the job?
A. I was scared shitless. If the guy had pled guilty, I argued mitigation. This is what the other public defenders were doing. When a guy was not guilty, I set it down for a jury trial . . . I didn't know anything about juries: How it goes? Where it goes? Sometimes I asked for a court trial. I didn't know . . . I was getting shit on so bad it was ridiculous. I was looking really bad. I was getting chopped down. I just had the courage to stand there, and even when I didn't know what the procedure was—and the prosecutor said: "This is what's done; this is what is not done." I just spread my legs apart and just stood there and I took it and I learned . . . I just didn't have the time to keep up and research this volume of cases that I had. You try and interview these people. You just try and keep those files straight. Appointments were being made, and the public defender was appointed when you weren't even there and you didn't even know you had a case. You'd have to run down to the clerk's office at the end of the day, go through all those cases to find out what cases you had. They would appoint a public defender when you weren't even there; they do it today sometimes. I'd go nuts just trying to find out who I was representing, never mind studying the law. [3]

Q. Could you describe what happened the first few days on your job? What are your most vivid recollections?
A. I wanted to quit. I think the first day wasn't too bad because I didn't really do anything, I was just wandering around. ——was the only other attorney here at the time. I think the second and third day, in the morning, I went downstairs. ——had cases upstairs. I was all alone. I don't remember who the judge was, no one very bad. Then they started passing cases for the public defender, and I started running around and trying to fill out the applications, and they were pulling the cases up before I was

> done, setting bond. I was just . . . my head was swimming. I was extremely depressed and I . . . I just wanted to say, "This can't go on. You can't do it like this." [7]

These comments convey a sense of the public defenders' and private attorneys' initial impressions of the court. Ironically, the private attorney has the time to discuss cases with others, but often is hard put to find someone to assist him. Public defenders, on the other hand, have experienced colleagues but do not have time to avail themselves of their advice. Both public defenders and private attorneys feel lost, confused, uneasy, surprised, distressed, and ineffective.

Thrust into the world of the local criminal court, newcomers essentially react in one of two ways. Some attempt to proceed in accordance with their expectations, adopting a full-fledged adversary posture.

> In my first case, my gosh, I filed something like a twenty-five-page motion for production and inspection with a fifteen-page brief, and they looked at me, you know, like what are you doing? What's going on? [45]

> *Q*. What predisposed you to go in and try a case or enter a plea of abatement when you could have stood on that line and got a twenty-five-dollar fine for breach of peace?
> *A*. Because in law school they didn't teach us about that kind of shit. All I had was my old law school professor saying: "You go in there and you file this and you file that, and you raise this issue and . . . [31]

> I got burned a number of times [when new] because I'd jumped into cases, you know, when I really wasn't prepared. I wanted to try everything. [25]

This stance promotes the perception common among court veterans, that the new attorney is an unrealistic idealist.

> *Q*. Are there any important differences between new attorneys and attorneys who have been around awhile?
> *A*. A lot of them [new attorneys] are very confident fellows who are not going to put up with crap from anyone. A lot of them come in like real battlers. [52]

> A lot of these kids . . . We've always felt that they come in just out of law school, and they don't really know what it's all about . . . come in with the idea that, this attitude, that all our clients are innocent, and we're gonna charge off on a white steed and tilt all kinds of windmills. [24]

> The new attorney sees his case as if it is the only one, and his defendant shouldn't be "sold out" by his attorney. They are not being realistic. [56]

> They're out of law school; they were told by books or professors or somebody else, "Here are the motions you've got to file to protect your client's rights," and this is their indoctrination. They don't know any better. They've never been to court with work, and they don't want to make any mistakes. They don't want people calling them incompetent, and they think this is what they have to do to do a good job, and it's not necessarily true. [15]

Other newcomers lack the confidence to file motions and set cases down for trial. They agree with their more forceful peers that this is how one ought to proceed, but, concerned over their own inexperience, they opt tentatively for a more conservative tack. They choose to go along until they build up their own confidence. In a way, they want to extend their period of adaptation. Given the pot-luck quality of assistance they receive, they feel they need more time before striking out forcefully on their own.

> *Q*. At first you didn't want to try [a case] because ...
> *A*. Let's say I was reluctant to try a case, not that I wouldn't try a case ... But, whereas today I wouldn't try a case because I know simply more about the practice of law, in the beginning, my reluctance to try a case was my fear. All right. Because I was afraid ...[11] [55]

> I think part of it is I feel my lack of experience. I think that's one factor. I realize I don't have a great expertise in criminal law. And where some people may say: "Go ahead and file all these motions and fight on every ground," I don't want to do that till I'm sure of where I'm stepping and what I'm doing. When I file a motion I want to make sure I know what the grounds are and I've done the research for it. [7]

The differences between these two styles ought not be exaggerated. Both groups of defense attorneys share a preference for an adversary approach, and both also recognize their own inexperience. The differences are more a matter of degree than kind, and probably are best understood as a function of the individual's personality. In any event, seasoned court personnel tend to assume that all new defense attorneys fit the first style, and their efforts to educate the new defense attorneys reflect this assumption. Though the adversary actions of the more aggressive attorney may bring him into conflict with established court personnel at an earlier stage, his cautious peer will eventually receive the same messages.

Learning about the Defendant's Guilt

In the process of handling their cases, new defense attorneys learn that the reality of the court differs from what they had expected; through rewards and sanctions, they are also taught to proceed in a certain fashion. This is the point

I emphasized at the outset, one that I now want to develop more systematically. A degree of artificiality characterizes what follows, for I will sort what is learned and what is taught, and discuss them separately. In point of fact, newcomers are thrust into the court and have neither the time nor the awareness to separate these educational phenomena. Nonetheless, I think greater clarity ensues if we treat these separately and sequentially, bearing in mind, though, that the adaptation process is not as "neat" as the discussion suggests.

The most important thing the new defense attorney learns is that most of his clients are factually guilty. His raw material is not typically the railroaded innocent defendant; instead, it is an individual who, in all likelihood, is guilty as charged, or at least is guilty of an offense related to the charge.

> *Q*. Are most of the people you defend guilty?
> *A*. Of something. Yeah.
> *Q*. That's one of the things that surprised me. Did you expect that?
> *A*. I think in a sense it did surprise me. I expected there would be more opportunity to argue about guilt . . . and there isn't very much opportunity. [57]

> *Q*. So factually you are saying most people are guilty?
> *A*. They are guilty, but some don't feel guilty in their own sense. In their own community . . . breach of peace with their wife for them is like when you have an argument with your wife, but their arguments involve violence, cuttings.
> *Q*. Coming from law school, and you say you wanted to do trials, did this . . .
> *A*. Oh, it hurts, it hurts. Sure, it's like wanting to race cars and you're stuck in a VW. You want to race Ferraris but you're putting VW's together . . . but you do the best you can. [53]

Newcomers have difficulty coming to grips with the factual culpability of most defendants. They begin their jobs with a vague notion that "many" defendants are innocent. After several months in the system, they offer estimates that about 50 percent are guilty. The figure contrasts with the 90 percent estimate given by almost all experienced defense attorneys. It takes time for the newcomers to learn about, to accept, and to be comfortable with the factual guilt of their clients.

They learn of the defendant's guilt in several ways. Attorneys with primarily circuit court practices handle mostly misdemeanants. These clients often perceive their own cases to be relatively minor, and they frequently and freely admit their guilt during the first or second meeting with the attorney. As we shall see shortly, they are more concerned about "getting it over with" than with disputing their own guilt. Thus, one way defense attorneys learn of the factual culpability of the defendant is simply from the defendant himself.

In superior court cases, defendants are less likely to own up to the offense in their initial contact with the defense attorney. Experienced defense attorneys posit that the defendant's reluctance is based on the belief that a defense attorney will work harder for a client that he assumes innocent. Whatever the explanation, the defendant at first offers a story that exculpates him. The newer the defense attorney, the more likely he is to believe the defendant's version of what happened. It is only when he confronts the state's attorney with the defendant's story that he learns that there is more to the matter than the defendant first led him to believe.

> As you go into the facts more and more they [the defendants] change their stories. The first time their stories are very different from the police report. You hear things like "I never said that" . . . that is very common. We are supposed to take the facts as they give them to us. But then the state's attorney gives us more information, and we tell the defendant the state's claim. We find then that they "omitted" certain features of the case. You keep talking the case over with them, and get closer and closer to what actually happened. [60]

Sometimes the defendant maintains his innocence even in the face of the state's evidence. Again the newcomer is more likely to believe the defendant, and again he is likely to be disappointed.

> I used to believe anything anybody told me, and I'd be representing some guy, and he would be telling me: "I'm not guilty, I'm not guilty." I'd feel out the state's attorney and find that he'd offer some reduced charge or low sentence or a suspended sentence, and he'd [the defendant] jump at it. It would bother me. I'd say, "Well Jesus, the guy is pleading guilty and he is not guilty; he shouldn't be doing that." Then I would get the presentence report, and I'd look up the offender's version of the offense, and the guy would be telling the probation officer what he did, how he committed the crime, and so on . . . Now I listen to everybody with more of a jaundiced eye, or grain of salt, or something. [22]

Skepticism in evaluating the defendant's story, then, is something new attorneys learn. Over time they become veritable cynics.

> Yeah, well, you know . . . the first year you practice law you believe everything your client tells you. The second year you practice, you believe everything that the other side tells you. The third year you don't know who's telling the truth. Most people tend not to believe their clients that much, justifiably. [11]

> I've gotten more cynical, insofar as I am less gullible than I used to be, and I'm less apt to rely on what they [the defendants] have told me, but by the same token, I'm a little less cynical, in that it doesn't bother me that much. I don't expect that much from them as individuals, so I don't get so excited at them . . . [3]

The point to stress here is that defense attorneys learn that most of their clients are indeed factually guilty. The newcomer's naiveté in believing the defendant's claim of innocence is replaced by cynicism. The defense attorney realizes that it is his lot to begin with defendants who are, in all probability, factually guilty.

In our system, however, factual guilt and legal guilt are not necessarily the same thing. To say that most defendants are factually guilty is not to say that the state can establish this guilt in court. At each step of its investigation, police and prosecutors are bound by legal strictures. Searches, confessions, lineups, and so on, must be conducted in a prescribed fashion. Absent adherence to these formal rules, the evidence obtained is inadmissible in court, and once excluded can render the state's case unprovable. Though the individual may be factually guilty, he may be set free because the state failed to comply with the rule of law.

As we have seen, newcomers expect that many of their cases will be characterized by these disputable legal issues. They believe that cases can be won or lost on the basis of their own legal acumen. Again, they learn that the reality differs from their expectations.

Statistical estimates vary, but experienced defense attorneys agree that of the approximately 90 percent of the defendants who are factually guilty, most have cases devoid of any legally disputable issue. These cases, as one defense attorney phrased it, are "born dead." (37) The defendant is factually guilty and has few avenues for legal challenge.

> We make an initial determination of what's needed to complete the file. I suppose what I'm saying is we make a determination whether we've got a defense, and many times we don't. When somebody's apprehended in the midst of a break, caught in a store or a house, you have to go some to explain what you're doing there at two or three o'clock in the morning. We get a fair number of these. If you are apprehended fleeing the scene of the crime, you are going to be hard pressed to explain why he's running away from the scene . . . [23]

> I'm not going to try a case where, as I told you in the beginning, the state usually has you right by the . . . in nine out of ten cases they . . . as I said, your client, generally he's guilty, they usually have the evidence. [38]

In an attempt to check whether actual cases fit these descriptions, I reviewed the files of eighty-eight defendants represented by the public defenders of one of the superior courts. Though it is difficult to develop criteria for evaluating whether or not the state has a strong case, my overall impression of these files comported with what the respondents indicated. In many of the cases, the defendant was simply caught red-handed, or a codefendant was prepared to testify against him, or the defendant had sold heroin to an undercover agent without any evidence of entrapment in the record, and so on. There did not appear to be much the defense attorney could do to win the case.[12]

The newcomer, then, learns two unexpected things about the cases he is assigned. Most of the defendants are factually guilty and have no legal grounds to challenge the state's evidence. These are aspects of the reality of the local criminal court that the defense attorney learns about, independent of any rewards or sanctions.

It is only after the newcomer has worked in the court for several months or longer that he is able even to begin to characterize his cases in this fashion. Time constraints are such that he does not have the time to ponder their nature. Many decisions have to be made, many strategies have to be decided upon, many choices about how to proceed have to be considered, and these all converge upon him at once. To complicate things further, the rewards and sanctions of the local criminal court are also brought into play.

Testing the Adversary Position: Preliminary Motions, Legal Motions, and Trials

At the same time that he is learning piecemeal about the factual culpability of most defendants and the futility of legal challenge, the new defense attorney is forced to decide how to proceed in given cases. His options are twofold: he can opt for an adversary posture (motions and trials), or he can engage in plea bargaining. These are not unrelated; the sanctions of the former approach contrast with the rewards attached to plea bargaining. He is taught the risks of being an adversary and the benefits of being a plea bargainer.

His education begins almost immediately. In every case the defense attorney needs certain information that the prosecutor possesses. This material includes the police report, the defendant's record, the basic facts of the case, and so on. As indicated earlier, there is a formal way to obtain some of this material—through filing a Motion for Discovery and a Bill of Particulars. The new defense attorney assumes that these motions are in order in every case. What he is taught, though, is that the prosecutors resent these motions. Prosecutors prefer to communicate the information orally and informally, thus relieving themselves of the burden of preparing typewritten responses in every case. Since they assume that the case will be settled by a plea bargain, they feel a formal response to be an unwarranted waste of time. A secondary concern of the prosecutor is that by not having to reply formally, the facts of the case are not "frozen." This is to say that once the prosecutor responds to a Bill of Particulars or Motion for Discovery, he is bound by the facts given in his response. Thus, if there was an error in his file, or if in the process of responding to the motion an error was made, an astute defense attorney could later use this as grounds for dismissal of the case.

The hostility of prosecutors and judges to these time-consuming motions is communicated to the new defense attorney. First, the prosecutor or judge may simply call the defense attorney into his office and explain that the motions are needless formalities. If this advice is insufficient to dissuade the newcomer, sanctions such as ''hassling'' the attorney by dragging the case out over a long period of time, closing all files to the attorney, and even threatening to go to trial on the case, ensue. The following remarks, by circuit and superior prosecutors respectively, illustrate the hostility to these motions, and the sanctions that are brought to bear.

> And then we have the open-file policy for public defenders. They can look at all the files they want. There was a time when some new public defenders started filing Bills of Particulars. Now, if I am going to show you all my notes, why would you file a Bill of Particulars? If they hassle us like that, close the files to them. Let them file their bills, and we'll argue the Bill of Particulars. Don't forget, they've got ten cases here and ten cases upstairs, and they've got to run up and down those stairs. Me, I'm in this one courtroom. I call the names, and I argue them. You know what I mean? So, they hassle you like that . . . Same with private attorneys. There is an easy way and a hard way for them to get their fees. One way you can make the lawyer earn his fee; the other way you can have the lawyer come in, grab his thing, and run. If he wants to be a ballbreaker, I say, ''File your motions, pal.'' He has to file a Bill of Particulars, and then he'll have to come back to argue it. Then if he wants to put in a not-guilty plea to the jury, he comes back again. He comes back, and I say, ''Oh, we have a case going on. You'll have to come back next week.'' So this guy is a private attorney, and he's running around trying to make money. He doesn't want to come to our court ten times for a lousy case. And with the public defenders, we control the docket in court, so you hassle them. You know, call one case, the guy upstairs runs downstairs, and back and forth. It's like a kid's game, but you know, I like to get along with people if I can, and I don't try to be obnoxious to people, but if a person hassles me, tries to make my life more difficult, I will make his more difficult. [9]
>
> *Q*. How about new attorneys? How do you establish . . .
> *A*. Well, what I try to tell every new attorney who comes in, because I was in the same boat once . . . I try to ''steer them straight.'' I'll call them in on the first case we're dealing with and say: ''Look, there are two ways to practice law here. You can file all the motions you want, harass me any way you want, but you and your client in the long run are not going to gain anything. Or, do you want to come in, I'll tell you what my file has, I'll show you what my file has, and we can talk about the case. It's your choice.'' Now, he may give me a hard time the first or second time around, but, you know, the aggravations can be going both ways, and eventually most people come to the point where they'll prefer to sit

> down and see what I have rather than go into court and make a big production of everything.

> *Q*. Let's say he does it the way that hassles you, and then he later comes in and wants to negotiate the case?
> *A*. Well, you know, let's face it, we're all human, and you may be tempted to say . . . Well, if it was a case that you would have settled for three to five [years] eventually, you may say: "All right, five to ten." If he doesn't want it, you will go on trial, and you know this attorney is scared to death to go to trial. He doesn't want to go to trial, and so you're shaking him up a little, and maybe it's a lesson you teach him. "Look, you've harassed me, now you're going to be harassed because I'm telling you, you're going to have to go to trial on the case. Number one, you can't win. Number two, you're really not prepared to try." [15]

A new public defender in Arborville's circuit court relates below the pressures not to file a Bill of Particulars and a Motion for Discovery that were brought to bear on him by prosecutors and judges.

> That happened again last week, myself and —— [a prosecutor]. I filed a motion for a Bill of Particulars, and right away he says: "You don't get to look in any files; you don't get to look in any files while I'm here." And when I asked him a question later, on another case or something, he said: "File your motion. You want to file a motion, file your motion. You don't get to see anything." They really try to intimidate you in many ways. Certain prosecutors try to intimidate you as if to say, "Don't you get near us with a motion or we're going to flex our muscles." [7]

> *A*. I went up to introduce myself to the judge, and there were some other attorneys in there. I don't remember, what did we talk about? There was no specific case or anything, but the judge said: "Well, we'll see you tomorrow and, well, just play along with everyone else. Don't file a lot of motions. The prosecutors are all good people, and you'll get good dispositions. Don't mess around like those legal-aid attorneys, filing all their motions. Don't file a lot of motions and don't make a lot of noise."
> *Q*. Does that make you reluctant to file motions in front of him?
> *A*. It made me mad, but I just was not in a position to say anything. Three or four attorneys were all there shaking their heads, private attorneys. One of them bragged that, "I've been here eight years and never filed a motion." What are you going to say to the judge, you know? [7]

Prosecutors and judges attempt to instill an antipathy to motions early in the new defense attorney's career. The Bill of Particulars and Motion for Discovery are not in and of themselves particularly difficult to respond to, but were all attorneys to file these motions, a tremendous amount of work would be generated. Thus, prosecutors try to demonstrate that informal cooperation leads to greater benefits and that persistence in filing even these rather minor motions can lead to numerous sanctions.

In situations where attorneys continue to file these motions in quantity, and/or where they also file motions challenging the arrest, the search, the jurisdiction of the court ("legal motions"), the sanctions brought to bear become more severe. Simple harassing of the defense attorney is replaced by an unwillingness to show him any files, by a refusal to plea bargain in any cases, and by a real threat to go to trial in every case. The sanctions escalate because the sheer number of motions presents a real threat to the prosecutor's and judge's time; and the quality of the motions, that is, complex challenges on legal questions, necessitates research by the prosecutor and separate court hearings presided over by the judge. The following exchange with a circuit court prosecutor details the initial unwillingness of a new attorney to desist from filing motions, the prosecutor's subsequent refusal to plea bargain in any of the attorney's cases, and finally, the prosecutor's offer of an extraordinarily good deal to this very same attorney in an attempt (successful) to prove the virtues of cooperation.

Q. You said these fellows change. That's interesting. That's what I'm interested in. They come out of law school, and they're these great advocates, and somehow they come to realize that's not how the system should operate?
A. That's because the realities of the situation begin to crowd in on them. This young fellow I was telling you about. I sat down one day. I'm old enough to be his father. I met him socially, a personable young man. This occurred to me one morning. I came in and found motions this high, literally, and I knew I didn't have the time nor the interest to read them, and so I sat him down and said to him: "If you want to make money in the practice of criminal law, you're never going to do it by filing motions. If you have a reasonable defense in a case, you tell me what it is; you don't have to file a single motion with me. I'll dispose of the case. And if you don't have a reasonable defense, but it's a question of penalty, then I'm perfectly willing to talk to you about that, too. All you do when you file motions like that is that you get my back up. I'm immediately antagonistic, and the reason for that is self-preservation, because if every lawyer who handles criminal cases in this court were to do this to me I could never get my job done, so I have to do everything I can to discourage you from doing this.
Q. What was his reaction?
A. He went right on. So finally one day he really got the treatment from me.
Q. You mean you were less likely to negotiate with him?
A. I didn't even want to talk to him. I wouldn't bargain with him. I would not discuss anything with him. So finally we were down to the wire one day here, going to try some cases, and he says to the judge and me . . .

> the judge was trying to resolve some of the cases on a plea bargain basis . . . "You know, I sit here in this courtroom and I watch the prosecutor change that charge and nolle another, and the prosecutor's office doesn't offer anything to me. I think they've got it in for me." And I said: "That's exactly what happened."
> *Q*. Did he start switching then?
> *A*. He was making a lot of noise about wanting to try these cases, that he wasn't interested in plea bargaining. I offered him a deal—I shouldn't say deal—I offered him a disposition that I thought would be attractive to him and his client, and since then we've been able to work things out a lot better. [42]

I witnessed a similar lesson being taught a "brash" new attorney insistent upon filing preliminary motions in every case and raising legal challenges at every turn. I had interviewed this attorney the previous day, and he reported that he had encountered numerous harassing ploys in response to his filing motions. He also admitted that he had become less brash about his actions, recognizing that the motions were incurring the collective wrath of court personnel.

The morning after our interview, I was in the state's attorney's office arranging a follow-up interview. Into the office walked this very same new attorney, armed with a Bill of Particulars, a Motion for Discovery, and three motions challenging the search of his client, arrested only two days before for sale of marijuana. The attorney, having already been taught that his motions would not be met with shouts of glee, presented them to the state's attorney in an almost apologetic fashion. He mumbled several times that he was filing them "just to protect the record." The state's attorney picked up the motions, glanced at them, and then turned to his audience (a county detective, a secretary, and me), proclaiming: "Look at this, Latin stuff, blah, blah, blah. A person can't even read this stuff, all these words. It's like Adlai Stevenson. No one can read this and understand it." His performance for the audience completed, he turned to the new attorney and announced, "I'm going to trial on this case." By now the attorney was even edgier. "I'm doing this just to protect the record," he said. "I just need some information." The state's attorney turned to the county detective, ordering him to get the file. In contrast to the innumerable other interactions between the state's attorney and defense attorneys that I had witnessed, this one did not involve the state's attorney's showing the file to the attorney. He glanced at it briefly and told the attorney the charge, the defendant's age, and the defendant's home address. This was the only information he divulged.

With a rather smug expression on his face, he called me over to his side. "See what I mean. This is the new breed" [meaning the new attorneys he had been telling me about who insisted on filing motions]. The unfortunate victim of this hostility, the attorney, was now extremely uncomfortable, mumbling over and over that he just wanted to talk to the state's attorney. The state's attorney continued to ignore his pleas, however, repeating his threat about going to trial on the case. It was plain that he was enjoying his little show, enjoying belittling the motions, enjoying his show of power, enjoying the discomfort of the defense attorney. Eventually he indicated that he might consider speaking with the attorney at some later time; the attorney, chastened and thankful, humbly thanked him and beat a quick retreat. Subsequent conversations with him indicated that he had indeed learned a lesson.

Though these sanctions (and the rewards associated with cooperation) move many a new attorney away from the adversary direction, some persist in acting out their expectations by raising motions and trying cases. Regardless of the pressure they encounter, they insist on filing the motions and in setting cases down for a trial. Again, they are taught that this avenue—trials—has serious sanctions attached to it. Specifically, the newcomer is taught one of the central norms of the local court: there is a penalty attached to going to trial and losing; conversely, there is a reward accorded the defendant who forsakes his right to trial and pleads guilty.

Several explanations for this reward/penalty are set forth by court personnel. Some argue that the defendant who pleads guilty saves the state the time and expense of a trial, and thus is entitled to a reward. Others argue that pleading guilty is the first step in the defendant's rehabilitation, and that this ought to be recognized by a shorter sentence. Proponents of this argument contrast the contrite defendant admitting his guilt with the recalcitrant accused who insists upon a trial and then is found guilty. The latter refuses to own up to his complicity in the crime, perhaps perjures himself if he takes the stand, and all in all deserves a more severe sentence for rehabilitative purposes.

An additional argument justifying the reward for pleading guilty revolves around the proposition that in every case there is the possibility of acquittal at trial. In many cases this may be a remote possibility, but, nonetheless, juries can be unpredictable. The defendant who pleads guilty sacrifices his chance for acquittal and deserves a reward for not gambling on the jury. If he insists on a trial and is found guilty, he gives up nothing and deserves nothing in return. Thus, under this formulation, he is not being penalized for trial, but simply is not being rewarded for forsaking possible legal issues.[13]

A final explanation for the penalty for trial revolves around the judge's aversion to being reversed on appeal. To hear critics develop this argument, judges hate nothing more than to be reversed; therefore, they pressure for a plea, which, in turn, precludes the necessity of deciding potentially reversible issues during a trial. The judges justify their reward for a plea by pointing to the benefits for the system in having the defendant admit his guilt, without the option of subsequent appeals. The appellate courts are saved time and expense; the defendant does not spend his prison time planning appeals; and finally, because he has admitted his guilt, and the case is closed, he can begin on the road to rehabilitation.

It is not necessary for us to evalutate these arguments at this point. For our present purposes, it is sufficient to note that the new defense attorney is taught to believe that there is a penalty attached to going to trial. Whether or not such a penalty actually exists is a question that we will address in chapters five and six; the point here is that the newcomer *perceives* that there is a penalty extracted for trials.

Most attorneys first hear about the penalty from their peers, for it is unlikely that the newcomers are actually involved in trials immediately. The following two exchanges with attorneys working in the court for only a few months are illustrative.

> *Q*. Some people say that if the defendant goes to trial he'll receive a more severe sentence.
> *A*. Yeah. That has not happened to me yet, but from everyone I've spoken to, it seems to be common knowledge that if someone is convicted after a trial, that the judges, in their sentencing, tend to remember the fact that this person was probably offered a good deal, or a deal, earlier on in the proceedings, and they have put the state to a great expense, kept the jury . . . I've heard from other attorneys that very often a judge will take that into consideration and be more harsh on someone after a trial than he would be if he'd pled guilty without a trial. I can't speak from personal knowledge about that. I haven't gotten to it yet.
> *Q*. But that's kind of your apprehension about taking cases to trial . . .
> *A*. It's something I take into consideration. Not just the penalty but the charge also. If he's charged with a felony and they offer a misdemeanor, and you go to trial on the felony . . . [7]

> *Q*. Let's say you are offered a misdemeanor by the prosecutor . . .
> *A*. Oh, you mean after you . . . Yeah, yeah, then they go the maximum. If you go to trial, then it's the original charge and they ask for the maximum penalty.
> *Q*. How do you know that?
> *A*. I just know it from hearsay, what I've been told. Well, generally, you know, if I were a prosecutor, and I'd offered you a deal on something, and you wouldn't take it, well, fuck you. If you are going to go, go, go all the way. I mean I can't see a lawyer doing anything half-ass. If he's going to go, he's going to go [that is, if the prosecutor is going to go to trial]. It's a lot of preparation for him; it's bringing witnesses in. I think the judges feel that way also. The jury list is long; the amount of time required for a trial is phenomenal; and the administration costs . . . You know, they figure we're no longer going to give anybody a break. We're just going to give them whatever the facts merit. [53]

When an atttorney's case finally reaches trial, he is taught firsthand about the pressures the judge brings to bear to encourage a plea of guilty. In the examples that follow, defense attorneys report that judges called them into chambers and threatened to give their clients higher sentences if those clients did not accept the prosecutor's offer, or the judge's compromise offer. The experience left the newcomer bitter.

> Oh yeah. This case that I started; about five times, at least five times during the course of picking the first six jurors, the judge called me up to the bench or took a recess and called me into the office and told me: "Look, you gotta take a year, you gotta take a year." [An offer below the state's but substantially above what the defense attorney wanted.] Which was incredible, and I said, "I'm not going to do it anymore, my client thinks I'm working for you because I keep coming back with these messages." [33]

> *Q*. Do you have any particularly vivid recollections about your first trials?
> *A*. I've been given what is known as the Black Jack in the judge's chambers, at least what I call the Black Jack, and several really prominent attorneys who practice criminal law call it the Black Jack . . . and that's when you go into the court ready to try your case and pick a jury, and you can't agree with the prosecutor on a plea, so he says: "Well, the judge wants us to come in and talk about the case in his chambers." You go to the judge's chambers and the judge says: "What's the matter, can't you guys get together?" "Your Honor, I can win this case, I have a good defense, they should nolle this case." The judge says: "Well, counsel, you certainly have the right to try this case; however, I want to bring to your attention a case very similar to this I sat on recently, and the counsel there really was incompetent and shouldn't be practicing criminal law, and he lost and I had to give his client time in jail even though if he had pled him to the same charge, they really didn't have to go to jail. But because he felt he had to try a case that should never have been tried, he really had to learn a lesson, and his client had to learn a lesson," and so forth. "But I think we could work out a little better plea than the one the prosecutor has offered. Mr. Prosecutor, can't you reach a little bit better?" "Well, yes, I think we can drop it down to such and such." Well, what are you going to do? You have to go back and tell your clients: "Look, if we get convicted on this charge, even though ordinarily you wouldn't, but the judge doesn't want to try the case. So you can go in and give this plea, and you will not go to jail. You'll get a suspended sentence or a fine. The judge has pretty much indicated what you will get. Do you want to take the chance?" And brother, there are not many who want to take the chance, something like .00001 will take that chance.
> *Q*. That's incredible. This happened to you in a number of trials?
> *A*. Well I haven't had too many, and it's happened in most of the ones I've had. Many of the older lawyers I speak with always tell me, you

know, this is what the judge said: "Well, if you lose, this guy is going away, and he's going to get time." [45]

The Other Option: Informal Cooperation and Plea Bargaining

Earlier, I indicated that there were two strategies the defense attorney could pursue. One, raising procedural and legal motions, and setting cases down for trial, comported with his expectations. Even the brief preceding examination of the sanctions attached to this approach is sufficient to suggest that when the newcomer opts to be an adversary, the system is prepared to teach him, bluntly, that the client may suffer. Informal discussion of the contents of the prosecutor's file is preferred to formal responses to a Bill of Particulars; informal handling of legal questions is preferred to technical legal challenges; negotiated settlements are preferred to trials. Failure to cooperate leads to harassment, closing of all the files, refusal to plea bargain on all of the defense attorney's cases, and finally, to higher sentences for the defendant. These rules of the local criminal court are taught to the newcomer as he feels his way about.

But there is a second route open to him, one that is certainly implied in the discussion of sanctions for motions and trials, and one that we will now examine in greater detail. Specifically, I refer to plea bargaining. I postponed moving directly to plea bargaining, since it least comports with what the newcomer expected to be doing. Yet, as we will see, it in short order becomes his predominant activity.

Recall that the newcomer is surprised by the factual culpability of most of his clients and by the absence of legal challenges in many of their cases. In common parlance, this "throws him for a loop." Contrary to his expectations, the opportunities for brilliant strokes at trial do not seem promising. When he attempts to venture forth in the adversary direction, he quickly encounters the sanctions described above; and his efforts seem difficult to justify in any event, since the cases are often of the "born dead" variety.

These considerations—sanctions for an adversary approach on one hand, and weak cases to begin with on the other—propel the defense attorney to consider the plea bargaining option. Further persuading him to plea bargain are two factors he had not previously recognized: the eagerness of many defendants to plead guilty and the willingness of prosecutors and judges to mete out seemingly light dispositions in return for the defendant's plea. It is worthwhile to consider these influences carefully.

Contrary to what the newcomer expects, defendants are often eager to plead guilty. In relatively minor cases, they simply want to "get it over with." They exhibit—to the surprise of their attorneys—little concern about having a criminal record. They have, after all, committed the offense, and are ready to bear the consequences, as long as the penalty is minor.[14] And they contrast the relative ease with which they can plead guilty with the costs in time and effort required to fight a case. A plea of not guilty and a subsequent trial require several court appearances. Defendants must wait around for a case to be called; sometimes court personnel or witnesses are not available, and further delay ensues; sometimes their own attorneys ask for postponements. Rather than expend the time and effort necessary for a trial, many defendants prefer to plead, especially if only a suspended sentence and fine are involved. The defendant's desire to "get it over with" is an important variable affecting the attorney's plea bargaining behavior.[15] The surprise, and, I think, sense of frustration the new attorney feels as a result of the defendant's attitude (and the factors that shape it) are indicated below.

Q. But you are saying that despite your initial inclination to try cases you are plea bargaining. Why aren't you trying your cases? Were there sanctions for being an adversary?
A. No, not at all, not at all. I think mainly because the way it is, having so many cases, and I found that . . . It's very frustrating on the part of so many of the people. So many of my clients, even when I suggest possible ways of fighting a case to the nth degree, are not interested in that. I find people say: "Just let me . . . can you get me a fine? I want to pay a fine and get it over with. I don't care about the illegal arrest. I don't care about . . ." [3]

The thought of a trial scares an awful lot of people. When I talk to them, "Today we enter a plea of not guilty or guilty. If we enter a plea of not guilty, we set it down for trial, you know, jury trial of twelve. If we plead guilty you'll be sentenced immediately." A lot of people will argue: "Well, I'm guilty, I don't want a trial. I did it." [7]

Q. Have you been pursuing the legal issues you find through motions and trials?
A. Right. As much as I can, although the system defeats that, too.
Q. How does that happen? I mean, one young attorney I interviewed said that to me. That he doesn't understand it. He wants to try cases; he thinks he's qualified to try cases, only the system defeats it, almost in those words.
A. Because either the defendant has been through the mill, and his objective will be to just get out of the courtroom and not have to come back, not caring how it's done. If you can get him to plead to . . . or get the prosecutor realizing that he's faced with a trial and all this garbage, then he can nolle the case, or let him plead to intoxicated or disorderly conduct with a suspended sentence, or a twenty-five-dollar fine. And it's your duty to tell the defendant that. You tell him that, you know, it's not a guarantee, but it's like 101 percent sure that you can walk out of here

today and not go to jail. They'll take it simply because they don't care about what the criminal record is. They have criminal records. [49]

Q. Did what you called "the eagerness of the defendant to plead guilty" strike you as strange?
A. Yes, it did . . . It did because I approached it as, you know, my parents; I'd be concerned with the record. To them it's just a way of life, and everybody has a few breaches of the peace, and everybody has a few disorderly conducts, carrying a dangerous weapon, and if you don't have one, well, you're almost strange. [53]

You know, when you try to fight a case, the people have to come back, you know, a second or third time. Today I conducted a case of . . . I think it was the second time, maybe it was even the third time, and the client is getting a little upset, and I told him: "Unfortunately, if you want to exercise all your rights, it's going to take time." You know, I explained to people, it's very quick and easy it you want to plead guilty, but if you want to maintain your innocence, unfortunately people have to come another time. It's awful. Everything is done to make it easy and comfortable, quick, for the person who wants to plead guilty. To the person who wants to fight his case, you file a motion to fight it; in two or three weeks he comes back. The police officer doesn't show up, and they've got to come back again. Back and back and back . . . [7]

Q. Would you feel that justice would be better served [if all cases went to trial]?
A. You get the feeling, you know, that somehow you're just caught in the quagmires of people playing the game and you say, God, you know, what is this? It doesn't seem rational by any means; it doesn't fit any textbook definition of anything. It's different. It's so completely different that maybe only an experienced person can understand, and maybe he doesn't trust it. One of the most important things I've found out about defendants is that they don't want to be bothered with anything. As I say, you know, it's like a bureaucracy in that they don't want to be bothered with anything. And if you had all these trials they'd be here for months, and they'd keep on having to come to court, and the kids would end up having kids. [49]

The defendant's desire to settle the case, then, becomes an important pressure on the attorney. Even in the handful of cases which have disputable legal issues, the eagerness of the new attorney to "go for broke" is tempered by the input he receives from his client to resolve the case quickly and expeditiously.

In addition to learning of the defendant's interest in a negotiated settlement, the new attorney also learns that seemingly lenient dispositions can be obtained from the prosecutor through plea bargaining. The newcomer is struck by the prosecutor's eagerness to enter into a deal that seems beneficial to the defendant.

> They [the prosecutors] are always doing most anything to dispose of cases. "You want to plead to this, we'll give you that. We'll drop this, we'll drop that. Plead so that we can move the file." This kind of thing . . . I don't like plea bargaining, but unfortunately it helps someone who's guilty. Everything is done to encourage someone to plead guilty. And if someone is guilty, or is just willing to plead guilty, they'll give him the courthouse. [7]

Furthermore, the attorney finds that he can obtain an even "sweeter" deal if he can pinpoint a legal defect in the state's case. We saw earlier that the prosecutor has sanctions he can bring to bear on the attorney who insists on a formal hearing for these legal questions. But, the other side of this sanctioning behavior is the prosecutor's willingness to "reward" legal defects with more lenient plea bargaining offers, eliminating (in his eyes) the need for a formal hearing. A number of newcomers reported that their efforts to challenge legal issues were frustrated when the prosecutor offered to nolle the case or to reduce the charge/sentence so much that it became too risky to refuse the offer.

> *A*. Usually we get very good first-offer-deals from the prosecutors. You don't have to go two, three, four negotiation sessions, or put it down for trial, or a motion, or something like that. It is easy to get a plea bargain out of them. And it's easy to take the deal. I've become, though, a little more difficult for them to compromise with because I am seeing repetitious police activity that I don't like. I'd like to attack the vice squad as much as I can down here, although it's a very difficult thing to do, because if it's not a bad case they'll throw the case out. I never had a hearing on a motion in the six months I've been here.
> *Q*. Every time it's been a nolle?
> *A*. About 75 percent of the time. They just nolle it if you've got a good point.
> *Q*. So you are saying you don't have to file the motions because they'll nolle the case?
> *A*. They nolle them . . . Well, like yesterday, I had four guys picked up for possession of marijuana. I took one of them. Boy, did he have a criminal record from California, four-and-a-half pages long, anything you can imagine, a lot of convictions, and he was only young. The vice squad busted him on a package of marijuana in the hallway behind the waiting room. They harassed the guys by arresting them. I looked at the case and told the prosecutor: "You're not going to get a conviction out of this mess. Why don't you throw them out?" So he threw the cases out. So you see, you don't even have to file motions. You don't even get a chance to file. [49]

> You see, you do come to the point where you work with the prosecutors, and the case really has good technical defects; it would be great to be able to go to court and win. But you give your information to the prosecutors, and they're going to nolle the case, and you're not going to have an opportunity to get the experience of putting on evidence and winning. [45]

The defense attorney also learns that there is another side to the penalties he experiences for persisting on seeing a case through to trial. He finds that as the trial approaches, the prosecutor's offer improves.[16] Sometimes these offers are so lenient that he is left with little choice but to accept them.

> *Q*. Let's go into your style of practice. You said you hated to plead people guilty when you first started. Did you sort of think that there would be more trials, was that it?
> *A*. I'd love to try cases every day. I'd prefer to do nothing but try cases. I enjoy it. But there isn't enough time, and you can't try everything that comes down the pike. And you find that the prosecutors . . . they don't want to try. When it comes right down to it, you push them to the wall, say, "I'm ready to go"; you go out there; you're ready to go; you've subpoenaed people; you've got your case ready. They back off. They will give you what you want to begin originally with. [36]

> *A*. I had a charge of interference with a police officer against two boys, and it involved a plainclothes cop who was sent into the place ahead of all the other officers. It is just too detailed to go into, but I put this kid under a sodium pentothal test, which is supposedly truth serum, and he came out great. We were going to go to trial, I wanted to go to trial and I had it all briefed out. We were going to whip a brief out during the trial and introduce a tape, you know, get the psychiatrist to testify. But they made such a fabulous deal for the guy; they gave him disorderly conduct. That's a ninety-day misdemeanor versus a potential five-year felony. So what are you going to do? And of course he got fined fifty dollars, and that's all . . . he didn't even get a sentence.
> *Q*. Well, let's talk about that a minute. Could you have beat it going to trial?
> *A*. I'm pretty sure we could have.
> *Q*. But the risk was too great?
> *A*. The client doesn't want to take the risk.
> *Q*. Oh, the client . . .
> *A*. Yes, see, they make the decision. The client makes the decision. They want to rely on your judgment, and if I told him the way I felt, personally, then we would try a lot of cases. But my professional judgment is that the best avenue for them, under the circumstances is to take a plea. This is what we all face. Sometimes we get the greatest cases, and we know it and the prosecutor knows it. Sometimes he'll just nolle it. If he

won't nolle it he gives them a plea which, you know, like the Godfather, you can't refuse. [45]

Q. So in a typical circuit case, you'll get the case, see what you can get, negotiate, maybe continue it a while, sit down with the prosecutor, maybe set it down for the jury, and figure you'll negotiate at a later point. You're saying that rarely do you think of a trial?
A. The closest I ever came to a circuit court trial, —— was the prosecutor, this girl had a pretty bad record, and my case was the first ready case, and we were still doing some bargaining, and —— said he wanted her to do six months in jail, and I really . . . I did get scared then. I really thought he meant business. About an hour later he was offering me three months, and I was off preparing my witnesses while he was off doing some other bargaining. He finally offered thirty days, and I said no, that I was ready to start at 2 P.M. At 2 P.M. a panel was sworn in and brought back out, and —— said, "Will your client take a suspended sentence?" I said: "——, you should have said that two hours ago." We took it, with a small fine. It was after that that I realized what the game was. That made such an impression on me, because there was a case where I was 100 percent convinced I was going to trial. There was no question about it. I was firmly convinced we were going to trial, and after that I just kind of threw my head back and laughed, and I said, "You're never going to do a trial in this court."[17] [33]

There is a degree of inconsistency in the remarks that we have examined concerning motions and trials. We saw earlier that prosecutors brought sanctions to bear on the attorney who persisted in filing motions and seeing a case through to trial. Now the same attorneys report that prosecutors capitulate in the face of legal motions and the threat of trial and offer even better deals. How are these remarks to be reconciled?

I think the explanation rests at least partially on the attitude prosecutors and judges have toward motions and trials. As we will see in chapters five and six, prosecutors and judges distinguish between "frivolous" and "serious" motions and trials. The frivolous motion and trial are characterized as those without much chance of success, those built on relatively insignificant technical contentions, and those without much merit. Prosecutors associate the filing of frivolous motions and persistence in proceeding with frivolous trials with new attorneys and with (politically) radical attorneys. When prosecutors assign a motion to this category, they are inclined to stress the sanctions they possess and to emphasize that the defense should take the deal, or else. If, however, the motion or trial is perceived as serious, then the prosecutors recognize that they may have trouble proving the case, and they are inclined to "sweeten" their offers and emphasize their powers to reward the cooperative defendant.[18]

Newcomers experience both of these prosecutorial and judicial reactions.

Thus they sometimes find sanctions brought to bear for their proceeding with motions and trials; other times they find that these adversary strategies lead to more successful deals for the defendant. When asked about their adaptation and early experiences, this mixed set of reactions to their own attempts at being an adversary is reported.

The newcomer himself may or may not recognize the inconsistency. His observations are not the product of a well-thought-through position. The adaptation process is such that he does not have the time to sit back and attempt to piece together what he has learned and what he has been taught. He reacts and is reacted to on the basis of the steps he takes on particular cases. He gains bits and pieces of insight in each of these ventures, but has little time to put these thoughts and experiences together. This pattern of adaptation helps account for the somewhat inconsistent views about motions and trials expressed by newcomers. Furthermore, it aptly characterizes the way the newcomer actually learns the techniques of plea bargaining.

Learning How to Plea Bargain

Thus far, I have examined the forces that move the newcomer in the plea bargaining direction—be they sanctions, rewards, or simply the obvious and uncontestable guilt of the defendant. Little has been explicitly said about the newcomer's learning how to negotiate cases. This omission was intentional. The newcomer is not placed in a classroom and told: "Here is how we plea bargain. Do this, do that . . . " Instead, he feels his way about, testing the efficacy of motions, of trials, of formal over informal approaches. If the pressure from his client, or from the prosecutor or the judge or from his own evaluation of the case is such that he feels a plea bargain is called for, he plea bargains. No set of carefully reasoned strategies guides him in these negotiations. These only develop over time.

The new attorney tests the plea bargaining waters gingerly. If he has colleagues who can assist him in evaluating the merits of the prosecutor's offer, he eagerly seeks their advice.

> *Q*. How did you learn to negotiate a case?
> *A*. I went over it with other lawyers. You know, it's like many problem-solving situations; hopefully, you know what the strengths in your position are, what the weaknesses are, what the risks are, what the exposure is, and you learn very quickly that there is a bargaining process. How do you learn? I went to people in the firm who had been practicing, and I asked them questions. They gave me answers. I watched the process at work. I watched the judges to avoid . . . Yeah, one of the things you have to learn about practicing law around here, that basically there is a lot of luncheon conversation, it's a very intensely practical education. [3]

Less fortunate solo practitioners report that they were often taken advantage of in their early plea bargaining encounters.

Q. Did you ever get bagged while you were learning?
A. Yeah, I got burned a number of times. I had a case where my guy got six months in jail. Now, with the same case I would get a suspended sentence. You've just got to learn through experience what a case is worth. [67]

A. I think at first there were cases where I took a bad disposition because of lack of experience and because the prosecutors were being miserable because of my having filed motions. Today that same prosecutor, the same charges, I would laugh at him. I'd tell him his offer was a joke. This is one of those things you pick up as you go along.
Q. You mean not taking bad deals?
A. Yeah. I wouldn't say a bad deal. The deal I got this fellow was, in my mind, extremely good, but it wasn't, in my mind today, as good as I could have gotten him right now. [45]

Q. How did you learn to plea bargain?
A. By getting my head scrambled a few times. You learn from experiences. [68]

Both the attorney who can seek out colleagues (private attorneys in firms, and public defenders) and the solo practitioner need to develop a sense of "what the case is worth." How are they to judge a prosecutor's offer which falls substantially below the maximum the charge allows? Is it a good deal? Could it be better? Is it in line with what other attorneys receive?

Newcomers learn to answer these questions through experience. All outside advice is sought and cherished. But, without exception, every attorney interviewed indicated the necessity of developing his own "feel for a case." This feel for a case is precisely what the newcomer lacks and what the experienced attorney prides himself on. Essentially, it is an impressionistic multiple regression model carried in the attorney's head. It is a way of sorting and weighing the sundry factors that enter into a disposition. Attorneys believe it can be learned only through experience in negotiating cases. Once an attorney has a feel for cases, he knows whether to try or plea bargain a case; if he chooses plea bargaining, he knows how to weigh factors as diverse as the defendant's record, the facts of the case, the prosecutor's personality, the prosecutor's willingness to go to trial, the judge's reactions to specific types of crimes, the precedents in terms of prior dispositions for this type of offense, and so on. He is confident that he can predict early what disposition is obtainable. An attorney's feel for a case breeds a certain sense of efficacy, a sense that he knows what can be accomplished in a given case.

You know, I think I know what I'm doing. I'm a lawyer; I've been a lawyer for a few years; I've specialized in criminal law. I can analyze a case; I can tell a defendant in a few minutes just what's going to happen, what should be done and all. [55]

I look at a file and I know I can beat it. So I know that maybe I'll have it continued, with a plea, and file motions, maybe one or two or three times, but I'm going to get it [nolle or dismissal]. Then on the other hand, you know, this guy has to plead to something. You know that after you talk to him and read the sheet. You know he'll have to plead to something. [2]

I can take twenty-five files and look them over and, maybe without even speaking to the defendant, predict what is likely to happen. It's difficult to think that you could do that, but you can read a police report and the facts of the case, and because you have read so many and know that this guy should do this, and the prosecutor should do that. You have a good idea completely ahead of time. [49]

Q. How does a new attorney learn what a case is worth?
A. Well, the new guy is in trouble. He's got to learn the hard way, get battered around . . .You've got to put together a lot of things. You got to start off with the offense and the circumstances surrounding the events, naturally. Then you got to take the defendant, his record, his proximity to his last involvement, the kinds of last involvements, his family situation, anything good that you have going for you. These are the textbook things to look for. Then you got things that aren't in the textbooks. The month of the year. I've always made it a practice to do great things in December. The courts are closing; you want to get people out of the jails. It's the season, to a certain extent. I always save some of my real problems for the last day of court before Christmas recess. Nobody's going to turn me down. One of the things you'll also acquire a feel for, you get to know the people that you're dealing with. We all have our hang-ups. Some prosecutors get very upset with certain types of crimes, certain types of defendants. Sometimes they had the guy before, so they know him too well.
Q. But take —— [a new public defender]. How will he learn all of this?
A. Plea bargaining is difficult to participate in successfully until you've tried it out for a while. A lot of it has to do with personalities. And I think that, although plea bargaining is much maligned and much criticized, plea bargaining is an art that should be reserved for experts. That's a fact, because if you aren't careful, the victim may be the client. It's not as simple and it's not as cut-and-dried as you think. Sometimes the plea bargain requires striking at the appropriate moment. [23]

> I know what I want out of a case. That's the difference now than when I was younger, when I started. I know what a good result is and when I get it.[19] [10]

To argue that all experienced attorneys acquire a feel for a case through the give and take of actual plea bargaining negotiations is not to say that these feelings on a given case are equivalent or that all attorneys plea bargain in the same fashion. On the contrary, plea bargaining styles and skills (and, therefore, estimates of how well one can do in cases) vary tremendously among attorneys. The differences can be explained by personality variables, by legal knowledge and legal skills, by the individual's credibility when he threatens trial as a means of improving the deal, and by a host of other factors that need not concern us here. Some attorneys are more successful than others, but their success is not necessarily a product of any one style. The same attorney may try a different approach and get the same result.[20]

The upshot of all this is that there is no single model of the successful plea bargainer that the newcomer can emulate. He must learn to plea bargain by working through cases on his own, refining his approach until he finds one that he is comfortable with. As his confidence in his style increases, he will become confident that he knows where he is going on a particular case, that he knows what deal will eventually emerge, that, in short, he has a feel for the case. An apt summary of how the newcomer learns the techniques of plea bargaining was provided by one of the respondents.

> *Q*. How did you learn to plea bargain? How did you learn what a case is worth and what you could get?
> *A*. Well, there are no courses given on it. It's like . . . Well, I guess you could analogize it to making love. You know, it's something you can't teach; you can't put it in a book; you can't give a lecture on it. But, like making love, you do it enough times, you learn to like it, and you'll get good at it. [36]

Adaptation to Plea Bargaining: The Evaluative Component

It is important at this point to step away from the particulars of what the newcomer learns about plea bargaining and to consider the overall results of the process of adaptation. To clarify the changes in attitude and behavior the "typical" newcomer evidences as he gains experience in the system, I will contrast the attitudes of defense attorneys to plea bargaining and trials during three stages of their careers. We will be interested in the development of an evaluative judgment about the relative efficacy of the adversary approach versus the efficacy of plea bargaining.[21]

Adapting to Plea Bargaining: Defense Attorneys

The Initial Period of Adjustment: The First Few Months

This is the period in which the defense attorney first encounters plea bargaining. Overall, his reaction is negative. He resents the informal cooperation associated with plea bargaining, preferring a more formal, adversary approach. He is still under the sway of what one might call the "presumption of trial." By this I mean that he presumes each case to be triable, and presumes that he will see it through to trial. Case pressure or the defendant's wishes may ultimately thwart his designs, but his feel for the case is almost always conceptualized in terms of legal motions and eventual trial. The excerpt that follows is typical of the attorney's attitude during this very early period. It is quoted at length to convey the tone as well as the content of the newcomer's early reactions.

Q. Did you expect more cases to go to trial? Did you think that trial work is what you would be doing?
A. I thought that [trials] would be the ideal system. But you also see that there is pressure put on the defendants to cop out . . . and then there's the case load. But there isn't vigorous and aggressive defense practiced here.
Q. You say the ideal system would be, you imply, if everyone went to trial?
A. Not everybody. There are some people . . . some guilty people benefit from plea bargaining sometimes, in terms of getting a better sentence. But, there are many cases, even where someone is guilty, where you could put up a good fight and they could be acquitted, but that's not done here.
Q. Do you feel that you are being pushed to plea bargain?
A. No, not exactly. I'm aware that it goes on, and I'm aware that this is the route that most people choose because, I don't know, because it's easier. But look, like, I came here, and no one ever filed a Motion for Discovery. The thing was to send the investigator to the state's attorney's office or to go begging yourself, and say, "Oh, please give me a copy of your police report." . . . I don't see why that should be a matter of their grace. I'm very uncomfortable working that closely and being that dependent on the state's attorney's office. I mean, your defendant has independent rights, and you have to assert them as his attorney. I don't believe in relying on the good graces of the state's attorney.
Q. What steps are you going to take to rectify that or change that?
A. Well, in cases I'm working on, I'm not depending on the good graces of the prosecutor. I'll do it very much by the books. If you want something, you motion for it and you argue for it.
Q. Isn't that kind of half ass? I mean, if you can walk up there and look at their file, why file a Bill of Particulars? Why not get it informally?

A. I think it's better to do it formally for the sense, you know, you're getting it, it's on the record, the judge has heard it, it's been argued, and I think you get more respect that way.
Q. Do you have any particularly vivid recollections of your first few days on the job?
A. I was amazed at the hand-in-glove operations of the defense attorneys and the prosecutor's office. It destroyed me.
Q. You mean the fact they are so friendly?
A. Not necessarily friendly, just working together, which, as I said, I was not comfortable with. Also, when I first heard sentencing, when I heard the deals they worked out, and someone would get three to seven, and everyone would say: "Oh fantastic," you know, really light . . .
Q. Do you think, then, that you won't be negotiating these deals?
A. There was this one case . . . It was first-degree murder, and they offered to cop him out to manslaughter. And they were offering a five to ten or something, and the reason he didn't cop was he had a record and he was afraid that he'd have to serve the maximum. On the other hand, in this fight he had lost an eye. He was in the hospital, and he's sick, and he's kind of old, you know; I thought if he went before a judge and whipped out his glass eye, the judge was really not going to go too heavy on him, you know, because he got cut first. So that was a case where I thought he was stupid to go to trial, and finally his nephew told him he was nuts, and he changed his mind. But even then he [the defendant] had the satisfaction of starting the trial, of picking eight jurors.
Q. But overall do you think you'll be plea bargaining most of your cases?
A. I think that you should think that every case is going to turn out to . . . I mean, if you have someone who gave the statement to the police, there was a witness, they signed it, he was advised of his rights, and his mother watched, you're not sure that it's going to end in a trial. Maybe you're less sure than in other cases where the state's case is not as strong. But I think you should think that a trial is going to be a possibility and that you're negotiating to find out whether that, in fact, is true. You're not negotiating instead of a trial; you want to find what their attitude is . . . [20]

The Transition: Three Months to a Year

In this second adaptational stage, the newcomer's resolve to remain a firm adversary begins to crumble. He learns that most of his clients are guilty and that the opportunity to challenge the state's case on factual and legal grounds is limited. Furthermore, he experiences the sanctions associated with a formal adversary approach and the rewards that result from informal cooperation.

The attorney plea bargains more in this period, but he is uneasy and troubled by his own actions, and tends to attribute his participation in the plea bargaining system to the sanctions the court has at its disposal, to the case pressure under which he labors, and to the increasingly friendly ties with prosecutors that he is developing. He is satisfied with the results obtained—indeed, he is surprised at how lenient the dispositions are—but he is unhappy with the means he uses to achieve these results. Responses typical of the attorneys' attitudes during this transitional period follow.

Q. Are you doing the kind of job that you envisioned you would be doing?
A. I didn't envision that everybody would want to plead . . . or that so many cases would be nolled and so many people would plead out as easy as they do. I didn't envision that. I thought things were a little more clear-cut and legally defined. You know, there are so many compromises, you get sick of it sometimes . . . I don't know. We're not defense counsel. We are, but not in any traditional concept of what a defense counsel is. We certainly get the results. How we get them is completely different, unorthodox. No one would expect that this is how it's done. I've been amazed at exactly how this system works.
Q. And you must have been . . .
A. I am . . . I tell you, amazed even by how few people go to jail. I mean, we get some pretty bad clients, and they don't go to jail.
Q. You get these guys off?
A. Yes, it's amazing. You know, you get this feeling sometimes that you are like a mechanical man gaining a productive deal for the client, bargaining and dealing, and dealing and bargaining. And the deals are good.
Q. Let's say you had unlimited time to handle each one of your cases any way you wanted. There's no pressure on you.
A. Even from a client?
Q. With the exception of the client, okay. What would you do differently?
A. Probably not too much different. I mean I'd file . . . I don't know. If I filed more motions I'd probably . . . Sometimes it's hard to separate my eagerness for wanting to get experience from my eagerness to want to defend these clients by doing what's best for them. If I only had a few cases I could cause havoc in the court, I could have a ball down there.
Q. But that would be for your own experience?
A. It would probably be more for my own experience. I guess I'd still end up negotiating. [49]

Sometimes I call myself a criminal case adjustor. We are not lawyers. We are just like adjustors for insurance companies. We go in and try to settle the case, take a stack of files in and try to settle them. And we do okay, but . . . [71]

Q. Well, let's take your inclination before you took the job. You were sort of a civil libertarian. You could get up there now and make a motion for this and that. Cite cases. Yet you say that you are somehow fitting into the system.
A. Yeah. Unfortunately, I'm afraid I have. There's a big conflict going on, that has been going on in my mind . . . about working here as part of

the system. It's just so pervasive and so big and so awesome that there's just no way you can function in it constantly. If you have to be part of it, you know, five days a week, I really don't know if it is possible to be the complete adversary that you can be if, you know, you only had a few cases. You see the same prosecutors, the same judges and . . . I can see myself molding into the system a little more than I like to admit, and probably I'm not as much of an adversary sometimes as I should be. I think it's sad; I think it's unfortunate. I tell myself that maybe if I had a little more experience under my belt, if I was a little more sure of myself on legal grounds and . . . maybe it would be a little different. I'm not sure.

[The attorney next spoke of the pressures from his own clients to plead, the fact that plea bargaining appeared to benefit the guilty defendant, and the sanctions the prosecutor and judge level against the defendant who is convicted by trial. Since his comments are comparable to those examined earlier, I will not report them here.]

But, you see, you run into this. Let's say you have a defendant charged with a five-year felony. And very often the prosecutor will recommend a misdemeanor. And I explain that to the person. I really, I honestly try not to convince him to plead guilty, you know, encourage him to plead guilty. And if someone is innocent and maintains their innocence, I have encouraged people to plead not guilty. Sometimes people just want to get something over with, but I'm sure that sometimes our biases come through. Sometimes these are such hairline things, the way you . . . if I use the wrong word, or the way I phrase it to a person may get them scared that they'll get a lot of time.

Q. So you'll work out the deal with the prosecutor and leave the choice up to the defendant. But you think that at times he should take the deal?

A. When I first started here, —— [the preeminent "radical" attorney of Arborville] said to me: "Well, I've heard a lot about you, it's great to have you." Every time I see him now I feel as if he must be saying: "Well, he really got sucked into the system." I think he's one extreme, you know, the libertarian extreme . . . filing motions in every case. I think there are certain times in which that can work against him, and it may not be the best thing for the client. Because that brings you to the question what is . . . what is the duty of a criminal lawyer, you know, is his paramount concern the best interests of the client? Now you could conceivably have a case where the best interest of the client may be to get good dispositions for him or to get him help in a drug program, something like that.

Q. Well, let me be devil's advocate again. The job of an attorney is not to be a social worker but to be a defense attorney.

A. Right.

Q. Give the defendant every legal defense possible . . .

A. Right.

Q. Are you saying then that you've come to tilt more in the "social work" direction?
A. I'm afraid I am saying that, yeah. Yeah, that's what we very often feel like, combination social workers, administrators, employees pushing papers around. And it's hard to put your finger on just what went wrong, you know.
Q. Well what happened? You've been here a few months and you've changed already. Did you just get swept along, or . . .
A. Part of it is my inexperience. I don't have a great expertise in criminal law.
Q. Are you sure that when you ultimately obtain this greater knowledge of criminal law that you will be able to change the way you've . . .
A. No, I'm not sure.
Q. I don't think the way you are is necessarily bad, but it seems to trouble you.
A. Yeah, it has been troubling me. I don't know, you know . . . I blame it on time a lot. I don't know. Maybe that's a scapegoat. I guess the pressures . . . maybe they're subtle, that if you work along with the system and if you cooperate, you do get better dispositions for those clients who are guilty . . . I don't know. I dislike the system intensely, it's really awful and I guess I am—and I hate to admit it—but I guess I am part of it. It's like moving cattle, herding cattle through the stocks. There's just no time to stop and think or consider anything.
Q. Do you find that, when you bargain and now, your bargaining with the prosecutor is kind of a friendly thing? Does it become acrimonious sometimes, or is it by and large friendly?
A. It's by and large friendly. Perhaps a little too friendly. That's one of the irritating things about it; it's on an extremely friendly basis. I sit down and talk about this case and that case, and we work out deals.
Q. Despite the absence of sanctions and the fact that you're getting good dispositions, you're not completely comfortable with the way you are acting?
A. No. Not entirely . . . I know, I know there's a conflict, and it's been bothering me. I don't really, you know . . .
Q. I mean you're not worried about . . . you don't even worry about being fired or how that would look on your own record?
A. No, no, no. No, I'm not worried about that, about getting fired or anything like that.
Q. So you can do whatever you want?
A. Essentially, yes, I can.
Q. But, in fact, you are not doing anything different than anybody else?
A. Right.
Q. It's a real dilemma.
A. It's a real dilemma. [7]

The Defense Attorney as Plea Bargainer: The Final Stage

It generally takes at least a year for the defense attorney to reach this third stage. By this time he has handled a large number of cases, most of which were eventually resolved by a plea bargain. He has found that the dispositions he achieved through plea bargaining—given the charges against the defendant—were reasonable at worst, and extremely favorable at best.

His doubts about not being more of an adversary have been at least partially assuaged. He finds that if he has a good legal or factual issue, he can be an "informal adversary," presenting the issue to the prosecutor in a closed-door meeting. If he is convincing and his credibility is well regarded, the prosecutor will accept his contention and nolle the case and/or make the appropriate reduction in charges and sentence. The informal approach precludes the time-consuming filing of motions, preparation of briefs, and so on. And by obviating sanctions imposed for pursuing motions and trials, it limits the risks to the defendant.

The attorney still has some lingering uncertainties and qualms about his actions. He would enjoy trying cases, acting out his own conception of what an attorney "really" does. But he recognizes that he must temper his personal desires by what the defendant wants and by what best benefits the defendant. One thing that stands out above all else, one thing that outsiders fail to realize but, nonetheless, something the newcomer has learned, is that plea bargaining benefits most defendants. The attorney himself may not normatively subscribe to plea bargaining, but he is forced to concede that it is the preferable way to resolve at least some of his cases.[22]

Finally, the attorney's mind-set has been subtly altered. Whereas he had operated previously under what I called the presumption of trial, he now follows what we might call the "presumption of plea bargaining." When he obtains a new case, he no longer conceives of it as a potential trial or as a potential forum for his adversary skills. Instead, he thinks in terms of what he can do with the case, what his "feel for the case" suggests. What charges will be dropped? What is the likely sentence? What plea bargaining strategy should he follow?[23] At an earlier stage, the attorney would have approached the case as a potential trial, a trial that might not materialize because of subsequent plea bargaining offers, but, nonetheless, the trial and adversary approach were foremost in his mind. In this third stage, the attorney views the trial as the last resort. He thinks first of plea bargaining, of working it out, of hustling it through the circuit court, of strategies for negotiating sentences in the superior court. Only if these fail, if he is left with no other choice, does the trial reemerge as an option.

I have attempted to capture the attitudes of attorneys in this third period in the selections that follow. The first set of comments reflects the experienced attorney's belief that plea bargaining benefits the defendant. It is interesting that each of these attorneys criticizes inexperienced outsiders who attack plea bargaining without really understanding it.

> So you get a guy with three or four files. On one of them, they're going to be guilty of something and they have you nailed. So what you try to do is plead on the one he did and get the others nolled. The fact that cases don't go to trial for someone outside the system, that's always a benchmark to say, "Well, gee, that's not an aggressive lawyer . . . those defendants aren't getting a break," but in our court system, it's almost the other way around. It's almost that the state is folding or that somehow . . . [2]

> See, these people live in an ivory tower, these Yalies and . . . I'm not criticizing . . . the Yale law school; they live in an ivory tower. To them, everybody, I guess, must be innocent, and they feel that the poor are downtrodden, and there's so many things that must go through their minds. They're wrong. The system today primarily works for the benefit of the accused. [31]

> I'll stand on our dispositions anytime, take any comparison . . . you'll find they reflect a pretty good effort and pretty good results, at least from the standpoint of people who are in a position to evaluate a disposition. If you want to evaluate dispositions from the standpoint of newspapers, that's a waste of time. But if you want to get people who are knowledgeable and who know what sentencing is like, who know what offenses call for, they'll be pretty well agreed that our dispositions are pretty good, at least from the standpoint of the defendant.[24] [23]

The next set of responses illustrates the change in attitude toward motions and trials that the attorney evidences. These remarks are particularly striking when contrasted to the newcomers' responses to the same issues.

> *Q*. Looking back now, from when you began to now, have you made any significant changes in the way you handle criminal cases?
> *A*. Yeah. I would say that when I first started I was motion oriented, motion filing and things like that. It's less true now. I file motions when I think I have to, but . . . I think I have to review what I'm doing because maybe I'm not filing as much . . . When you've been dealing with people for five years, there's almost an awareness of . . . they know and you know what you're going to do in a particular situation, so if there's a weak case, the prosecutor knows that I'm going to file a motion to suppress, and I think I don't file it anymore because I know when I look at that case I'm going to go in, and the prosecutor is going to nolle it.
> *Q*. You mean because he knows you would file the motion?
> *A*. When you've been in a place four or five years, you get certain things done. Before, you would have had to file motions and stuff. Now . . . I'll

tell you . . . I'm a lawyer, and it is interesting to file motions, and . . . when you get a teaching job, you know, you're not going to like, after a few years, your introductory courses. You'll want some good graduate courses where you're challenged. It may be part of my problem that I'm not challenged as I was before. Because of a lot of reasons. I'm just getting results, just by them agreeing to something I asked for. It's fun to write a brief. It's fun to argue a motion. [2]

Q. Right now you're performing another job . . . I mean you're settling cases?
A. Yeah. Right. Why try if you don't have to? Especially when your client's guilty. Why try it? It's an academic situation. You know, you get what you want. Remember what you want. The major premise is the clients want to walk away. I don't have to go in and practice for practice's sake, you know, I've had that. I know what the law is all about. [13]

I don't particularly want to try cases. You always got so damn much to do, we've got so much work. Why, every time a trial starts and collapses, why, it's almost a sense of release. I can get back here and get my head a little bit above water. So not too many people really want to try cases, except young prosecutors, and they want to make a name or just get the practice or whatever. Or maybe also young defense attorneys who also are eager to try cases. [37]

Finally, I include a lengthy exchange with one court veteran. His remarks indicate poignantly the degree to which the "presumption of plea bargaining" holds sway.

Q. You expected [when new to the court] more trials?
A. Yeah, I think I did. I'm sure I did. I've had a couple of trials in the superior court and a couple in the circuit court . . . and some hearings and court trials. But certainly I've had a lot fewer trials than I expected initially. After a while you get not to expect trials and get surprised when they come up, almost chagrined when they come up. On one hand, you look forward to trials because that's what the system, in the back of my mind, is still about, trials, and that's kind of exciting, a chance to think on your feet and really be what you've always conceived of as a lawyer. On the other hand, the risks are so great and the actual trials are so rare that there's a certain amount of trepidation, a large amount.
Q. That comes with time?
A. I think it fair to say that I welcomed trials initially . . . But it's a funny situation with our system . . . I think substantial justice is worked out a good percentage of the time; you kind of reach the right results for the wrong reasons. That's the kind of argument that runs back and forth in my mind. The illusion of justice is not so . . . but the actual substance of it we work out.
Q. What about motions? Have you changed?

A. Well, I was capable of filing every motion in the book, and I filed a lot of them. But I found that as a technique it is preferable to go in there and let them know you are capable, but see if you can reason it out first.
Q. So for the same case now, you probably wouldn't file the motion?
A. Probably not, I think, you see, I've also built up, and I say this with all due modesty, I've built up a lot of credibility in the court. They know that whatever I say in there is the truth, and that's so. I've never, not to my knowledge at least, said anything that wasn't true. I suppose I've taken some representations that were given to me and passed them on to the court, and maybe they weren't so, but I certainly never knowingly said anything that was wrong. I usually check out what I say pretty carefully. And after a while they get to know that, and they know that if I come in there and I say something, that it's so, and they'll rely on that representation, and a case like that would be nolled right off the bat. I think that having that kind of credibility and being able to back it up with the ability to go all the way is what makes me effective . . . You know something though, people ask me "do you think you're a good lawyer?" and I still answer that in the negative. I think I am an effective lawyer, a very effective lawyer, but I know, for example, that I don't know law nearly as well as —— does. I mean he really knows his law, much better than I do. I think I get at least as good results as he does, but from the point of view of really knowing my stuff, I don't think I'm in the same class he is.
Q. Let's go back to this philosophy. At the beginning you saw the prosecutor as the enemy, and you were the defense counsel. And was the question to do the best for your client, or was the question to fight it out at a trial?
A. The question I always felt was to do the best for my client. I felt that was the goal, and I guess I slowly began to realize that I was aware of going to trial; I always had that in the back of my mind, and I felt myself, after a period of time, I don't know exactly when it occurred, kind of dismissing trial as a likelihood. Well, I began to say, "This is what is going to happen in this case. They are going to drop this charge probably, or they'll drop this one, and you're going to have to plead out to this one ultimately." I began to see that as the pattern and began to stop thinking of trials as a realistic possibility.
Q. Now there are a couple of levels that could probably be true on?
A. I think I probably resisted it at first, but after a while it became a way of looking at things. It becomes like a game, going in there and talking to the prosecutor and coming out with the deal. And what do you think . . . I was always impressed with the majesty of the process, and I watched Perry Mason; what do you think when you find out it's nothing like that at all . . . and what does the client think? I mean, we do okay, we do great. I've had clients walk out of there laughing. And I've walked out of there laughing, too. I can think of some cases that are just ridiculous dispositions that I had no business getting.
Q. You started calling it a game after about a year?

A. Yeah. I would guess about a year that I really became aware of the fact that it was a game that was played by certain rules. I went in there with a certain attitude and a certain amount of bluff involved, and the prosecutor had a certain attitude and he was bluffing this and that, and he would ask for a certain amount of time and this and that, and the guy was going to jail. And after a while of playing the game, you know what's going to happen . . . you kind of know what the results are going to be, what you have to play, and how you have to play to get it. I began calling it a game, and I became more and more aware that results were a function of one's personality as much as one's knowledge of the law. That's when I got into this thing about the difference between being an effective lawyer and a good lawyer. So much of the game is personality.
Q. This was being an effective lawyer, playing this particular game? Is your conception of a good lawyer different? Is that something different, or does that necessitate a different system?
A. Yeah, it probably necessitates a different system. There's not much point, I don't think, in being a good lawyer in this type of system. Why bother reading all your Supreme Court decisions? It's good to have a couple of them handy, so that you can throw them out and intimidate somebody, but there is no point in being a constitutional law scholar to play this kind of game. Same with motions. Throw your motions in and you argue it and you're probably going to lose, but maybe you win. I find that if you do have the case, and you make the argument to the prosecutor, you can very often get a nolle and you save yourself the whole bother of filing the motion, of having the hearing, of getting the transcript, and all that crap. If you've got a good case, you lay it out in advance and you get a nolle. That may be a cheap way of doing it because a nolle isn't as good as a dismissal, at least not for a year it's not, but again, I think it's good enough. I've never kicked out a nolle.
Q. Now, you have associated trials with the dignified method of proceeding, and you have said that plea bargaining, that you found what you were doing didn't have dignity. Yet you opted for the less dignified way?
A. Yeah.
Q. Right now if I gave you a case, you would continue to go the "undignified route"?
A. Probably.
Q. Because you feel the dignified route—the trial—is less effective?
A. It's less effective.
Q. You've been using loaded words like dignified, suggesting that the trial is somehow . . . that it is the good approach. In the best of all possible worlds, do you . . .
A. I'm not saying it's necessarily good. I've gone back and forth on this and . . . plea bargaining is not a bad thing. If a person committed an offense, is charged, and has indeed committed the offense, I don't see why he should be made to go to trial if he wants to admit his guilt. I also don't see anything wrong with his lawyer, his representative, trying to work out for him the best possible disposition he can get. The problem

comes with the capacity for abuse, with the risk that innocent people will plead guilty. I think this is overrated as a problem because you never see . . . most defendants who plead guilty . . . I know some of them say they were forced . . . but most of the time it's just not true.
Q. So generally you'd opt for plea bargaining?
A. Well . . . let me say this. It isn't so much that I'm going to get screwed at trial . . . it's just that I can do so much without going to trial. It isn't even the fear of what happens to you after trial so much as the fact that it's almost an irrelevant consideration. The fact is that in the plea bargaining system—which is not so much an alternative to trial as *the* system—you get good results by plea bargaining. [33]

By outlining the changes that take place in each of these three adaptational stages, I do not mean to imply that every new attorney necessarily shares the same experiences, nor that each necessarily changes in the direction indicated.[25] Obviously, there is going to be variation from these general patterns; furthermore, attorneys will tend to emphasize different aspects of how and why they changed. But I think the three-stage analysis is at least suggestive of the way most of the interviewed attorneys changed, and the extensive quotations in each section offer some additional insight into the ways the attorneys themselves reconciled their change in attitude and behavior.

Summary and Conclusions

The new defense attorney knows little about the plea bargaining operations of the court. He expects to try many of his cases and attributes the plea bargaining he sees in the court to poorly motivated or overworked court personnel. He sees himself as Perry Mason: filing motions, going to trial, being an adversary throughout. Though it is uncommon for him to articulate his expectations in precisely this fashion, he assumes that a sizable percentage of his clients are innocent and/or that they have disputable legal claims in their cases.

When the attorney begins handling actual cases, there is no formal socialization program to guide him. He must fend for himself. He searches out information from anyone who is willing to offer it and receives bits and pieces of advice. These are not aggregated for him into any overall perspective on the court. He grabs what he can, digests these pieces, but is unable to formulate a well-thought-out framework for his actions. In part, this is because he simply does not have the time; he is too busy worrying about the particulars of the cases he is handling. Also, he simply lacks the knowledge to piece together the sundry bits of information he collects. The adaptation process, then, is experiential. The newcomer learns by trial and error, by exploring one, and then another, option. He rarely sits back and thinks about what he is doing. Indeed, it is instructive to recall that the subjects often thanked me for the interview. They welcomed the opportunity to be forced to think systematically and theoretically about their experiences.

As the newcomer's experience with actual cases increases, he learns that the reality differs substantially from what he expected. He finds that most defendants are guilty and that frequently their cases do not provide grounds for legal or factual challenge. Often, to the defense attorney's surprise, the defendant readily admits his guilt, or at least admits it after a good deal has been proffered by the prosecutor. Relatedly, the defense attorney is also surprised by the pressure the defendant brings to bear to negotiate the case. In the circuit court, defendants often simply "want to get it over with"; in the superior court they are more concerned with a "good deal," particularly one not involving "time." But in both courts, they seem eager to avoid trial.

At the same time that the attorney is learning about the factual culpability of his clients and is being pressured by them to arrange a deal, he is pursuing (or asking about) motions and trials. It is at this point that he is taught that there are court-imposed sanctions on the attorney insistent upon being an adversary. He is taught (or told) that the prosecutor's file will be closed to him if he continues to file Bills of Particulars and Motions for Discovery; that the prosecutor will refuse to plea bargain if he files legal challenges; and that the sentences will be harsher if the defendant is convicted after trial. The latter in particular stands out in the newcomer's mind: without exception, newcomers believe that there definitely is a penalty for going to trial and a reward for plea bargaining.

These rewards for plea bargaining are especially surprising to the newcomer. The deals appear excellent in and of themselves, and when juxtaposed with the weakness of the defense the newcomer could present, they appear irresistible. But the newcomer is still unsure. He still has lingering doubts about forsaking an adversary posture. He is not sure what to do.

Defendant pressure and advice from others convince him to accept the prosecutor's offer. He acts hesitantly at first and with greater confidence in succeeding cases. What is happening—almost unknown to him—is that he is sharpening his own plea bargaining skills. He is working out a niche for himself in plea bargaining negotiations, becoming more confident that his strategy and tactics in these negotiations, his informal adversary approach, if you will, is leading to excellent deals for his client. He begins to develop a "feel for a case," an ability to predict what will happen if he negotiates successfully. The attorney's confidence in his predictive ability is such that he is willing to wager that he can successfully predict the outcome of most cases at a very early stage.

Subtly, the defense attorney has adapted to the plea bargaining system. He no longer is preoccupied with his failure to raise motions and to try most cases. He presumes a plea bargain will be obtained in every case, and only if that option fails does the trial reemerge as a possible approach.[26] Sometimes he will have a hearing on a motion and go to trial on a case simply to retain his credibility in the plea bargaining negotiations; the threats of motions and trial are potent weapons in his arsenal, and it is occassionally necessary for him to prove that he is capable of using them. But in most cases he expects quite correctly that a deal will be negotiated without recourse to these formal weapons.

It is important to emphasize that much of what has been said about the defense attorney's adaptation to plea bargaining does not rest on a case-pressure foundation. For example, I have argued that the defendant's factual culpability coupled with the absence of contestable legal and factual issues bears importantly on the attorney's decision to plea bargain. There is no compelling reason to believe that cases in low volume jurisdictions exhibit different properties than those in high volume jurisdictions, and thus there is no reason to believe that the attorney's reactions to these cases differ.[27] The properties of the cases themselves will have the same effect on attorneys in high- and low-volume jurisdictions.

It is possible, however, to argue that other aspects of the adaptation process (for example, pressure from judges and prosecutors on motions and trials) will vary with increases in volume. These differences, in turn, would lead to a different perspective on the adaptation of new defense attorneys, one more dependent on case volume. In Centerville, the low volume jurisdiction included in this study, this proved not to be the case. The attorneys' adaptation in this low volume jurisdiction could be explained in essentially the same way as could the adaptation of attorneys in high volume areas.[28] Though there were some differences on the margins, what the attorneys learned and how they learned it, varied only minimally in high and low volume courts.

5 Adapting to Plea Bargaining: Prosecutors

Expectations and Orientations

The new prosecutor shares many of the general expectations that his counterpart for the defense brings to the court.[1] He expects factually and legally disputable issues, and the preliminary hearings and trials associated with these. If his expectations differ at all from the naive "Perry Mason" orientation, it is only to the extent that he anticipates greater success than the hapless Hamilton Burger of Perry Mason fame.

The new prosecutor's views about plea bargaining parallel those of the defense attorney. He views plea bargaining as an expedient employed in crowded urban courts by harried and/or poorly motivated prosecutors. He views the trial as "what the system is really about," and plea bargaining as a necessary evil dictated by case volume. The following exchange with a newly appointed prosecutor is illustrative.

> *Q*. Let's say they removed the effects of case pressure, provided you with more manpower. You wouldn't have that many cases . . .
> *A*. Then everybody should go to trial.
> *Q*. Everybody should go to trial?
> *A*. Yeah.
> *Q*. Why?
> *A*. Because supposedly if they're guilty they'll be found guilty. If they're not guilty they'll be found not guilty. That's the fairest way . . . judged by a group of your peers, supposedly.
> *Q*. So you think that plea bargaining is a necessary evil?
> *A*. Yeah.
> *Q*. Would justice be better served if all cases went to trial?
> *A*. That's the way it's supposed to be set up. Sure. Why wouldn't it?
> *Q*. Would prosecutors be more satisfied?

A. Probably.
Q. If cases went to trial?
A. Sure.
Q. Why?
A. Because they could talk in front of twelve people and act like a lawyer. Right. Play the role. [28]

It should be emphasized that these expectations and preferences of the new prosecutor are founded on the minimal law school preparation discussed earlier. The newcomers simply do not know very much about the criminal justice system.

Unlike defense attorneys, however, the new prosecutor is likely to receive some form of structured assistance when he begins his job. The chief prosecutor or chief state's attorney may provide this aid;[2] if the prosecutor's office is staffed by a number of prosecutors or state's attorneys—that is, if the newcomer is not the only assistant prosecutor—it is more common for the chief prosecutor to assign to one or more of his experienced assistants the responsibility for helping the newcomer adjust. Since the newcomer's actions reflect on the office as a whole, it is not surprising that this effort is made.

The assistance the newcomer receives can be described as a form of structured observation. For roughly two weeks, he accompanies an experienced prosecutor to court and to plea bargaining sessions and observes him in action. The proximity of the veteran prosecutor—and his designation as the newcomer's mentor—facilitate communication between the two. The experienced prosecutor can readily explain or justify his actions, and the newcomer can ask any and all relevant questions. Certainly, this is a more structured form of assistance than defense attorneys receive.

However, new prosecutors still feel confused and overwhelmed during this initial period. Notwithstanding the assistance they receive, they are disoriented by the multitude of tasks performed by the prosecutor and by the environment in which he operates. This is particularly true in the circuit court, where the seemingly endless shuffling of files, the parade of defendants before the court and around the courtroom, the hurried, early morning plea bargaining sessions all come as a surprise to the new prosecutor.

Q. What were your initial impressions of the court during this "orientation period?"
A. The first time I came down here was a Monday morning at the arraignments. Let's face it, the majority of people here, you don't expect courts to be as crowded as they are. You don't expect thirty to thirty-five people to come out of the cell block who have been arrested over the weekend. It was . . . you sit in court the first few days, you didn't realize the court was run like this. All you see, you see Perry Mason on TV, or pictures of the Supreme Court, or you see six judges up there in a spotless courtroom, everyone well dressed, well manicured, and you come to

court and find people coming in their everyday clothes, coming up drunk, some are high on drugs, it's . . . it's an experience to say the least. [9]

Q. Could you describe your first few days when you came down here? What are your recollections? Anything strike you as strange?
A. Just the volume of business and all the stuff the prosecutor had to do. For the first week or two, I went to court with guys who had been here. Just sat there and watched. What struck me was the amount of things he [the prosecutor] has to do in the courtroom. The prosecutor runs the courtroom. Although the judge is theoretically in charge, we're standing there plea bargaining and calling the cases at the same time and chewing gum and telling the people to quiet down and setting bonds, and that's what amazed me. I never thought I would learn all the terms. What bothered me also was the paperwork. Not the Supreme Court decisions, not the *mens rea* or any of this other stuff, but the amount of junk that's in those files that you have to know. We never heard about this crap in law school. [51]

As suggested in the second excerpt, the new prosecutor is also surprised by the relative insignificance of the judge. He observes that the prosecutor assumes—through plea bargaining—responsibility for the disposition of many cases.[3] Contrary to his expectations of being an adversary in a dispute moderated by the judge, he finds that often the prosecutor performs the judge's function.

It is precisely this responsibility for resolving disputes that is most vexing to the new superior court state's attorney. Unlike his circuit court counterpart, he does not generally find hurried conferences, crowded courts, and so on. But he observes that, as in the circuit court, the state's attorney negotiates cases, and in the superior court far more serious issues and periods of incarceration are involved in these negotiations. For the novice state's attorney, the notion that he will in short order be responsible for resolving these disputes is particularly disturbing.

Q. What were your initial impressions of your job here [as a state's attorney]?
A. Well, I was frightened of the increased responsibility. I knew the stakes were high here . . . I didn't really know what to expect, and I would say it took me a good deal of time to adapt here.
Q. Adapt in which way?
A. To the higher responsibilities. Here you're dealing with felonies, serious felonies all the way up to homicides, and I had never been involved in that particular type of situation . . . I didn't believe that I was prepared to handle the type of job that I'd been hired to do. I looked around me and I saw the serious charges, the types of cases, and the experienced defense counsel on the one hand and the inexperience on my part on the other, and I was, well . . .

Q. Did you study up on your own?
A. No more than . . . Before I came over here I had done some research and made a few notes, et cetera, about the procedures. I think I was prepared from the book end of things to take the job, but, again, it was the practical aspects that you're not taught in law school and that you can only learn from experience that I didn't have, and that's what I was apprehensive about. [15]

These first weeks in the court, then, serve to familiarize the newcomer with the general patterns of case resolution. He is not immediately thrust into the court but is able to spend some time simply observing the way matters are handled. The result, though, is to increase his anxiety. The confusion of the circuit court and the responsibilities of a state's attorney in the superior court were not anticipated. The newcomer expects to be able to prepare cases leisurely and to rely on the skills learned in law school. Yet he finds that his colleagues seem to have neither the time nor the inclination to operate in this fashion. As the informal period of orientation draws to a close, the newcomer has a better perspective on the way the system operates, but still is on very uneasy footing about how to proceed when the responsibility for the case is his alone. In short, he is somewhat disoriented by his orientation.

The Prosecutor on His Own: Initial Firmness and Resistance to Plea Bargaining

Within a few weeks after starting his job, the prosecutor and the state's attorney are expected to handle cases on their own. Experienced personnel are still available for advice, and the newcomer is told that he can turn to them with his problems. But the cases are now the newcomer's, and, with one exception,[4] he is under no obligation to ask anyone for anything.[5]

The new prosecutor is confronted by a stream of defense attorneys asking for a particular plea bargain in a case. If the prosecutor agrees, his decision is irreversible. It would be a violation of all the unwritten folkways of the criminal court for either a defense attorney or a prosecutor to break his word.[6] On the other hand, if the prosecutor does not plea bargain, offers nothing in exchange for a plea, he at least does not commit himself to an outcome that may eventually prove to be a poor decision on his part. However, a refusal to plea bargain also places him "out of step" with his colleagues and with the general expectation of experienced defense attorneys.

Like the new attorney, the new prosecutor is in no hurry to dispose of the case. He is (1) inclined toward an adversary resolution of the case through formal hearings and trial, (2) disinclined to plea bargain in general, and (3) unsure about what constitutes an appropriate plea bargain for a particular case. Yet he is faced with demands by defense attorneys to resolve the case through plea bargaining. The new defense attorney has the luxury of postponing his decision for any given case. He can seek the advice of others before committing himself to a particular plea bargain in a particular case. For the new prosecutor, this is more difficult, since he is immediately faced with the demands of a number of attorneys in a number of different cases.

When the new prosecutor begins to handle his own cases, then, he lacks confidence about how to proceed in his dealings with defense attorneys. He often masks his insecurity in this period with an outward air of firmness. He is convinced that he must appear confident and tough, lest experienced attorneys think they can take advantage of him.

Q. What happened during your first few days of handling cases on your own?
A. Well, as a prosecutor, first of all, people try to cater to you because they want you to do favors for them. If you let a lawyer run all over you, you are dead. I had criminal the first day, on a Monday, and I'm in there [in the room where cases are negotiated], and a guy comes in, and I was talking to some lawyer on his file, and he's just standing there. Then I was talking to a second guy, and he was about fourth or fifth. So he looked at me and says: ''When the hell you going to get to me?'' So I says: ''You wait your fucking turn. I'll get to you when I'm ready. If you don't like it, get out.'' It's sad that you have to swear at people, but it's the only language they understand—especially lawyers. Lawyers are the most obstinate, arrogant, belligerent bastards you will ever meet. Believe me. They come into this court—first of all—and we are really the asshole of the judicial system [circuit court], and they come in here and don't really have any respect for you. They'll come in here and be nice to you, because they feel you'll give them a nolle. That's all. Lawyers do not respect this court. I don't know if I can blame them or not blame them. You can come in here and see the facilities here; you see how things are handled; you see how it's like a zoo pushing people in and out . . . When they do come here, lawyers have two approaches. One, they try to soft soap you and kiss your ass if you give them a nolle. Two, they'll come in here and try to ride roughshod over you and try to push you to a corner. Like that lawyer that first day. I had to swear at him and show him I wasn't going to take shit, and that's that. The problem of dealing with lawyers is that you can't let them bullshit you. So, when I first started out I tried to be . . . It's like the new kid on the block. He comes to a new neighborhood, and you've got to prove yourself. If you're a patsy, you're going to live with that as long as you're in court. If you let a couple of lawyers run over you, word will get around to go to ——, he's a pushover. Before you know it, they're running all over you. So you have to draw a line so they will respect you. [9]

At first I was very tough because I didn't know what I was doing. In other words, you have to be very wary. These guys, some of them, have

> been practicing in this court for forty years. And they'll take you to the cleaners. You have to be pretty damn careful. [51]

The new prosecutor couples this outward show of firmness toward attorneys with a fairly rigid plea bargaining posture. His reluctance to offer incentives to the defendant for a plea or to reward the defendant who chooses to plead is, at this point in the prosecutor's career, as much a function of his lack of confidence as it is a reflection of his antipathy toward plea bargaining. During this very early stage he is simply afraid to make concessions. Experienced court personnel are well aware that new prosecutors adopt this rigid stance.

> *Q*. Have you noticed any differences between new prosecutors and prosecutors that have been around awhile?
> *A*. Oh, yes. First of all, a new prosecutor is more likely to be less flexible in changing charges. He's afraid. He's cautious. He doesn't know his business. He doesn't know the liars. He can't tell when he's lying or exaggerating. He doesn't know all the ramifications. He doesn't know how tough it is sometimes to prove the case to juries. He hasn't got the experience, so that more likely than not he will be less flexible. He is also more easily fooled. [32, circuit court judge]

> I can only answer that question in a general way. It does seem to me that the old workhorses [experienced prosecutors] are more flexible than the young stallions. [69, superior court judge]

> *Q*. You were saying about the kids, the new prosecutors, the new state's attorneys. Are they kind of more hard-assed?
> *A*. They tend to be more nervous. They tend to have a less well-defined idea of what they can do and what they can't do without being criticized. So, to the extent that they are more nervous, they tend to be more hard-assed. [37, private criminal attorney]

> *Q*. What about new prosecutors? Do they differ significantly from prosecutors who have been around awhile?
> *A*. Initially a new prosecutor is going to be reluctant to nolle, reluctant to give too good a deal because he is scared. He is afraid of being taken advantage of. And if you are talking about the circuit court, they've got the problem that they can't even talk it over with anybody. They've got a hundred fifty cases or whatever, and they make an offer or don't make an offer, that's it. Maybe at the end of the day they may get a chance to talk it over and say: "Gee, did I do the right thing?" The defense attorney, when the offer is made, has the opportunity to talk to somebody plus his client before making a decision. So I think it takes the prosecutor a longer time to come around and work under the system. [33, legal aid attorney]

It is not difficult to understand why the new prosecutor is reluctant to plea bargain and why he appears rigid to court veterans. Set aside for the moment the prosecutor's personal preference for an adversary resolution and consider only the nature of the demands being made on him. Experienced attorneys want charges dropped, sentence recommendations, and nolles. They approach him with the standard argument about the wonderful personal traits of the defendant, the minor nature of the crime, the futility of incarceration, and so on. When the new prosecutor picks up the file, he finds that the defendant probably has an extensive prior criminal record and, often, that he has committed a crime that does not sound minor at all.[7] Under the statute for the crime involved, it is likely that the defendant faces a substantial period of incarceration, yet in almost all circuit court cases and in many superior court cases, the attorneys are talking about a no-time disposition. What to the new prosecutor frequently seems like a serious matter is treated as a relatively inconsequential offense by defense attorneys. And, because the newcomer views the matter as serious, his resolve to remain firm—or, conversely, his insecurity about reducing charges—is reinforced.[8]

Illustrations of this propensity for the new prosecutor or state's attorney to be "outraged" by the facts of the case, and to be disinclined to offer "sweet" deals, are plentiful. The following comments by two circuit court prosecutors and a superior court state's attorney, respectively, illustrate the extent to which the newcomer's appraisal of a case differed from that of the defense attorney and from that of his own colleagues.

> *Q*. You used to go to —— [chief prosecutor] for help on early cases. Were his recommendations out of line with what you thought should be done with the case?
> *A*. Let's say a guy came in with a serious crime . . . a crime that I thought was serious at one time, anyway. Take fighting on —— Avenue [a depressed area of Arborville]. He got twenty-five stitches in the head and is charged with aggravated assault. One guy got twenty-five stitches, the other fifteen. And the attorneys would want me to reduce it. I'd go and talk to —— [chief prosecutor]. He'd say: "They both are drunk, they both got head wounds. Let them plead to breach of peace, and the judge will give them a money fine." Things like that I didn't feel right about doing, since, to me, right out of law school, middle class, you figure twenty-five stitches in the head, Jesus Christ. [9]

> *Q*. How did you learn what a case was worth?
> *A*. What do you mean, what it's worth?
> *Q*. In terms of plea bargaining. What the going rate . . .
> *A*. From the prosecutors and defense attorneys who would look at me dumbfounded when I would tell them that I would not reduce this charge. And then they would go running to my boss and he'd say, "Well, it's up to him."[9] Some would even go running to the judge, screaming. One guy claimed surprise when I intended to go to trial for assault in second, which is a Class D felony. Two counts of that and two misdemeanor

counts. It was set for jury trial. His witnesses were there. His experience in this court, he said, having handled two or three hundred cases, was that none has ever gone to trial. So he claimed surprise the day of trial. He just couldn't believe it. [51]

Q. Were you in any way out of step with the way things were done here when you first began handling cases on your own?
A. In one respect I was. I evaluated a case by what I felt a proper recommendation should be, and my recommendations were almost always in terms of longer time. I found that the other guys in the office were breaking things down more than I expected. As a citizen, I couldn't be too complacent about an old lady getting knocked down, stuff like that. I thought more time should be recommended. I might think five to ten, six to twelve, while the other guys felt that three to seven was enough. [56]

Implicit in these remarks are the seeds of an explanation for a prosecutor's gradually becoming more willing to plea bargain. One can hypothesize that as his experience with handling cases increases, he will feel less outraged by the crime, and thus will be more willing to work out a negotiated settlement. One assistant state's attorney likened his change in attitude to that of a nurse in an emergency room.

It's like nurses in emergency rooms. You get so used to armed robbery that you treat it as routine, not as morally upsetting. In the emergency room, the biggest emergency is treated as routine. And it's happening to me. The nature of the offense doesn't cause the reaction in me that it would cause in the average citizen. Maybe this is a good thing; maybe it isn't. [56]

Though there is merit in this argument—prosecutors do become accustomed to crime—it is hardly a sufficient explanation of prosecutorial adaptation to plea bargaining. Other factors, often far more subtle, must be considered if we are to understand how and why the novice prosecutor becomes a seasoned plea bargainer.

Learning about Plea Bargaining

In the preceding sections I have portrayed the new prosecutor as being predisposed toward an adversary resolution of a case, uncertain about his responsibilities, rigid in his relations with defense attorneys, reluctant to drop charges and to plea bargain in cases that he considers serious, and anxious to try out the skills he learned in law school. This characterization of the newcomer contrasts sharply with that of the veteran prosecutor portrayed in chapter 4. There the prosecutor was described as taking an active role in plea bargaining—urging, cajoling, and threatening the defense attorney to share in the benefits of a negotiated disposition. How is the veteran prosecutor of chapter 4 to be reconciled with the new prosecutor of the preceding section?

The answer lies in what the prosecutor learns and is taught about plea bargaining. His education, like the defense attorney's, is not structured and systematic. Instead, he works his way through cases, testing the adversary and plea bargaining approaches. He learns piecemeal the costs and benefits of these approaches, and only over a period of time does he develop an appreciation for the relative benefits of a negotiated disposition.

Rather than proceed with a sequential discussion of the newcomer's experience, I think it more profitable at this point to distill from his experiences those central concerns that best explain his adaptation to the plea bargaining system. Some of the "flavor" of the adaptation process is sacrificed by proceeding in this fashion, but, in terms of clarity of presentation, I think it is a justifiable sacrifice. Thus, I will discuss separately the considerations that move the prosecutor in the plea bargaining direction, and later tie these together into an overall perspective on prosecutorial adaptation.

The Defendant's Factual and Legal Guilt

Prosecutors and state's attorneys learn that their roles primarily entail the processing of factually guilty defendants. Contrary to their expectations that problems of establishing factual guilt would be central to their job, they find that in most cases the evidence in the file is sufficient to conclude (and prove) that the defendant is factually guilty. For those cases where there is a substantial question as to factual guilt, the prosecutor has the power—and is inclined to exercise it—to nolle or dismiss the case. If he himself does not believe the defendant to be factually guilty, it is part of his formal responsibilities to filter the case out. But, of the cases that remain after the initial screening, the prosecutor believes the majority of defendants to be factually guilty.

Furthermore, he finds that defense attorneys only infrequently contest the prosecutor's own conclusion that the defendant is guilty. In their initial approach to the prosecutor they may raise the possibility that the defendant is factually innocent, but in most subsequent discussions their advances focus on disposition and not on the problem of factual guilt. Thus, from the prosecutor's own reading of the file (after screening) and from the comments of his "adversary," he learns that he begins with the upper hand; more often than not, the factual guilt of the defendant is not really disputable.

> *Q*. Are most of the defendants who come to this court guilty?
> *A*. Yeah, or else we wouldn't have charged them. You know, that's something that people don't understand. Basically the people that are brought here are believed very definitely to be guilty or we wouldn't go on with the prosecution. We would nolle the case, and, you know, that is something, when people say, "Well, do you really believe . . ." Yeah, I

do. I really do, and if I didn't and we can clear them, then we nolle it, there's no question about it. [30]

But most cases are good, solid cases, and in most of them the defendant is guilty. We have them cold-cocked. And they plead guilty because they are guilty . . . a guy might have been caught in a package store with bottles. Now, he wasn't there to warm his hands. The defendant may try some excuse, but they are guilty and they know they are guilty. And we'll give them a break when they plead guilty. I don't think we should throw away the key on the guy just because we got him cold-cocked. We've got good cases, we give them what we think the case is worth from our point of view, allowing the defendant's mitigating circumstances to enter. [62]

Q. The fact that you're willing to offer a pretty good bargain in negotiations might lead a person to plead guilty even if he had a chance to beat it at trial. But if he was found guilty at the trial he might not get the same result?
A. That's possible. I mean, only the accused person knows whether or not he's committed the crime, and . . . . It's an amazing thing, where, on any number of occasions, you will sit down to negotiate with an accused's attorney . . . and you know [he will say]: "No, no, he's not guilty, he wants his trial." But then if he develops a weakness in the case, or points out a weakness to you, and then you come back and say: "Well, we'll take a suspended sentence and probation," suddenly he says, "Yes, I'm guilty." So it leads you to conclude that, well, all these people who are proclaiming innocence are really not innocent. They're just looking for the right disposition. Now, from my point of view, the ideal situation might be if the person is not guilty, that he pleads not guilty, and we'll give him his trial and let the jury decide. But most people who are in court don't want a trial. I'm not the person who seeks them out and says, "I will drop this charge" or "I will reduce this charge, I will reduce the amount of time you have to do." They come to us, so, you know, the conclusion I think is there that any reasonable person could draw, that these people are guilty, that they are just looking for the best disposition possible. Very few people ask for a speedy trial. [15]

In addition to learning of the factual culpability of most defendants, the prosecutor also learns that defendants would be hard pressed to raise legal challenges to the state's case. As was discussed earlier, most cases are simply barren of any contestable legal issue, and nothing in the prosecutor's file or the defense attorney's arguments leads the prosecutor to conclude otherwise.

The new prosecutor or state's attorney, then, learns that in most cases the problem of establishing the defendant's factual and legal guilt is nonexistent. Typically, he begins with a very solid case, and, contrary to his expectations, he finds that few issues are in need of resolution at an adversary hearing or trial. The defendant's guilt is not generally problematic; it is conceded by the defense attorney.[10] What remains problematic is the sentence the defendant will receive.

Distinguishing among the Guilty Defendants

Formally, the prosecutor has some powers that bear directly on sentence. He has the option to reduce or eliminate charges leveled against the defendant; the responsibility for the indictment is his, and his alone. Thus, if he nolles some of the charges against the defendant, he can reduce the maximum exposure the defendant faces or insure that the defendant is sentenced only on a misdemeanor (if he nolles a felony), and so forth. Beyond these actions on charges, the formal powers of the prosecutor cease. The judge is responsible for sentencing. He is supposed to decide the conditions of probation, the length of incarceration, and so on. Notwithstanding this formal dichotomy of responsibility, prosecutors find that defense attorneys approach them about both charge and sentence reduction.

Since charge reduction bears on sentence reduction, it is only a small step for defense attorneys to inquire specifically about sentence; and, because there is often an interdependence between charge and sentence, prosecutors are compelled at least to listen to the attorney's arguments. Thus, the prosecutor finds attorneys parading before him asking for charge and sentence reduction, and, in a sense, he is obligated to hear them out.[11]

It is one thing to say that prosecutors and state's attorneys must listen to defense attorneys' requests about disposition and another so say that they must cooperate with these attorneys. As already indicated, new prosecutors feel acutely uneasy about charge and sentence reduction. They have neither the confidence nor the inclination to usurp what they view as primarily the judge's responsibility. Furthermore, one would think that their resolve not to become involved in this area would be strengthened by their learning that most defendants are factually and legally guilty. Why should they discuss dispositions in cases in which they "hold all the cards?"

This query presupposes that prosecutors continue to conceive of themselves as adversaries, whose exclusive task is to establish the defendant's guilt or innocence. But what happens is that as prosecutors gain greater experience handling cases, they gradually develop certain standards for evaluating cases, standards that bear not just on the defendant's guilt or innocence, but, more importantly, on the disposition of the defendant's case. These standards better explain prosecutorial behavior in negotiating dispositions than does the simple notion of establishing guilt or innocence.

Specifically, prosecutors come to distinguish between serious and nonserious cases, and between cases in which they are looking for time and cases in which they are not looking for time.[12] These standards or distinctions evolve after the prosecutor has processed a substantial number of factually and legally guilty defendants. They provide a means of sorting the raw material—the guilty defendants. Indeed, one can argue that the adversary component of the prosecutor's job is shifted from establishing guilt or innocence to determining the seriousness of the defendant's guilt and whether he should receive time. The guilt of the defendant is assumed, but the problem of disposition remains to be informally argued.

Prosecutors and state's attorneys draw sharp distinctions between serious and nonserious cases. In both instances, they assume the defendant guilty, but they are looking for different types of dispositions, dependent upon their classification of the case. If it is a nonserious matter, they are amenable to defense requests for a small fine in the circuit court, some short, suspended sentence, or some brief period of probation; similarly, in a nonserious superior court matter the state's attorney is willing to work out a combination suspended sentence and probation.[13] The central concern with these nonserious cases is to dispose of them quickly. If the defense attorney requests some sort of no-time disposition that is dependent upon either a prosecutorial reduction of charges or a sentence recommendation, the prosecutor and state's attorney are likely to agree. They have no incentive to refuse the attorney's request, since the attorney's desire comports with what they are "looking for." The case is simply not worth the effort to press for greater penalty.

On the other hand, if the case is serious, the prosecutor and state's attorney are likely to be looking for time. The serious case cannot be quickly disposed of by a no-time alternative. These are cases in which we would expect more involved and lengthy plea bargaining negotiations.

Whether the case is viewed as serious or nonserious depends on factors other than the formal charge(s) the defendant faces. For example, these nonformal considerations might include the degree of harm done the victim, the amount of violence employed by the defendant, the defendant's prior record, the characteristics of the victim and defendant, the defendant's motive; all are somewhat independent of formal charge, and yet all weigh heavily in the prosecutor's judgment of the seriousness of the case. Defendants facing the same formal charges, then, may find that prosecutors sort their cases into different categories. Two defendants charged with robbery with violence may find that in one instance the state's attorney is willing to reduce the charge and recommend probation, while in the second case he is looking for a substantial period of incarceration. In the former case, the defendant may have simply brushed against the victim (still technically robbery with violence), whereas in the second, he may have dealt the victim a severe blow. Or possibly, the first defendant was a junkie supporting his habit, whereas the second was operating on the profit motive. These are, of course, imperfect illustrations, but the point is that the determination as to whether a case is serious or not serious only partially reflects the charges against the defendant. Often the determination is based on a standard that develops with experience in the court, and operates, for the most part, independently of formal statutory penalties.

The following excerpts convey a sense of the serious/nonserious dichotomy and also support the argument that charge does not necessarily indicate seriousness.

> *Q*. How did you learn what cases were worth?
> *A*. You mean sentences.
> *Q*. Yeah.
> *A*. Well, that's a hit-or-miss kind of an experience. You take a first offender; any first offender in a nonviolent crime certainly is not going to jail for a nonviolent crime. And a second offender, well, it depends again on the type of crime, and maybe there should be some supervision, some probation. And a third time, you say, well, now this is a guy who maybe you should treat a little more strictly. Now, a violent crime, I would treat differently. How did I learn to? I learned because there were a few other guys around with experience, and I got experience, and they had good judgments, workable approaches, and you pick it up like that. In other words, you watch others, you talk to others, you handle a lot of cases yourself.
> *Q*. Does anybody, the public, put pressure on you to be tougher?
> *A*. Not really.
> *Q*. Wouldn't these sentences be pretty difficult for the public to understand?
> *A*. Yeah, somewhat . . . Sure, we are pretty easy on a lot of these cases except that . . . We are tough on mugging and crimes by violence. Say an old lady is grabbed by a kid and knocked to the ground and her pocketbook taken as she is waiting for the bus. We'd be as tough as anybody on that one, whether you call it a breach of peace or a robbery. We'd be very tough. And in this case there would be a good likelihood of the first offender going to jail, whatever the charge we give him. The name of the charge isn't important. We'd have the facts regardless. [52]

> *Q*. So you think you have changed? You give away more than you used to?
> *A*. I don't give away more. I think that I have reached the point where . . . When I started I was trying to be too fair, if you want to say that, you know, to see that justice was done, and I was severe. But, you know, like —— [head prosecutor] says, you need to look for justice tempered with mercy, you know, substantial justice, and that's what I do now. When I was new, a guy cut [knifed] someone he had to go to jail. But now I look for substantial justice—if two guys have been drinking and one guy got cut, I'm not giving anything away, but a fine, that's enough there.
> *Q*. But you are easier now? I mean, you could look for time?
> *A*. Look, if I get a guy that I feel belongs in jail, I try to sentence bargain and get him in jail. We had this one guy, ——. He was charged with

breach of peace. We knew he had been selling drugs but we couldn't prove anything. He hits this girl in ——'s parking lot [large department store], and tried to take her purse. She screams and he runs. This was a real son-of-a-bitch, been pimping for his own wife. On breach of peace I wanted the full year, and eventually got nine months. Cases like that I won't give an inch on.[14] And the lawyer first wanted him to plead to suspended sentence and a money fine. I said this guy is a goddamned animal. Anybody who lets his wife screw and then gets proceeds from it, and deals in drugs . . . well, if you can catch the bastard on it, he belongs behind bars. [9]

After a matter of time you just see so much that you really . . . You must always remember there are always two sides to the story, even though somebody might've gotten belted with a pipe, and it is a serious offense, but there might be something in mitigation to that. You know, there are some statutes that are mandatory minimum time. Assault in the third degree with a dangerous weapon is mandatory time of one year. Now if we stuck to that statute and subsection, if we stuck to that, we'd be trying everything out there; there'd be a lot of people going away for a minimum of one year. But a lot of times we allow a little flexibility; we give them assault in the third but not with a dangerous weapon, and then we or the judge look at the facts. This kid today was an example, the kid who hit the guy on the wrist with a pipe. Now technically he was guilty of assault with a dangerous weapon; he could have been charged with assault in the third with a dangerous weapon, and the mandatory minimum one year in jail. But the kid had a clean record, the fight was no big thing, so I gave him assault in the third, under subsection one, which is not with a dangerous weapon, and we were looking for a suspended sentence. That's what the judge did, thirty days suspended. [5]

When the legislature last October changed the jurisdiction of the circuit court to include all five-year felonies, this, of course, kept out of this court [superior court] a number of what we could term minor felonies. By that I would mean all the forgery cases, the breaking and entering cases, possession of heroin cases. Those generally were the type of cases that would be associated first of all with junkies, and, secondly, were not looked upon too seriously because usually there is no violence involved in them. And assuming the person did not have a bad record or he was going to get into some sort of rehabilitation program, you could almost predict if a person did not have a substantial record, he was going to get a probationary period rather than confinement. [15]

You've still got to always differentiate between serious cases where there's incarceration involved, and nickel-and-dime cases where you're talking about records. And when you are talking about a record, or the amount of a fine, you know, the nature of the charge, the considerations are different in each of those types of cases. [10]

The second standard used by prosecutors and state's attorneys in processing factually and legally guilty defendants is the time/no-time distinction. There is an obvious relationship between the serious/nonserious standard and this one: in the serious case, time is generally the goal; whereas in the nonserious case, a no-time disposition is satisfactory to the prosecutor. But this simple relationship does not always hold, and it is important for us to consider the exceptions.

In some serious cases, the prosecutor or state's attorney may not be looking for time. Generally, these are cases in which the prosecutor has a problem establishing either the factual or legal guilt of the defendant, and thus is willing to settle for a plea to the charge and offer a recommendation of a suspended sentence. The logic is simple: the prosecutor feels the defendant is guilty of the offense but fears that if he insists on time, the defense attorney will go to trial and uncover the factual or legal defects of the state's case. Thus, the prosecutor "sweetens the deal" to extract a guilty plea and to decrease the likelihood that the attorney will gamble on complete vindication.

Of the prosecutors I interviewed, a handful expressed disenchantment with plea bargaining. They felt that their associates were being too lenient, giving away too much in return for the defendant's plea. They argued that the prosecutor's office should stay firm and go to trial if necessary in order to obtain higher sentences. They were personally inclined to act this way; they "didn't like plea bargaining." But when pushed a bit, it became clear that their antipathy to plea bargaining was not without its exceptions. In the serious case with factual or legal defects they felt very strongly that plea bargaining was appropriate. The sentiments of such an "opponent" to plea bargaining are presented below.

Q. So you are saying that you only like some kinds of plea bargaining?
A. I like to negotiate cases where I have a problem with the case. I know the guy is guilty, but I have some legal problem, or unavailability of a witness that the defendant doesn't know about that will make it difficult for us to put the case on. I would have trouble with the case. Then it is in my interest to bargain; even in serious cases with these problems, it is in the best interests of the state to get the guy to plead, even if it's to a felony with a suspended sentence.
Q. If there was no plea bargaining, then the state would lose out?
A. Yes, in cases like these. These would be cases that without plea bargaining we would have trouble convicting the defendant. But this has nothing to do with the defendant's guilt or innocence. Yet we might have to let him go. It is just to plea bargain in cases like this. It is fair to get the plea from the defendant, since he is guilty. Now, there is another situation; whereas in the first situation, I have no philosophical problems with plea bargaining. We may have a weak case factually. Maybe the case depends on one witness, and I have talked to the witness and realized how the witness would appear in court. Maybe the witness would

be a flop when he testifies. If I feel the defendant is guilty, but the witness is really bad, then I know that we won't win the case at trial, that we won't win a big concession in plea bargaining. So I will evaluate the case, and I will be predisposed to talking about a more lenient disposition. [40]

The significance of the "philosophical opponent" to plea bargaining embracing plea bargaining for certain cases will be discussed later. Suffice it to say here that this eagerness to negotiate some cases is important in understanding why policy proposals to eliminate plea bargaining are unlikely to obtain much support from court personnel. For the moment, I present their position only to illustrate the serious-case/no-time position.

The other unexpected cross between the standards—nonserious case/looking for time—occurs in several types of situations. First, there is the case in which the defendant has a long history of nonserious offenses, and it is felt that a short period of incarceration will "teach him a lesson," or at least indicate that there are limits beyond which prosecutors cannot be pushed.[15] Second, there is the situation where the prosecutor holds the defense attorney in disdain and is determined to teach the attorney a lesson. Thus, though the defendant's offense is nonserious, and the prosecutor would generally be amenable to a no-time disposition, the prosecutor chooses to hold firm. It is precisely in these borderline cases that the prosecutor can be most successful in exercising sanctions against the uncooperative defense attorney. The formal penalties associated with the charges against the defendant give him ample sentencing range, and by refusing to agree to a no-time disposition, the costs to the defense attorney become great. The attorney is not able to meet his client's demands for no time, and yet he must be leery about trial, given the even greater exposure the defendant faces. These borderline decisions by prosecutors, then, are fertile grounds for exploring sanctions against defense attorneys. It is here that we can expect the cooperative defense attorneys to benefit most, and the recalcitrant defense attorney to suffer the most. Relatedly, one can also expect prosecutors to be looking for time in nonserious offenses in which the defendant or his counsel insists on raising motions and going to trial. These adversary activities may be just enough to tip the prosecutor into looking for time.

In addition to its relationship to the serious/nonserious standard, the time/no-time standard bears on prosecutorial plea bargaining behavior in another way. As prosecutors gain experience in the plea bargaining system, they tend to stress "certainty of time" rather than "amount of time." This is to say that they become less concerned about extracting maximum penalties from defendants and more concerned with insuring that in cases in which they are looking for time, the defendant actually receives some time.[16] Obviously, there are limits to the prosecutor's largesse—in a serious case thirty days will not be considered sufficient time. But prosecutors are willing to consider periods of incarceration substantially shorter than the maximum sentence allowable for a particular crime. In return, though, prosecutors want a guarantee of sorts that the defendant will receive time. They want to decrease the likelihood that the defendant, by some means or other, will obtain a suspended sentence. Thus, they will "take" a fixed amount of time if the defendant agrees not to try to "pitch" for a lower sentence,[17] or if the defendant pleads to a charge in which all participants know some time will be meted out by the judge. In the latter instance, the attorney may be free to "pitch," but court personnel know his effort is more a charade for the defendant than a realistic effort to obtain a no-time disposition. The following excerpts illustrate prosecutorial willingness to trade off years of time for certainty of time.

> I don't believe in giving away things. In fact —— [a public defender] approached me; there's this kid ——, he has two robberies, one first degree, one second, and three minor cases. Now, this kid I made out an affidavit myself for tampering with a witness. This kid is just n.g. —— came to me and said, "We'll plead out, two to five." He'll go to state's prison. I agreed to that—both these offenses are bindovers. These kids belong in jail. I'd rather take two to five here than bind them over to superior court and take a chance on what will happen there. At least my two to five will be a year and three-quarters in state's prison. The thing is, if I want to get a guy in jail for a year, I'll plea bargain with him, and I'll take six months if I can get it, because the guy belongs in jail, and if I can get him to jail for six months why should I fool around with that case, and maybe get a year if I am lucky? If I can put a guy away for six months I might be cheated out of six months, but at least the guy is doing six months in jail. [9]

> What is a proper time? It never bothers me if we could have gotten seven years and instead we got five. In this case, there was no violence; minor stuff was stolen. We got time out of him. That is the important thing. [21]

> *A*. It makes no difference to me really if a man does five to ten or four to eight. The important thing is he's off the street, not a menace to society for a period of time, and the year or two less is not going to make that great a difference. If you do get time, I think it's . . . you know, many prosecutors I know feel this way. They have achieved confinement, that's what they're here for.
> *Q*. Let's take another example. Yesterday an attorney walked in here when I was present on that gambling case. He asked you if it could be settled without time?
> *A*. And I said no. That ended the discussion.
> *Q*. What will he do now?
> *A*. He'll file certain motions that he really doesn't have to file. All the facts of our case were spelled out; he knows as much about our cases as

he'll ever know. So his motions will just delay things. There'll come a point, though, when he'll have to face trial; and he'll come in to speak with us, and ask if we still have the same position. We'll have the same position. We'll still be looking for one to three. His record goes back to 1923, he's served two or three terms for narcotics, and he's been fined five times for gambling. So we'd be looking for one to three and a fine. Even though he's in his sixties, he's been a criminal all his life, since 1923 . . .
Q. But if the attorney pushes and says, "Now look. He's an old guy. He's sixty-two years old, how about six months?"
A. I might be inclined to accept it because, again, confinement would be involved. I think our ends would be met. It would show his compadres that there's no longer any immunity for gambling, that there is confinement involved. So the end result would be achieved. [15]

Justice Holmes, who is supposed to be the big sage in American jurisprudence, said it isn't the extent of the punishment but the certainty of it. This is my basic philosophy. If the guy faces twelve years in state's prison, I'm satisfied if on a plea of guilty he'll go to state's prison for two or three years. [42]

The experienced prosecutor, then, looks beyond the defendant's guilt when evaluating a case. He learns—from a reading of the file and from the defense attorney's entreaties—that most defendants are factually and legally guilty and that he generally holds the upper hand. As he gains experience in processing these cases, he gradually begins to draw distinctions within this pool of guilty defendants. Some of the cases appear not to be serious, and the prosecutor becomes willing to go along with the defense attorney's request for no-time dispositions. The cases simply do not warrant a firmer prosecutorial posture. In serious cases, when he feels time is in order, he often finds defense attorneys in agreement on the need for some incarceration.

In a sense, the prosecutor redefines his professional goals. He learns that the statutes fail to distinguish adequately among guilty defendants, that they "sweep too broadly," and give short shrift to the specific facts of the offense, to the defendant's prior record, to the degree of contributory culpability of the victim, and so on. Possessing more information about the defendant than the judge does, the prosecutor—probably unconsciously—comes to believe that it is his professional responsibility to develop standards that distinguish among defendants and lead to "equitable" dispositions. Over time, the prosecutor comes to feel that if he does not develop these standards, if he does not make these professional judgments, no one else will.[18]

The prosecutor seems almost to drift into plea bargaining. When he begins his job he observes that his colleagues plea bargain routinely and quickly finds that defense attorneys expect him to do the same. Independent of any rewards, sanctions, or pressures, he learns the strengths of his cases, and learns to distinguish the serious from the nonserious ones. After an initial period of reluctance to plea bargain at all (he is fearful of being taken advantage of by defense attorneys), the prosecutor finds that he is engaged almost unwittingly in daily decisions concerning the disposition of cases. His obligation to consider alternative charges paves the way for the defense attorney's advances; it is only a small jump to move to sentence discussions. And as he plea bargains more and more cases, the serious/nonserious and time/no-time standards begin to hold sway in his judgments. He feels confident about the disposition he is looking for, and if a satisfactory plea bargain in line with his goals can be negotiated, he comes to feel that there is little point to following a more formal adversary process.

Reducing Uncertainty and the Risks of Trial

The description of the prosecutor drifting into plea bargaining—learning to sort serious from nonserious cases, and becoming increasingly comfortable about discussing dispositions—partially explains prosecutorial adaptation to plea bargaining. It speaks only to the "learning to plea bargain" component of the prosecutor's adaptation. The prosecutor learns that defendants are guilty and that in nonserious cases a quick, efficient, and mutually satisfactory disposition is possible through informal negotiation. But why does the prosecutor develop a preference for certainty of time over maximum time? Why is he willing to trade off years of time in return for an agreement on a fixed period of incarceration?

The development of the "certain time" component of the time/no-time standard is best understood as a result of the sanctions prosecutors experience (or think they might experience) if they refuse to negotiate sentences. Recall that the prosecutors are dealing with serious cases and that the defense attorneys involved in these cases probably recognize that some time will be included in the disposition. The issue is whether the prosecutor ought to negotiate sentence or whether he ought to insist that the defendant plead as charged and take his chances before a judge. The latter option increases—or is perceived by prosecutors as increasing—the likelihood that the defendant will opt for trial. The defendant may feel that he has little to lose by gambling on an acquittal at trial. It is true that if he is convicted he will bear the additional burden of a "penalty for trial," and he will still face an uncertain future before a judge. However, in light of the prosecutor's refusal to negotiate a sentence in return for a plea, the defendant in the serious case may feel that the cost of the penalty (assuming that it will involve time) is outweighed by even a slight chance for acquittal.

The new prosecutor is not particularly disturbed by the possibility that his refusal to plea bargain over sentence may lead the defendant to trial. As we saw earlier, he feels uncomfortable about plea bargaining and is particularly disturbed by sentence negotiations. He believes that sentencing is the judge's responsibility, that a defendant either ought to plead as charged or go to trial, and that it is his job as prosecutor to establish the defendant's guilt in trial. Furthermore, he does not view the threat of trial as much of a threat at all; his case seems strong, and he is confident that there is little chance of victory for the defense.

What the new prosecutor is taught is that no matter how solid a case he has, there is always the possibility that he will lose at trial. And a defeat at trial means total loss; whereas, the defense attorney might have been willing to agree to some time as part of a plea bargaining agreement, after defeat the prosecutor has neither a conviction nor a period of incarceration.

Experienced prosecutors pointed to the unpredictability of juries as the foremost explanation for why a seemingly "sure" case is lost at trial. A number of prosecutors recalled their own early defeats in front of a jury, and maintained that they were taught a significant lesson from their experience: they became more willing to negotiate cases to insure a conviction and some period of incarceration. By a stroke of good fortune, I had the opportunity to witness firsthand a prosecutor being taught this particular lesson.

I had mentioned to a new circuit court prosecutor that I planned to be in his court on a particular day and that I would try to interview him then. When I arrived, he was presenting his final arguments to a jury. After the prosecutor's presentation, the court recessed for lunch, and he agreed to begin our interview during lunch and continue it while the jury deliberated. This provided an opportunity for me to probe the plea bargaining history of the case prior to a final jury verdict.

The defendant was alleged to have physically struck the driver of another car after a minor car accident. The charge of aggravated assault specified that the defendant ran after the victim with a lead pipe in hand, caught the victim, aimed the pipe at the victim's head, but delivered a blow that actually struck the victim's outstretched arm. The prosecutor considered this a very serious offense because a physical attack ensued and because, had the defendant been successful in hitting the victim's head, the charge might very well have been manslaughter or murder. In any event, this new prosecutor was confident. He had several witnesses to the incident, and there appeared to be no legal problems with the case. The prosecutor had lost his first jury trial and was confident that this one would be different.

The defense attorney for this case had attempted to plea bargain several times prior to trial. The only offer the prosecutor was willing to make was to reduce the charge to breach of peace, which, under the statute in effect at the time of the incident, carried a one-year maximum penalty. All requests by the defense attorney for a prosecutorial recommendation of a suspended sentence and fine were refused by the prosecutor. He wanted the one-year period of incarceration.

As the trial progressed, the prosecutor's confidence increased. The witnesses made firm identifications, and there did not appear to be any holes in the state's case. Indeed, the defense attorney took the prosecutor aside during the trial in a last-ditch attempt at plea bargaining. He implied that his client might take a short period of incarceration. Again the prosecutor refused.

During our interview, the prosecutor indicated that he was looking for at least a one-year incarceration and that after conviction he might even recommend a longer sentence. We were discussing this possibility when a clerk informed us that the jury had reached a decision.

The jury filed into the courtroom, and the foreman announced the verdict: Not Guilty. The prosecutor's gasp could not be heard amid the hugs and shouts of glee of the defendant, his family, and his attorney. His air of optimism was replaced with a shocked and pallid expression. He simply could not believe that he had lost.

Before resuming our interview, the prosecutor sought solace from the judge. He wanted to know what the judge thought about the defendant's guilt. Apparently the judge was sympathetic, telling the prosecutor that he disagreed with the jury's verdict, and that he would have sentenced the defendant to a jail term had he been convicted. But he also told the prosecutor that "these are the kinds of things that happen with juries. You just never know."

Eventually the prosecutor returned to his office, and I was able to discuss with him what had transpired. He offered a number of possible explanations for why the jury chose to acquit but remained unconvinced that there was any serious, legitimate factual defect in the case.[19] Essentially, he felt that the jury had acted irrationally.

However, attributing the acquittal to the irrationality of the jury did not seem to make him feel any better about the outcome. He chastised himself several times for not thinking more carefully about negotiating the case, especially after he had sensed that the attorney would take a brief period of incarceration. "Maybe I should have come down [in his plea bargain offer]. I think he would have taken a few months . . . Maybe I should have . . ." It was plain that he was rethinking his refusal to plea bargain over sentence.

When I completed the interview, I encountered another prosecutor whom I had interviewed several days earlier. In his interview, he had stressed the unpredictability of juries and had expressed his preference for negotiated dispositions. He had also noted that the two newcomers in the office had not yet been taught the risks of trial. At the time of this second encounter, he had already heard of the newcomer's defeat. "You see," he said to me, "that's why I don't like to try a case. He'll think twice about it next time."[20] [52]

The point of this illustration is clear. The newcomer is taught that there are risks attached to trying even the "sure" case. Whereas a plea bargain could yield a conviction and a certain period of incarceration, defeat at trial yields neither incarceration nor conviction. The prosecutor ''loses'' on both counts; his defeat is complete.

If the option of negotiating time was not available, perhaps these defeats would not weigh so heavily on the minds of the novice prosecutor. He could attribute his defeat to his inexperience, and maintain that such an outcome is an inevitable byproduct of his need to obtain trial experience.[21] But the option to negotiate time does dangle before his eyes in almost every case. He could have won a conviction; he could have extracted some time from the defendant had he chosen to negotiate. He had an option other than that of going to trial, an option he eschewed, but one that would have led to ''victory.'' Perhaps he lost the case because of his own inexperience at trial; but in all likelihood he will attribute that defeat, and subsequent ones, at least partially to the unpredictability of juries. He has had firsthand experience with the court veterans' adage that ''no case is 100 percent sure one way or the other.'' In subsequent cases, he will consider more carefully the possibility of a negotiated ''victory.''

I do not mean to suggest that defeat at one or two trials invariably leads every prosecutor to negotiate every case. Obviously, prosecutors will continue to try some cases, and they will employ their own calculi to estimate their chances of success at trial. But experiencing a defeat in a ''sure'' case, and/or hearing of such defeats suffered by one's colleagues, is sufficient to cause them to give substantial pause before rejecting the option of negotiating time.

Ironically, the opposite result—that is, a prosecutor's victory at trial—may also increase his willingness to negotiate time. Though victory yields a conviction, the prosecutor still is not assured of a fixed period of incarceration. After trial, the judge is more familiar with the facts of the case, and he is less likely to simply rubberstamp a prosecutor's recommendation. Thus, to an extent, the uncertainty whether the defendant will ''do time'' remains. Furthermore, even if the judge's sentence corresponds roughly to the prosecutor's recommendation, the sentence itself may not differ substantially from what the defense attorney would have accepted as part of the plea bargain.[22] The prosecutor's time and effort expended on trial may, then, only have a marginal impact on final disposition. The following excerpts are illustrative of these concerns.

> Because, don't forget, once you are convicted, all I can do is recommend to a judge; and the way the tendency is now—to kind of rehabilitate this one, and rehabilitate that one—I trust myself as to sentencing. [9]

> Now, any case, particularly a jury case, can be lost. Or, you can try a case, and try it for several weeks, and very often not get any result in terms of punishment for the defendant that you couldn't have plea bargained for in the beginning, and I just feel that to try cases for the sake of

> trying cases, and for the sake of giving the judge the say in what the individual is going to get, I just think, that from a practical point of view, it is absurd. What is the sense, from the state's point of view, in going to trial in a serious criminal case; of bringing in witnesses; tying up a judge for two weeks; bringing in twelve angry men, or fourteen, because you need two alternates; paying them; feeding them for a couple of weeks; tying up the sheriffs; transporting the guy back and forth from the jail—all of this for a trial, when the same result, or just about the same result, or just as good a result from everybody's point of view could have been worked out here at the desk. I just don't see it. The only reason I could see for doing it is, well, you could say, "It's the judge's prerogative to decide what an individual is going to get." Well, I just don't buy that. [17]

These considerations—continuing uncertainty about the judge's sentence and the related possibility that the trial will not make a difference in sentence—buttress the prosecutor's conviction that a negotiated disposition over sentence is a reasonable approach to follow. By venturing little and negotiating a time disposition, he avoids the chance of acquittal and conserves his resources. Contrariwise, a trial bears the risks of acquittal, is a substantial consumer of prosecutorial resources, and may not have an appreciable effect on sentence.[23] To paraphrase (and twist a bit) an old cliché: nothing ventured may be a lot gained; whereas something ventured may be nothing gained.

Case Pressure and Potential Backlog

Though they may do so during the first few weeks, the newcomer's peers and superiors do not generally pressure him to move cases because of volume. Instead, he is thrust in the fray largely on his own and is allowed to work out his own style of case disposition. Contrary to the "conspiratorial perspective" of the adaptation process, he is not coerced to cooperate in processing "onerously large case loads."

The newcomer's plea bargaining behavior is conditioned by his reactions to particular cases he handles or learns about and not by caseload problems of the office. The chief prosecutor within the jurisdiction may worry about his court's volume and the speed with which cases are disposed, but he does not generally interfere with his assistant's decisions about how to proceed in a case.[24] The newcomer is left to learn about plea bargaining on his own, and for the reasons already discussed, he learns and is taught the value of negotiating many of his cases. The absence of a direct relationship between prosecutor plea bargaining and case pressure is suggested in the following remarks.

> *Q*. Is it case pressure that leads you to negotiate?
> *A*. I don't believe it's the case pressure at all. In every court, whether

there are five cases or one hundred cases, we should try to settle it. It's good for both sides. If I were a public defender I'd try to settle all the cases for my guilty clients. By negotiating you are bound to do better. Now take this case. [He reviewed the facts of a case in which an elderly man was charged with raping a seven-year-old girl. The defendant claimed he could not remember what happened, that he was drunk, and that, though the girl might have been in the bed with him, he did not think he raped her.] I think I gave the defense attorney a fair deal. The relatives say she was raped, but the doctors couldn't conclusively establish that. I offered him a plea to a lesser charge, one dealing with advances toward minors, but excluding the sex act. If he takes it, he'll be able to walk away with time served [the defendant had not posted bail and had spent several months in jail]. It's the defendant's option though. He can go through trial if he wants, but if he makes that choice, the kid and her relatives will have to be dragged through the agonies of trial also. Then I would be disposed to look for a higher sentence for the defendant. So I think my offer is fair, and the offer has nothing to do with the volume of this court. It's the way I think the case—all things considered—should be resolved. [21]

Q. You say the docket wasn't as crowded in 1966, and yet there was plea bargaining. If I had begun this interview by saying why is there plea bargaining here . . .
A. I couldn't use the reason there's plea bargaining because there are a lot of cases. That's not so; that's not so at all. If we had only ten cases down for tomorrow and an attorney walked in and wanted to discuss a case with me, I'd sit down and discuss it with him. In effect, that's plea bargaining. Whether it's for the charge or for an agreed recommendation or reduction of the charge or what have you, it's still plea bargaining. It's part of the process that has been going on for quite a long time.
Q. And you say it's not because of the crowded docket, but if I gave you a list of reasons for why there was plea bargaining and asked you to pick the most important . . .
A. I never really thought about the . . . You talk about the necessity for plea bargaining, and you say, well, it's necessary, and one of the reasons is because we have a crowded docket, but even if we didn't we still would plea bargain.
Q. Why?
A. Well, it has been working throughout the years, and the way I look at it, it's beneficial to the defendant, it's beneficial to the court, and not just in saving time but in avoiding police officers coming to court, witnesses being subpoenaed in, and usually things can be discussed between prosecutors and defense counsel which won't be said in the open court and on the record. There are many times that the defense counsel will speak confidentially with the prosecutor about his client or about the facts or about the complainant or a number of things. So I don't know if I can

> justify plea bargaining other than by speaking of the necessity of plea bargaining. If there were only ten cases down for one day, it still would be something that would be done. [5]

> Maybe in places like New York they plea bargain because of case pressure. I don't know. But here it is different. We dispose of cases on the basis of what is fair to both sides. You can get a fair settlement by plea bargaining. If you don't try to settle a case quickly, it gets stale. In New York the volume probably is so bad that it becomes a matter of "getting rid of cases." In Connecticut, we have some pretty big dockets in some cities, but in other areas—here, for example—we don't have that kind of pressure. Sure, I feel some pressure, but you can't say that we negotiate our cases out to clear the docket. And you probably can't say that even about the big cities in Connecticut either. [46]

Prosecutors, then, do not view their propensity to plea bargain as a direct outcome of case pressure. Instead, they speak of "mutually satisfactory outcomes," "fair dispositions," "reducing police overcharging," and so on.[25] We need not here evaluate their claims in detail; what is important is that collectively their arguments militate against according case pressure the "top billing" it so often receives in the literature.

Another way to conceptualize the relationship between case pressure and plea bargaining is to introduce the notion of a "potential backlog." Some prosecutors maintain that if fewer cases were plea bargained, or if plea bargaining were eliminated, a backlog of cases to be disposed of would quickly clog their calendars. A potential backlog, then, lurks as a possibility in every jurisdiction. Even in a low volume jurisdiction, one complex trial could back up cases for weeks, or even months. If all those delayed cases also had to be tried, the prosecutor feels he would face two not so enviable options. He could become further backlogged by trying as many of them as was feasible, or he could reduce his backlog by outright dismissal of cases.[26] The following comments are typical of the potential backlog argument.

> *Q*. Some people have suggested that plea bargaining not be allowed in the court. All cases would go to trial before a judge or jury and . . .
> *A*. Something like that would double, triple, and quadruple the backlog. Reduce that 90 percent of people pleading guilty, and even if you were to try a bare minimum of those cases, you quadruple your backlog. It's not feasible. [5]

> Well, right now we don't have a backlog. But if we were to try even 10 percent of our cases, take them to a jury, we'd be so backed up that we couldn't even move. We'd be very much in the position of . . . some traffic director in New York once said that there will come a time that there will be one car too many coming into New York and nobody will be able to move. Well, we can get ourselves into that kind of situation if we

are going to go ahead and refuse to plea bargain even in the serious cases. [42]

Though a potential backlog is an ever-present possibility, it should be stressed that most prosecutors develop this argument more as a prediction as to the outcome of a rule decreasing or eliminating plea bargaining than as an explanation for why they engage in plea bargaining.[27] If plea bargaining were eliminated, a backlog would develop; but awareness of this outcome does not explain why they plea bargain.

Furthermore, prosecutors tend to view the very notion of eliminating plea bargaining as a fake issue, a straw-man proposition. It is simply inconceivable to them that plea bargaining could or would be eliminated. They maintain that no court system could try all of its cases, even if huge increases in personnel levels were made; trials consume more time than any realistic increase in personnel levels could manage.[28] They were willing to speculate on the outcome of a rule proscribing plea bargaining, but the argument based on court backlog that they evoked was not a salient consideration in understanding their day-in, day-out plea bargaining behavior.

It is, of course, impossible to refute with complete certainty an argument that prosecutors plea bargain because failure to do so would cause a backlog of unmanageable proportions to develop. However, the interviews indicate other more compelling ways to conceptualize prosecutorial adaptation to plea bargaining, and these do not depend on a potential backlog that always can be conjured up. Though the backlog may loom as a consequence of a failure to plea bargain, it—like its case-pressure cousin—is neither a necessary nor sufficient explanatory vehicle for understanding the core aspects of prosecutorial plea bargaining behavior.

A Perspective on Prosecutorial Adaptation

In this concluding section, I will explain the experienced prosecutor's behavior in light of what we have learned about his adaptation to the court. This approach allows us to integrate the adaptation material with the descriptive account of the experienced prosecutor's plea bargaining behavior presented in chapters 3 and 4.

Perhaps the most important outcome of the prosecutor's adaptation is that he evidences a major shift in his own presumption about how to proceed with a case. As a newcomer, he feels it to be his responsibility to establish the defendant's guilt at trial, and he sees no need to justify a decision to go to trial. However, as he processes more and more cases, as he drifts into plea bargaining, and as he is taught the risks associated with trials, his own assumption about how to proceed with a case changes. He approaches every case with plea bargaining in mind, that is, he presumes that the case will be plea bargained. If it is a "nonserious" matter, he expects it to be quickly resolved; if it is "serious" he generally expects to negotiate time as part of the disposition. In both instances, he anticipates that the case will eventually be resolved by a negotiated disposition and not by a trial. When a plea bargain does not materialize, and the case goes to trial, the prosecutor feels compelled to justify his failure to reach an accord. He no longer is content to simply assert that it is the role of the prosecutor to establish the defendant's guilt at trial. This adversary component of the prosecutor's role has been replaced by a self-imposed burden to justify why he chose to go to trial, particularly if a certain conviction—and, for serious cases, a period of incarceration—could have been obtained by means of a negotiated disposition.

Relatedly, the prosecutor grows accustomed to the power he exercises in these plea bargaining negotiations. As a newcomer, he argued that his job was to be an advocate for the state and that it was the judge's responsibility to sentence defendants. But, having in fact "sentenced" most of the defendants whose files he plea bargained, the distinction between prosecutor and judge becomes blurred in his own mind. Though he did not set out to usurp judicial prerogatives—indeed, he resisted efforts to engage him in the plea bargaining process—he gradually comes to expect that he will exercise sentencing powers. There is no fixed point in time when he makes a calculated choice to become adjudicator as well as adversary. In a sense, it simply "happens"; the more cases he resolves (either by charge reduction or sentence recommendations), the greater the likelihood that he will lose sight of the distinction between the roles of judge and prosecutor.

The interview results support the hypothesis that the prosecutor—not the judge—looms as the central and most important figure for case disposition in the local criminal court.[29] The remarks that follow are typical of the responses to my question to defense attorneys as to the relative importance of the prosecutor and judge.

> Well, I'm not sure that it ought to be the case that the prosecutor is more important than the judge, but it certainly is. He can frequently give you the benefit of the doubt on the degree of an offense, which makes a difference in terms of the maximum exposure. He can make the difference in terms of how many counts you get thrown at you. A burglary can be a burglary and can become a burglary plus a larceny, and if there's somebody brushed on the stairway or pushed out of the way on his way down, he'll add still another offense. And if in the process he pushes a police officer, you're going to have still another offense. It's not hard for the prosecutor to really give your guy about nine counts for the same offense if he wants, and it's all perfectly legal. And then there are his sentence recommendations also. [23]

> I'm sure that many judges would disagree with an assertion that the prosecutor is more important. But very few recommendations are not accepted

by the judges. So, in a practical, day-by-day way, justice is really being administered by the state's attorney's office and by the private attorneys and public defenders and not by the judges. The court just stamps these deals. [57]

Similarly, a prosecutor succinctly summarized the powers that accrue to his role in the court.

Q. You seem to be suggesting that you have a lot of latitude in deciding which cases to pursue and how to pursue them?
A. Of course we do. We differ amongst ourselves sometimes, since we each have our own backgrounds, but for the most part . . .
Q. But what you are really saying . . .
A. Is that we play God. [57]

If, indeed, the prosecutor reigns supreme in the local criminal court, his rule is generally a benevolent one. Contrary to suggestions in the literature that prosecutors develop a "mentality" that is biased toward harsh dispositions, my data reflect a consensus that prosecutors mellow over time.[30] With two important exceptions that we will explore below, prosecutors generally become inclined to negotiate more lenient sentences as they gain experience in the criminal justice system.

Q. Would you [an experienced prosecutor] make a prediction as to how —— [a relative newcomer to this court] would handle cases if I came back here in several years?
A. If he is still around, I'd say he'd mellow a lot, sure.
Q. Why?
A. Why, I don't know. You are aware of other factors and life itself. You know what I mean. You are not so conscious of what the book says. You know the book calls for a sentence of one year and a fine of up to five thousand dollars, but you're more willing to say, "Oh sure it does, but . . ." You recognize that a good many arrests are lousy. You know a good many things like that, and a lot of people are really up against it, and the jails are overcrowded, and you can't be sending everybody to jail, anyway. A lot of crazy things come into it, you know. [52]

—— and I [two relative newcomers to the court] would be pretty even in nolles and jail time. —— [a veteran] would be lower in jail time and higher in nolles. Maybe because we haven't been here that long and the system still hasn't sunk into our heads yet. We haven't mellowed, or whatever you want to call it. ——has been here eight years, and from all we've heard, he has changed. [4]

Several of the arguments already advanced in this chapter bear on this "mellowing process," and these need not be reconsidered here.[31] One additional explanation, however, does merit our attention at this point. Specifically, I refer to the development of personal ties between prosecutors and defense attorneys, and the impact of these ties on case disposition. As a newcomer to the court, the prosecutor fended off defense attorneys at every turn, leery that these court veterans were attempting to take advantage of him. But as the prosecutor increasingly engages in plea bargaining, he inevitably finds himself spending the better part of every day speaking with these attorneys. Furthermore, the population from which these defense attorneys is drawn is not very large; the public defender and a handful of private attorneys[32] process at least 80 percent of the court's cases.[33] In other words, the court community is not very large. Most plea bargained cases are negotiated by prosecutors and defense attorneys who know each other, who have worked together on innumerable cases in the past, and who expect to work together in the future.[34] It is not surprising, then, that personal ties of both respect and, frequently, mutual dependence develop between these two "adversaries." But the central question is: Of what import are these ties for understanding case disposition? Do prosecutors give defense attorneys good deals because they are good friends? Are these bonds of friendship (and/or mutual dependence) so strong that, as some have suggested, prosecutors forsake their responsibility to the state (or defense attorneys forsake their obligation to their clients) in an effort to serve the other's interest?[35]

As best as could be determined, the answers to these questions appear to be qualified "no's." I would not be surprised to learn that there have been isolated but on-going instances of particular prosecutors' and particular defense attorneys' tradeoffs based exclusively on friendship ties; there certainly are occasional deals made in which these ties are an influencing factor.[36] Also, I am sure that friendship has some bearing on marginal cases, cases in which a little bit of prosecutorial leniency can go a long way (for example, no time in relatively minor "serious" cases). But, for the most part, I do not think it accurate to explain prosecutorial mellowing (or plea bargaining) in these terms. Plea bargains are not consummated because of personal ties between the putative opposing sides.

On the other hand, I do think that the patterned interaction between prosecutors and defense attorneys bears on plea bargaining and prosecutors' mellowing in a more subtle way. Over time, defense attorneys develop expectations of what they consider to be a proper disposition of a case. After obtaining a specific plea bargain for a particular factual constellation and charge for one defendant, they treat this disposition as a "precedent" for subsequent negotiations in similar cases. Since they deal with the same prosecutor over a period of time, they can readily point to the action taken in the earlier case, and argue that a similar deal ought to be accorded the defendant in the case being negotiated. Prosecutors, in turn, admit that they are subject to these "habits of disposition," as the following excerpt illustrates.[37]

> You know, there is a human relations side of plea bargaining. You are dealing with another attorney, and you keep dealing with him over time. After a while it is as if you are dealing with him, giving him the disposition. It's not that you give him an unreasonably good deal, but you do try to be nice, and also to be consistent. You get into what I call "habits of disposition." Once you have given three to seven on armed robbery, then the next time that case comes up you also tend to give, or are asked to give, the same thing. So an established precedent for armed robbery is set up. These things have a way of going on and on, of being perpetuated over time. [56]

I think the opportunity for defense attorneys to cite relatively mild dispositions in roughly comparable "precedent cases," and the susceptibility of prosecutors to "habits of disposition" contribute to the already described mellowing of prosecutors. Prosecutors may simply not consider thoroughly the seriousness of a particular case when negotiating it with a familiar defense attorney who comes armed with ample "precedent cases." Thus, a good defense deal in one case can have a trickle-down effect in others and, to the extent that prosecutors are susceptible to claims of equity, can contribute to prosecutorial mellowing.

As noted earlier, there are two exceptions to the "prosecutors mellow over time" hypothesis. The first reflects the propensity of some prosecutors to become "harder" on certain types of crime. Though the prosecutor mellows overall—that is, he becomes inclined to settle for lighter sentences than he would have as a newcomer to the court—he singles out one or more types of crime as being particularly heinous/dangerous, and for these he determines to hold firm. In the language of the prosecutors, he has "got a thing" for these crimes. When he is asked to negotiate one of these cases, he is less likely to be willing to go along with a no-time disposition if the defense attorney argues it is a minor matter, and less likely to grab certain time if it is discussed as a serious case. In these instances, the prosecutor is looking for substantial time, and though he probably will end up plea bargaining the case, he will hold out for a more severe disposition.

The tendency of prosecutors to feel particularly strongly about certain types of crime (and for different prosecutors to feel strongly about different types of crime) ought not to surprise us. It directly parallels the oft-noted tendency of judges to single out certain types of offenses.[38] I stress it here because (1) it represents an exception to the mellowing hypothesis; (2) it may explain why some observers have mistakenly believed prosecutors harden with increased experience in the court (they harden selectively but overall are easier); (3) it suggests that "prosecutor shopping" may be as important, if not more important, than "judge shopping" (the latter has received primary attention in the literature).[39] Several examples of this prosecutorial selectivity follow.[40]

> I like to see higher sentences in robbery, assault, but probably not burglary than my associates do. I agree with most of them on drugs and sex cases. So in the robbery or assault case I argue for greater sentences. [56]

> Each prosecutor has different feelings. Some people are very hard on some types of offenses, and others don't feel they're very serious at all. I've got a thing about purse snatchers, particularly ones who pick on the older women, the older women who they feel can't identify them or, even if they can, won't identify them because of their age and because they're afraid. A lot of these old women get knocked down and injured severely, and, you know, it's permanent injury at that age. I feel very very tough about somebody like that who comes in. I won't bend a finger to help them. Others feel more seriously about alcoholic-related crimes, others about drug-related offenses. You know, everybody's got their own feelings. Some people feel very strongly on larceny, shoplifting, which I rate very low. [5]

The second exception to the "mellowing hypothesis" relates to sanctions imposed by prosecutors on defense attorneys who raise motions and who take cases to trial. Earlier in this concluding section, I argued that prosecutors have emerged as the central figures in the local criminal court, and that they presume that a plea bargain will be expeditiously arrived at in every case. This expectation is predicated on their belief that most defendants are factually guilty and have little cause to challenge the state's case. Veteran prosecutors scoff at the notion that plea bargaining coerces innocent defendants to plead guilty.

> Defendants would be the first ones not to want it [the elimination of plea bargaining]. They are always saying: "I don't want the trial, the jury. I want to plead guilty, and get a 'rec.'" And most defendants are guilty. One of the things that I have learned over the years is that I've rarely had a guy go to prison that wasn't guilty. Once in a rare while maybe. But, by and large, most of them are guilty, know that they are guilty, and plead because they are guilty. Most of the cases in this court are cases of guilty people. [62]

> What you are saying is that there is the possibility of an innocent person suffering a conviction and maybe even a short, or reduced, prison term. It's possible, depending on what you are dealing with, because they didn't want to take the chance of an increased prison sentence. Naturally, that is the danger that everybody hollers about in plea bargaining. I think it is a very artificial danger, a very uncommon danger. I've seen in the course of my prosecutorial career two cases where I felt the guy was innocent—the defendant was innocent—and one of those cases was not prosecuted, and in the other my judgment was overruled by somebody senior in the office. The person was prosecuted and acquitted. You never

> can be really sure whether somebody is guilty or innocent, but . . . I don't know what goes through the minds of many of these defendants, but every time that a plea is taken, they are asked in open court whether or not they committed the crime, and whether or not the facts and their involvement in the crime are as the state had stated. Now that's the moment of truth. If a person is so swayed by the possibility of a greater jail sentence or greater exposure that he'll lie at that point . . . I just don't believe that most of them do. [17]

In the prosecutor's eyes, the guilty defendant without any substantial legal defense ought to plead guilty. If he so pleads, a reward can justifiably be attached to his decision. But if the defendant's attorney insists on pursuing what the prosecutor perceives as pointless legal motions, and/or a pointless trial, the prosecutor feels that the reward should be canceled or that a penalty should be attached to the sentence ultimately meted out. The attorney is wasting the court's time with "frivolous" pursuit of an acquittal, and he has to bear the costs of these dilatory actions. The prosecutor's initial willingness to negotiate a reasonable disposition (under the assumption of an expeditious resolution of the case) is replaced by a feeling that the attorney chose to raise these motions, chose to go to trial, and now must suffer the consequences. The prosecutor does not believe that an innocent defendant will feel coerced into pleading because of the "here today, gone tomorrow" nature of the plea bargain offer. Though theoretically possible, the "coerced to plead" argument is undercut by his own observations that the defendant is guilty and that no innocent defendant is coerced into pleading.

The excerpts that follow (by a prosecutor, defense attorney, and two judges) deal with prosecutorial sanctions leveled against perceived frivolous motions and trials.

> There are situations where you make an offer and the attorney will laugh at you, and, you know, I don't mean literally, but in practice, and then over a period of the next three or four months he'll kill you with motions, he'll lose everything, and there's a point where you just want to say: "To hell with you. Now you'll try it. You either plead guilty to this or you try it." And that has happened, and human nature being what it is, I can't disagree with our taking that approach. And you know, it is the defendant who ends up suffering, not defense counsel. [5]

> You know, judges and prosecutors, they just feel that there's no necessity to the trial, no point to it. Let's say it's a minor case; they feel that the guy isn't going to jail. The guy can walk out with a fine or a suspended sentence, and why the hell is the lawyer fooling around? Why should we all stay here all day through a boring trial with nobody around and nobody enjoying it and . . . So if you go to trial on those cases you can really piss them off. [45]

> I think human nature being what it is, sure, some people get penalized for motions and trials. Why not? You're dealing with human beings. You're dealing with a judge sitting down there; he's got a splitting headache, and the heat and the volume of noise, and everything else, and along comes a frivolous motion that some lawyer decides to file. It serves no real purpose because if he knew what he was doing he would have gone into the prosecutor and looked at his file. Sure, judges will penalize this guy and so will prosecutors. He should look at the prosecutor's file and see what the prosecutor's got, and if it looks like a pretty good case, he should work it out. This is what a good lawyer would do. And by good lawyer, I mean the kind of lawyer I'd send someone in my family who was in trouble to. I'd send them to somebody who—number one—had good rapport with the prosecutors. He'd use his head, and if the client was guilty he'd get them the best possible deal. [8]

> By a good criminal attorney, I mean the kind of guy who checks their clients' stories out, checks the arrest, finds out everything that has to be found out about the case, and if they are convinced that their guy is guilty, they come in and plead him guilty. They don't pussyfoot around. These boys will go into a prosecutor's office and say: "Look, my guy is guilty as hell. You've got him ten ways to heaven. Can you give me a break?" That guy will get a break, as opposed to the fellow who comes in, "I'm going to file motions to this, and motions to that," and so forth. That guy, the prosecutor will make the charge stick. [14]

The "frivolous" motion and trial, then, call forth a prosecutorial response inconsistent with the mellowing hypothesis. Prosecutors extract penalties from defendants for pursuing this type of an adversary strategy, and the result is a disposition that exceeds the one prosecutors would have settled for had the case been plea bargained at an earlier stage.

It should be emphasized that not all motions and trials invariably incur the prosecutor's wrath and the resultant penalties that stem from it. In chapter 4, I noted that if the prosecutor thinks that a serious, contestable issue exists in the case, he will be disinclined to penalize the motion or trial. He feels that it is legitimate for the attorney to "take a shot" at victory if there are substantial grounds to believe a victory is possible. Similarly, the prosecutor may not penalize the attorney if the attorney explains why he must—in a particular case—adhere to an adversary format. For example, the attorney may argue that he knows the claim made in a motion has absolutely no chance for success at trial, but that he expects to appeal the case and needs the issue on the record. Similarly, prosecutors seem sympathetic toward the attorney who maintains that his client is being "unreasonable" and is insisting that he file the motions and go to trial. As long as the attorney's track record for most of the cases he handles comports with the prosecutor's expectations, the prosecutor will tolerate the adversary posture in a particular case and will be unlikely to sanction the defendant. The acceptance of certain defense motions and trials without prosecutor penalty is discussed in the following interview excerpts.

> *Q*. But if the case goes to trial, are you looking for a a higher penalty than you were willing to bargain for in advance?
> *A*. I will, well . . . You have got to take the factors into consideration, like the guy's record. You have got to look at that. I can't see penalizing a guy because he went to trial in one case. If I have a 50 percent chance of winning, and he maintains his innocence, and he has a good record, I am not going to penalize a guy for that.The guy had a chance at trial. When I have a guy who is caught in the cellar of a house that was broken into, and he has stolen items in his jacket and he has a record for burglary and robbery, and he's never spent a day in jail, if he pled out, and saved me the time of trial, I might recommend six months. But if he goes to trail and is convicted, he should do two years in prison, and I would recommend two years. [9]

> One thing you have to recognize—and we take this into account—is that a lot of lawyers can't control their clients. A lot of lawyers can control their clients. And a lot can't. And there are certain clients that can't be controlled. So you get certain cases that have to be tried. The guy may be guilty as hell, but he wants a trial. What you'll try to arrange is to try it before the court [judge trial rather than jury trial]. And you let the lawyer try to give his client his money's worth. The lawyer may even get up during the thing and make all kinds of flowery objections; he'll bang the tables a few times. Now, if we know and the judge knows that he's just going through the motions, fine. No problem if we know that this attorney is stuck with one of these types of clients. [11]

> You may offer a particular disposition to counsel and he may reject the offer and tell you: "You know, I've got to attack the search warrant. I feel it's defective on its face." And I'll say: "Go ahead." He loses that, he comes back and he says: "Is that offer still open?" You know, 999 times out of 1000 you're going to say yes, because the guy was open and sincere with you, and he told you that he felt there was a legal point that he should attack to protect himself . . . There's also the situation where the attorney feels the offered disposition is a good option and a good deal and he tells his client that he thinks it should be accepted. But if the defendant says no, the defense counsel is stuck with that, and if he comes back to us and says: "Gee, I recommended it to him but he wouldn't take it." Well, then we know that that's what the situation is. And we'll treat it differently than if the defense counsel flooded us with frivolous motions, and it was his decision to try the case. We understand what he is up against. [5]

> So naturally the prosecutor is going to resent the attorney who keeps

> filing frivolous motions. The files are open to him, and there is no need to file these motions. Now, there are highly unusual situations where the defense attorney is trying to create a record, and if someone comes in and says: "I'm sorry, I have to burden everybody, but in this situation I have to create a record," then the prosecutor understands the motions. The defense attorney might want to pin the prosecutor down on something, and if the reason is understood, it won't be considered unnecessary, and won't affect the offer. [26]

Though these excerpts are presented to demonstrate that prosecutors do not automatically punish all motions and trials, they are also illustrative of a central theme of this chapter—the emergence of the prosecutor as a central figure in the local criminal court, a figure who presumes that a plea bargain will be obtained in most cases, and that he has the responsibility and power to negotiate cases. He will tolerate motions and trials if the defense attorney justifies them to him. In other words, he expects the case to be plea bargained, but he will allow deviations in isolated instances.

The prosecutor has come a long way from his status as a novice eager to establish the defendant's guilt at trial, eager to leave sentencing to the judge after trial. He now believes that the issue of the defendant's guilt is generally a foregone conclusion, and that prosecutor and defense attorney ought to direct their efforts to the nature of the final disposition. From the evidence examined thus far, it appears that the prosecutor is extraordinarily successful in realizing these new goals. Most cases are resolved in plea bargaining sessions between prosecution and the defense. The issue that remains for our consideration can be succinctly placed in question form: What has happened to the judge? In the following chapter, I attempt to answer this question.

6 Adapting to Plea Bargaining: Judges

Prior Experience in the Criminal Justice System

A judge's prior experience in the court system influences his adaptation to plea bargaining. If the judge has extensive background working with criminal cases, he develops a posture toward plea bargaining during an earlier stage in his career, and this posture bears significantly on his subsequent judicial activities vis-à-vis plea bargaining. Alternatively, if his experience with criminal matters is limited, he is forced to adjust to plea bargaining upon assuming his judicial office. Thus, in addition to the general adaptation problems faced by all new judges, the "inexperienced" newcomer has to grapple with, and develop a policy toward, plea bargaining.

Table 10 classifies the thirteen judges included in this study by the extent of their prior experience with criminal cases. Only three of the judges had substantial prior experience in criminal courts (one had been an assistant state's attorney, one a circuit court prosecutor, and one had a private practice specializing in criminal cases). The five judges with "moderate" experience had handled some criminal cases in the city court system, the old structure for processing misdemeanors that was replaced by the statewide circuit court system in 1961. Their experience was most limited, however, encompassing a year or two of part-time work as a prosecutor, or work with a small number of cases as private attorneys in these city courts.[1] None of the judges in this category considered himself to be particularly experienced with criminal justice matters. All of them ranked their expertise prior to appointment as resting in areas other than criminal justice. Finally, five of the judges had very little prior criminal court experience. The only circuit court judge included in this category had been a private practitioner prior to appointment, and had rarely been inside the criminal court. The four superior court judges were elevated from the court of common pleas—the intermediate court between the circuit and superior court, which deals exclusively with civil matters. Though their experience prior to assuming a judgeship may have qualified them for a common pleas appointment, being a common pleas judge removed them entirely from criminal matters. Upon appointment to the superior court, they literally had not handled any criminal case for all the years spent on the common pleas bench. Furthermore, none of these judges had any significant criminal experience prior to the common pleas appointment.

Overall, then, most of the judges included in this sample were not distinguished by an extensive grounding in criminal law. This conclusion comports with Carp and Wheeler's finding for federal district court judges: "Ignorance of criminal law was the most common complaint of our interviewed judges."[2]

Table 10 Classification of Judges by Prior Experience in the Criminal Justice System

	Weak Background	Moderate Background	Strong Background
Circuit court	1	5	2
Superior court	4	0	1
Total	5	5	3

One need not search long or far for an explanation of why judges come to the bench unprepared for criminal matters. Unlike the British system, in which judges receive specific training for their jobs,[3] our system (at least in states with strong traditional party organizations) primarily relies on political recruitment of judges, with little consideration given to the judge's actual behavior once he is appointed or elected.[4] A judgeship is a prize awarded to an individual for loyal service to the party. As one attorney viewed it, "Judges are merely lawyers who know politicians" (13). In somewhat more colorful language, another attorney noted: "A judge is just a lawyer who knows the governor. And don't forget that, young man. You can put a robe on a horse's ass, but he's still a horse's ass."[5] And finally, the judges themselves were frank to admit that their participation in local politics accounted for their appointment to the bench.

> Any judge who tells you that he was not politically appointed is trying to b.s. you. We're all politically appointed, and if you don't know the right people, well, you can forget about it. [69]

I have no intention of getting bogged down in the often polemical and vitriolic discussion of the merits and lack thereof of political recruitment of judges.[6] It is sufficient to note that specific qualifications for the judicial office are given short shrift in the political appointment process. Advocates of political recruitment would argue that the general skills of an attorney are sufficient to allow the newly appointed judge to master specific substantive problems as they crop up. Even if he is "weak" in criminal justice, his background—or so the argument runs—in law and politics is sufficient proof that he is a competent generalist able to shift his skills into different arenas. For our purposes, it is enough to recognize that a background in criminal justice is not required of candidates for appointment to the bench. A handful have this experience; most do not. Apparently, careers in areas other than criminal law more frequently characterize politically active attorneys, and it is from this pool of attorneys that judges are eventually chosen.[7]

Early Experiences

Generally, a period of a month or two, but, in a handful of cases, an even longer period[8] intervenes between the announcement of a judicial appointment, and the candidate's actual assumption of his job. This period is used—with varying degrees of success—to review areas of law that the newly appointed judge feels unprepared to handle, and to seek advice from other judges about the problems he is likely to encounter. The extent of time the appointee can devote to this preparation varies with his responsibilities during this period. For example, a number of the interviewed judges were private practitioners at the time of their appointment. For them, most of the transitional period was spent "tying up loose ends" at the practice, disposing of outstanding cases, and so on. Very little time could be devoted to considering the demands of the judicial role. On the other hand, individuals with more time to prepare—those judges elevated from the common pleas to the superior court—were able to read in the areas of law that they felt least prepared to handle, and most frequently this meant reading criminal law.

> *Q*. So, on common pleas you also didn't do any criminal work. How well prepared were you then, when you found out that you were elevated to the superior court?
> *A*. I knew beans about criminal law and the superior court, absolutely nothing. I knew that I'd get a criminal assignment, and here I was completely ignorant about criminal law. I had a couple of months before my advancement took effect, so during that time I just read criminal law, basically—the Horn books and anything I could get my hands on. [35]
>
> I realized right after the announcement of my advancement that I would have to reeducate myself, learn the basic theory of criminal administration to conform more to the present time. I knew that the strict law-and-order stuff that characterized the cases and the way things were done when I was younger was out. Let me give you an illustration. Back in the

> old days, in the old town courts, this goes quite a bit back, when I was a kid, I remember we used to have two cops, one was called Bemie, the other Femie. One was about 6'4'', the other 6'2''. They both looked like they could have played on any pro football team, and they didn't have much trouble. These two guys alone used to keep the peace in ——. And they knew the bad ones and they knew the good ones, and they did not necessarily arrest you because you were violating the law. They didn't arrest kids, they just whacked them on the head or on the butt, or they would call the old man up and say, ''Give your kid a licking because he was doing this or that.'' I remember one time we were in Finnegan's alley, and they used to have a place in back of it, and the boys used to go there and gamble. Of course, the cops knew it, and they wouldn't do anything about it until they got a lot of complaints from the wives that the husbands were losing too much money. So old Bemie and Femie decided to break the joint up. They hit the door—it came off the hinges—they ran in there, picked the guys up, banged their heads together, dropped them to the ground, called the paddy wagon, dumped them in the paddy wagon, took them to jail, and they got fined the next day. That was search and seizure. Well, that's an extreme case, but it's illustrative of the theories under which I was taught and brought up, and these were considerably different than what we have today. So, for the time I had before actually being on the bench, I went through the process of reeducating myself. I read everything I could of the modern concepts. I studied decisions—I used to read them by the hundreds, you know, supreme court decisions. I read them all. [32]

The only preparation for assuming formal judicial responsibilities uncovered in my research were these piecemeal efforts by judges to ''get a handle'' on areas of law with which they were totally unfamiliar. The extent to which a judge makes even this effort depends on the time at his disposal and, I suppose, on his inclination to be prepared. Unlike the program that exists for federal judges, Connecticut offers no institutionalized program of formal seminars for its new judges.[9] The only formal assistance provided is a series of written guidelines on court procedures and jury instructions. To say that these fall short, both with regard to describing the state's criminal laws and, more importantly, with regard to describing actual criminal court practices, is to put the matter mildly.

Upon assuming formal responsibilities as a judge, the newcomer may receive some additional assistance. Depending on the jurisdiction to which he is assigned, he may be permitted to sit with other judges for several days and observe how they process cases.[10] Additionally, several newcomers reported that they received advice about ''judging'' from other veteran judges they came into contact with; similarly, veterans reported on advice they gave to newcomers. The following comments are illustrative of the type of information communicated.

Q. If a new judge was appointed to the court today, what advice would you give him concerning the criminal side?
A. Well, my first piece of advice . . . I can tell you because I've done this with Judge ——. He's going to be a good judge, by the way. I said to him . . . I gave him three pieces of advice. First of all, I told him that for the first year he should let no evening go by except Saturday night without studying. I said: "Study, study, study, and study, because until you know your job, your best intentions and your common sense isn't going to be totally decisive." The second thing I told him to remember is that we are the lowest level [circuit court judge]. This is the court of original jurisdiction, and we are handling the lives of people; therefore, we have to balance the volume of cases against justice in the ultimate sense. So I said: "Don't try to treat these cases as if each case was a supreme court case because no one will get any justice. So what you have to do is start learning your practical way of proceeding as quickly as you can so you can recognize in minutes the junk from the substantive cases and then concentrate on the substantive and never mind the junk." And the third piece of advice that I gave him was, "You must not permit your judgment to be toned by trying to be popular. That does not mean you throw your weight around, or anything like that. But remember that when decisions are made, there will be those who will like them and there will be those who don't like them; you can't please both sides. So if you're going to worry about being more popular or whether that some day a decision is going to be held against you, then you're going to find that you're going to be making more than your proportionate share of bum decisions." And then I told him, I guess I gave him four pieces of advice: "You're going to make mistakes. You are not God, and you're not a computer. It's not a question of feeding information into you and pressing a button and out comes the perfect decision. You've got to accept the fact that you will make mistakes. You just hope that your mistakes will be few, and if you can get a batting average of about five hundred or six hundred I think you'd be doing fine. So try, if you're going to make a mistake, try to make a mistake on the side where you're not hurting somebody really bad." [32]

I was new and I came into Judge ——'s chambers. He had a big sign, KYBMS, and he looked down at me and said: "You know what that means?" "No," I said. "Keep Your Big Mouth Shut." Then he said, "Follow that advice and you'll get along very well," or words to that effect. And what he meant, of course, was don't pop off on the bench. There is a necessity for every new judge to develop patience, and that's what the legend implied, really, be patient. You have to learn to be patient, to keep your big mouth shut and listen. [18]

It is doubtful whether these sorts of little homilies reassure or assist the new judge. But even if we assume that they do (albeit in a very limited sense), it is instructive to recognize that not every new judge is a beneficiary of even such limited guidance. The veteran judges who did give advice along the lines indicated in the above excerpts frequently prefaced their responses by saying that they "just happened to see Judge ——." Similarly, newcomers reported how they grabbed morsels of advice from veterans, but that it was a very haphazard sort of thing. They saw so-and-so at lunch (we will return to luncheons shortly), and he told him about the problems new judges face; or he bumped into so-and-so, and he told him to read criminal law. Snippets of information may be communicated in these interactions, but again, no systematic insight into the operations of the court is communicated.

In light of the rather shallow experience judges bring to the bench, it is not surprising that almost all the judges included in my sample reported that they were nervous, uneasy, and often unsure of themselves when they began hearing cases on their own.

> *Q*. Do you have any particular recollections of your first days on the bench?
> *A*. Well, it all seemed kind of awesome. You don't realize as a lawyer what the judge is really doing, how many papers you have to sign; the paperwork was amazing to me. And the speed with which they expect you to decide, that upset me. Really, I guess I was just thrown into it, and I had to pick it up on a hit-and-miss basis. It wasn't easy. [63]

> I was very nervous. As a judge, I realized you had to think of different things than a lawyer thinks of. A lawyer stands in front of the bench with a client, and he's thinking in terms of how he can best put his client's case. You're thinking as a judge more in terms of procedure, in terms of the mechanics of the process, all of which never concerned you before because these things went on automatically without your thinking about them. So this aspect of it was hard. Then, I will admit that I was nowhere as near familiar with the penal code as I had to be. So I found myself looking at it as a fellow's name was called. "Line number 26, John Jones." I would look down on the docket and see that he was charged with Burglary 2 and Assault 3, and then, while he would be walking up to the bench, I'd be looking at my own papers to see what Burglary 2 is, what kind of felony, et cetera. What's his exposure? I didn't want to sit there mumbling about whether it was a felony or a misdemeanor. [25]

> I was shocked by some of the stuff I saw. I had my first assignment in —— [large city]. I never knew what a drug charge was until I went to ——. We never had any of it down in my area. I never represented a man on a drug charge. Never represented anybody on a drug-related crime. Then I walked into ——, and there it was—wham, bamm. I never had any experience with it, and there it was in front of me. [14]

> Of course, I was very apprehensive. That's one of the big things you feel, apprehensive and nervous. You don't know whether you can handle the job; you don't know whether you can handle the lawyers; you don't know whether you can handle your courtroom. There's a lot of things you're apprehensive about. When you're sitting up there, you're like God, and you know, when you're down in front of a judge you can argue with him and you can ... You're an advocate; you can put your case on the record the way you want it. But up there it's a completely different picture, and naturally you are concerned about whether you could do it. [35]

Interviews conducted with judges during this initial period (and with judges who had not yet heard any cases) support these reports of judicial uneasiness. As I have already noted in chapter 4, I was struck by how little judges knew about local court operations. Often they were unable to answer my questions simply because they had no idea of the issues involved. For example, and we will return to this shortly, they knew so little about actual plea bargaining dynamics that they could not answer my questions about accepting a plea, rewards for pleas, and so on. Instead, the judges eagerly sought my insights into these areas. In a sense, they turned the interview around, seeking to learn from my observations what their jobs entailed. They had been reading appellate cases to brush up on criminal law, and they had asked colleagues for advice whenever practicable. However, they realized that through these efforts they had only touched on the problems they would encounter, and that they had gained only minimal insight into the sundry demands awaiting them. I think my interview disconcerted them, sensitizing them anew to their lack of experience and to the potential problems this could pose for them.

Furthermore, the judges felt isolated. They knew they would encounter serious problems, but foresaw no structured means of obtaining assistance. Several of the judges remarked rather wistfully that it was unfortunate that clerks were not assigned to individual judges in Connecticut.[11] When I pressed these judges about how they would eventually master the problems facing them, the response generally was a shrug, or a comment about "working it out somehow." One judge remarked rather despondently: "I guess you could say that I will be getting a baptism by fire. I guess that's how it will all work out."[12] (39)

I have intentionally dwelled on the issues of judicial preparedness and early on-the-bench feelings because these convey in a general but important way the flavor of the newcomer's adaptation to the court. Like the defense attorney and the prosecutor, the judge is thrust into the local criminal court and is expected to muddle through largely on his own.[13] The implications of this mode of adaptation for judicial plea bargaining activities will be explored in the following section.

Judicial Adaptation to Plea Bargaining: Drifting Along

To understand how the novice judge adapts to plea bargaining, it is important to stress a rather obvious difference between the new judge and the attorneys for the defense or prosecution. Unlike the defense attorney or prosecutor, the judge's position is reactive. This is to say that he is an arbiter of sorts, ostensibly sitting to resolve adversary disputes. The new prosecutor has to decide whether or not to decrease the charge and/or whether to recommend a sentence; the new defense attorney must decide whether to accept a plea or insist on trial. The new judge, on the other hand, need not make these decisions. He can, and does, sit back and wait for issues to come to him. He reacts to plea bargaining decisions made by prosecutors and defense attorneys, and, at least when he is new, has little input into these decisions.

The fact that the judge's role (at least as a newcomer) is a reactive one bears on his adaptation to plea bargaining in two significant ways. First, a plea bargain normally comes before him as a fait accompli. Experienced prosecutors and defense attorneys have reached an agreement, and all that remains is for the judge to grant his imprimatur. The temptation for the new judge to accept the decision worked out by the "adversaries" is great. After all, if the opposing sides feel that a just decision has been arrived at, ought not the judge endorse their decision?

The second way the judge's reactive posture shapes his adaptation to plea bargaining is not unrelated to the first. "Agreed recs" are only one of the many issues that may confront the new judge. A particular case can raise questions about bail, legal motions, change of plea procedures, and, if trial is likely, problems of jury selection, instructions, judicial rulings, and sentencing. For the novice judge, decisions in any of these areas loom as difficult; they represent possible sources of public embarrassment. Thus, as each problem arises, the judge is likely to seek assistance. What is of immediate interest to us is the coloration cast over the adaptation process by this attempt to master the instant issue.

In effect, judges adapt to the court on a case-by-case basis. As a problem crops up, they seek guidance and information. Little time is set aside for systematic consideration of the general problem; instead, issues are examined in the context of a specific case, resolved for that case, and replaced by a new problem in a new case. Judges are content at this stage "to keep their heads above water," to muddle through without making too many serious errors. As suggested in the following excerpt, a premium is placed on adjusting to the sytem as it is.

> *Q*. Were any of the actions you took in those early cases "out of step" with the way other judges might have handled the issue, or out of line with what court personnel expected?

> *A*. No, I don't think so. I think you have a tendency as you go from circuit to circuit to pretty much go along. As a newcomer, I think most judges feel this way. Sometimes you find things are being done that you don't like, and I think that after I'm on the court longer, I'll be more apt to spot these types of things and . . . You know, when you're new, *you're not very familiar with what is going on, you're just trying to accommodate yourself to everything that's going on around you, and it flows in on you so quickly that you don't have too much time to think about it*. [63, italics mine]

Unfamiliar with the procedural routines of the court, untutored in criminal law, and unnerved by the prospect of sentencing defendants, the new judge feels severely burdened by the constant flow of requests for his authoritative decisions. He attempts to cope with these requests in several ways. If the question is a simple legal issue but one that, nevertheless, the judge is not confident about answering, he may call a recess (ostensibly for a coffee break), and hurriedly research the question himself. If the problem is more complex, he has the option of asking the opposing parties to submit briefs on the matter. Judges also ask for and/or receive advice from prosecutors and fellow judges. Prosecutors reported that it is not uncommon for them to explain court practices to the novice judge .

> *Q*. Let's say a new judge is appointed to this court. Do you help him to adjust to the way things are done around here?
> *A*. Well, generally speaking, the other judges will give him some sort of informal indoctrination. Secondly, he may call you to chambers and ask advice, and you'll give it to him. Also, if things really get out of hand, when you find that the court is just not functioning, you may knock on his door and say: "Judge, I'd like to speak to you for a few moments," and give him your thoughts on cases in general. I don't think you necessarily go in and say, "I think you were wrong on this case, or right on this case"; but you'd say, "Look, here's the way this has been employed here by all the other judges. If you want to change it, it's up to you, but I think you should be aware of this." [15]

> If he's got questions, I answer them. But I don't go into his chambers and tell him he is all wet. I do, however, tell him our policy on certain crimes. You see, it's hard for us to work with an inexperienced judge. We're under more tension, since we are not sure of what he is going to do, whether he'll be erratic in sentencing, and so on. So we go into him and try to clarify the way things are done. [62]

Similarly, new judges shop for assistance from their more experienced colleagues whenever possible. The most frequently mentioned setting for the exchange of advice was the daily luncheon gathering. Not surprisingly, judges generally lunch together; many judges consider it improper to be seen eating with defense attorneys or prosecutors. New judges report that they discuss their problems with particular cases—especially sentencing problems—during these luncheons.[14] Sentencing defendants seems to be one of the most vexing problems the newcomer encounters, and the informal luncheon is one of the few opportunities available for seeking guidance on this problem.[15]

> *Q*. But isn't there something you can read to help you with sentencing?
> *A*. Really there isn't. Today at lunch, —— [a new judge] was saying to —— [an experienced judge] that he was having a lot of trouble deciding on sentences, that he simply did not know how to sentence. [70]

> Every noon we have lunch together. Sometimes there are ten of us there, and we discuss everything over lunch. Those lunches, we're always talking over each other's problems. [29]

> I have done the best that I could to help —— [a new judge] with sentencing. I know that he's worried about it because he was telling us how much trouble he has had fixing on a sentence. I told him at lunch just the other day that you just can't look at the maximum, let's say, twenty years, and use that to judge. After a while, you get the knack for where a sentence should fall. [69]

> When you are sitting with someone, you go out to lunch together all the time, whoever the judge is, and you know, when you go out to lunch the tendency is, yes, you talk about family part of the time, but you talk about your work most of the time. Probably 70 to 80 percent of the time when you have lunch you are talking about cases, and I think during this time you can observe what another person's attitude is, and I'm a listener anyway; possibly being new, you are listening to hear what their feelings are. I have been picking up a lot this way. [63]

The judge's reactive posture fosters this case-by-case search for advice, this somewhat frenetic grasping for information from prosecutors and veteran judges. As I have indicated, the new judge is eager to adapt to the system as it is, satisfied to "keep his head above water." As far as plea bargaining is concerned, he accepts the agreed recommendations that come before him; they require little effort on his part, and they remove the sentencing burden from his shoulders. He is not involved in working out the plea bargain, nor does he devote much time to thinking about plea bargaining and the significance of his role for plea bargaining. Unlike the new defense attorney or prosecutor, he has a host of problems to confront. These problems may not always be those involving typical case dispositions (for example, if the new judge is assigned to a trial, or if he is assigned to do sentencings in cases without agreed recommendations), but they certainly pose substantial difficulties for the newcomer.[16] Thus, he will concentrate on handling these and give short shrift to areas such as plea bargaining, which seemingly rest within the prosecutor's and defense attorney's realm. During his first few months on the bench, then, the judge does not really learn very much, and is not taught very much, about plea bargaining. Deals are churned out, and the judge goes along with them. In effect, he drifts into the plea bargaining system without taking a very active part in it.

I do not mean to suggest, however, that the judge learns nothing about plea bargaining in these early months on the bench. Obviously he sees the product of the plea bargain, the agreed recommendation; and snippets of information about the underlying plea bargaining dynamics that generated these products are probably communicated to him. During these first few months on the bench, though, these snippets remain isolated bits of information, only some of the many inputs about the judicial role that the newcomer receives. The judge simply does not have the time and the requisite information about plea bargaining to develop a systematic posture toward these negotiated dispositions.

However, as he gains experience on the bench, the judge's information about plea bargaining increases. He is exposed to enough plea bargains in court, and engages in enough off-the-bench, informal chit-chat with his colleagues, with prosecutors, defense attorneys, clerks, and so on that one would not expect it to be any other way. The judge works in an organization that depends primarily on the plea bargain, and eventually the dynamics of the process are communicated to him. More significantly, one would hypothesize that the judge will develop an evaluative posture toward plea bargaining. This is to say that, though the judge may not necessarily participate in plea bargaining, the requirement that he sanction the deals suggests that over time he will have to come to grips (in a normative sense) with the notion of negotiated dispositions.

Learning about the Defendant's Guilt

As a newcomer to the court, the judge is resolute in his determination to be neutral about the issues involved in a case. Indeed, setting aside his prior experience as an adversary (either in civil or criminal matters) is one of the more difficult attitudinal adjustments that the judge claims he must make.

> When I became a judge, the first thing I had to learn is that you've got to look at the case in an entirely different way than as when you're a lawyer, when your vision is only from one side. Here, as a judge, I was faced with two sides, and I had to look and balance two sides. That takes time. [32]

I think judges are sincere in their claim that they strive to have cases unfold on a judicial *tabula rasa*. They are serious about their role obligation as neutral arbiters, and most new judges expend considerable effort consciously struggling for this neutral posture. For criminal cases, this neutrality can be interpreted to mean that judges (1) presume that the defendant has a right to trial and (2) presume the defendant innocent. These, then, are—if not expectations—at least mind-sets to which the newcomer feels a responsibility to adhere.

But no matter how conscientiously the new judge views this responsibility, his experience in the court militates against maintaining these mind-sets. Though he may consciously strive to "think neutral," he is confronted with, and thrust into, a reality in which most defendants plead guilty. As he struggles to adjust to his multifaceted role, the parade of defendants with guilty pleas in hand remains a constant feature of the environment. The circuit court judge almost daily encounters a steady stream of defendants marching up to the bench, pleading guilty, and, through their attorneys, arguing that mitigating circumstances ought to weigh in the judge's sentence. Similarly, though the superior court judge sees fewer defendants, he finds that most defendants charged with the more serious superior court offenses also plead guilty. He hears them admit culpability in court on sentencing day, and he reads their version of the offense in the presentence report. Significantly, he also presides over a number of trials that are interrupted some time between jury selection and the end of the case by the defendant's deciding to cop a plea. These defendants who insisted on trial, who persisted in maintaining their innocence, suddenly "sing a different song." Their attorney informs the court that the defendant desires to plead, and under questioning by the judge, the defendant admits to the crime, specifying all pertinent details. The confession is sufficiently accurate to convince the judge that there is no doubt about the defendant's factual culpability.

Judges gradually begin to find it difficult to presume most defendants innocent. Certainly, cases crop up in which the judge has his doubts about the defendant's factual culpability, but over time the judge becomes inclined to feel that most defendants are indeed guilty of the offense, or of a closely related matter.[17] This judicial assumption of factual guilt is illustrated in the following excerpts.

> *Q*. Are most of the people who come before you as a judge guilty?
> *A*. I would say so, yes.
> *Q*. Did that come as a surprise to you when you were new?
> *A*. At first it did, but I lost that fairy-tale approach pretty quickly after I started. Ninety-nine percent of the people in this court are guilty of something. If not the precise charge which is pending against them, they are guilty of something. Yes, I have that feeling as a judge. Most of them are guilty. [26]

> *Q*. Some of the defense attorneys don't seem to fight very hard for their clients and . . .

A. Sometimes you can't fight. They're up against a guy that's guilty, what is he going to fight for? So the attorney tries to get the defendant the best deal . . . You know, most of them apparently are guilty, so he works to get them the best deal he can. When you see an attorney who is a nice fellow, he figures, well, it pays off, and I think he is right. The few lawyers that are constantly agitating, I mean, in the end that isn't going to accomplish much. Their clients are guilty, and they won't get the breaks that the others get. I think one of the bad things is that in the end result sometimes the client suffers because of his lawyer. How are they going to benefit if their attorney is a pain in the neck? [8]

Yes, I think that most of the attorneys are pretty realistic in their approach to the disposition of a case. What they try to do, what they learn after they get some experience, is that most of the people who are here are guilty in some degree. So an attorney who cooperates will get the best possible bargain for his client on a plea of guilty. [14]

Q. What about the risk that a defendant may plead guilty because the inducements are so great, and yet he might be innocent?
A. This is the strongest argument against plea bargaining, the argument that an innocent man pleads guilty because the penalty is so light that he doesn't want to take the risk of a greater penalty.
Q. Right.
A. I agree that that's a good argument against plea bargaining, but in my experience, the times that that happens you can count on the fingers of two hands. So I think that the number of times that that happens is so minute that I don't think it's a relevant factor in judging whether plea bargaining should take place. That's my opinion. [32]

Judges, like the other actors we have examined, learn from personal experience (and to a lesser extent from conversations with their colleagues) that most defendants are guilty. This mind-set develops gradually, almost unconsciously, as their experience with cases increases. As the judge muddles through in an environment in which most defendants eventually plead guilty, he gradually comes to assume that most defendants are guilty. The significance of this perception rests in the development of a related judicial assumption, namely, that most defendants *ought* to plead guilty.

Distinguishing among Guilty Defendants

In the excerpts presented above, judges speak of "realistic" attorneys, who advise their guilty clients about the futility of motions and trials. Comments such as these must be interpreted carefully. The judge is not necessarily arguing that all factually guilty defendants ought to waive legal challenges and trial and plead guilty. Instead, as discussed briefly earlier, his position is more subtle. He recognizes that most defendants are guilty. However, he also readily admits that some of them have credible legal challenges and justifiable bones for contention at trial. When these "real" issues exist, most judges have no qualms about the defendant's pursuing motions and a trial (even if the judge thinks the defendant factually guilty). But these same judges maintain that only a small percentage of the factually guilty defendants' cases are of this order. In most cases, they think the defendant ought to plead because he is factually *and* legally guilty.[18]

Thus, the judge's assumption that most defendants are guilty does not in itself explain his attitude toward guilty pleas. Instead, this assumption must be coupled with the judge's perception that there is no realistically contestable issue "justifying" a motion or trial for most of the guilty defendants. And it is from these defendants that the judge expects a guilty plea. Insistence by these defendants on motions or trials in light of the obvious futility of such efforts (from the judge's perspective) can be interpreted as nothing other than a frivolous exercise, an exercise which needlessly consumes court time and resources. It simply does not make sense to go through the formal routines when the conclusion is foregone.

As judges gain experience in the criminal justice system, they become increasingly confident about their ability to sort cases by the "contestability" of the issues. If there is a realistically contestable issue at stake in a case, they are unlikely to react with hostility if the defendant formally pursues the issue. If, on the other hand, the issue is perceived as frivolous, the judge feels that the reward for plea bargaining ought to be denied—or, put differently—that a penalty for these motions and trial ought to be extracted. We have already considered this reward/penalty argument, and, thus, it is sufficient at this point to illustrate this judicial attitude by means of several excerpts.[19] The comments that follow reflect the distinction judges draw between frivolous and serious matters (the first two deal with motions, the following four with trials), and the rewards and penalties that they associate with cases that fall within the two categories. The final excerpt is particularly instructive, for it includes a discussion of the reward/penalty problem within the context of a specific case.

Q. Some commentators have argued that judges are primarily concerned with moving cases as quickly through the court as possible.
A. Well, wait a minute, wait a minute. There is a big difference. Judges want cases prosecuted, and they want them prosecuted without undue delay. If the delay is caused by legal maneuvering that is legitimate, we are not going to complain. But if the delay is caused by legal maneuvering that is illegitimate, then, well, we are not going to be happy about it.
Q. Is "illegitimate" equivalent to frivolous?
A. Right.
Q. But conceivably legal?

A. Yes. When I say that, I am talking about a situation where somebody is arrested, and all of a sudden defense counsel files a motion for something or other, and you know on the very face of the damned thing that it is a foolish motion. It is a legitimate motion, but a foolish motion, and so it is a waste of time. And that doesn't please a judge.
Q. Do you think the defendant is hurt by these motions?
A. It can hurt them in the sense that if I know the attorney, if I have had dealings with him in the past, if I know that he is procrastinating—or, if not procrastinating, a guy who is fishing to get himself a good deal—then he'll get a reputation for this type of thing.
Q. And does that hurt him?
A. It hurts them when they come in on plea bargaining. And it hurts them when they have permission to come and speak with me about their cases, because . . . A judge, well, it's like a hypochondriac with a doctor. A doctor will get to the point where he wants to throw the patient the hell out of the office. And if you have a lawyer who does this kind of stuff, you'll want to throw him the hell out of your office too. You know, one time out of his forty complaints he might be right, but how much do you have to take?
Q. So the attorney may be doing a disservice to his client by filing these motions?
A. Well, the judge who gets these motions—when I saw that motion that —— filed this morning I knew right away what the hell he was doing—he wasn't doing his client a service; he was doing him a disservice. You know, you get a feeling about a lawyer, and sometimes, you hate to say it, but sometimes you get sore at the lawyer and you take it out on his client. [14]

Some of these attorneys spend a lot of time on frivolous motions. A lot of their stuff is frivolous, that's the problem. These are lawyers who have a theory. They get a client and try to make a war, and I'll tell you something, it hurts their clients. [8]

Q. What about the notion of a penalty after conviction at trial? Will the sentence be higher than if the defendant had pled guilty?
A. Well, I think that perhaps that could be true, not in the sense that you are punished for trying the case, but I think most judges feel that there is some merit to the claim, like George Washington stepping forward and admitting he chopped down the cherry tree. In other words, the defendant who says, "I'm sorry" deserves that consideration; as opposed to the man who says, "No, I'm not guilty," and then the proof turns out to be overwhelming that he's guilty and he was simply trying to see if he can get away with it. So, I would say that the average judge . . . let me speak for myself . . . if there is a jury trial and I hear the case and the man had a reasonably good defense, there's no repercussions in my own mind as far as penalty is concerned, none whatsoever. That's his right; we should allow him a trial. But if a man, by the evidence, is overwhelmingly

guilty, and he's just relying on the fact that the jury might let him off and free him, and he's found guilty, at that point I do not give him that consideration which I would have, had he stepped forward and said: "Look, I did it, and I'm sorry." And I think that's a legitimate philosophy, because if you give no consideration to the man who steps forward and says, "I am guilty and I'm sorry," as opposed to the guy who tries to get off, then it's unjust to the man who steps forward and says: "I'm sorry."[20] [32]

There's no penalty for the defendant who goes to trial when he honestly thinks that he shouldn't be found guilty, when he has a good defense to offer. It's a different case, though, when he is just trying to pull some fast one on the court, when the case is obviously so one-sided that no rational person would think he could be acquitted, then he'll get clobbered. [18]

If someone has a trial and it's apparent that there is some question of a good defense, where you can understand why this case was tried, then the sentence is probably no harsher than it would have been if he'd entered a plea. It's a delight to have a good trial, handled by a good attorney. He knows what he is doing and comes up with sharp things during the trial. I sit there very often in a trial, and I'll make notes on questions I would ask if I was defending the client, just for my own . . . and I check them off as they are asked. I really delight in some guy picking up some angle that I never thought of. There's no problem for the defendant in these types of cases. But I think there are times when you can see a completely frivolous trial which is, you know, the whole thing is a waste of everyone's time. Take the case of the guy who is caught with his hand in the till, and there's no question but that he's guilty. And the case is still tried, and his hands are still in the till, and he hasn't been able to get them out, and you wonder why he's wasted everyone's time in going through the trial. You know, what does he accomplish? Now if he's got a technical issue . . . it may not be a factual issue, but if he's got technical grounds, and it looks like a legitimate attempt, then I'm not talking about that. I think he should take his trial. Who knows? [8]

A. I sent a kid to jail the day before yesterday for ten days, a black kid who had a prior record, and he threatened repeatedly to kill a police officer who was trying to break up a disturbance, thereby creating his own disturbance with forty to fifty people around egging him on. I put him in jail for ten days.
Q. This was after a trial?
A. Yes.
Q. Would the disposition have been the same if the defendant had pled?
A. No, no it wouldn't have. Under certain circumstances there should be a penalty for trying a case. The circumstances are these: If a fellow tries a case where he is obviously guilty, where it's sheer folly to

> try the case, and yet the accused is insisting on trying the case, he deserves to be penalized for the trial because he takes up court time, there is expense involved, and so on. On the other hand, in a situation where he had a good defense, where it is close question, and he happens to be found guilty, I would not penalize him for trying a case like that. He's got a right to try a case where he has got a reasonable position, and it just happens not to prevail. If this kid had pled guilty, if he had negotiated his diposition, there is absolutely no question that he could have walked out without jail time. If that case were to come before me on a plea of guilty, and it were represented to me that this fellow, in the heat of the moment, had made a threat; nevertheless, had regretted it later on, was penitent, had expressed his regrets to the police officer that he never had any intention of carrying out that threat, and there was a recommendation for a twenty-five dollar fine or a fifty-dollar fine, or something like that, I would have gone along with that. But here is a fellow who two police officers testified—they were sequestered—testified exactly the same, that this fellow had made violent threats, appeared to have the intention of carrying them out, disappeared in the house, threatened to kill them repeatedly, used vile language, caused a disturbance, and so on, and this fellow gets on the stand and denies he ever said anything of the kind. Absolutely denied it. And then he accuses the police officers of being out to get him. This fellow deserves to be penalized for trial. [26]

Judicial attitudes toward negotiated dispositions emerge as a result of what judges learn about the characteristics of the defendant's case in the criminal court. I am arguing that independent of any felt sanctions (for example, pressures to "move the business"), judges come to believe that only certain cases are "worthy" of trial. For the overwhelming majority of defendants, a guilty plea is the appropriate way to proceed. There is simply no point to engaging in futile ceremonial trials for cases in which there is no reasonable expectation that the outcome will differ from what is obvious at the outset, namely, that the defendant is factually and legally guilty.

This perspective on judicial adaptation strips away the effects of rewards and sanctions on the judge and allows us to consider in "pure" form the development of judicial attitudes and behavior toward plea bargaining. We can see how judges would move in the direction of according rewards for the guilty plea and/or penalties for the trial without recourse to explanations resting on the rewards and sanctions the judges themselves feel.

However, it is artificial to consider judicial adaptation exclusively in terms of learning about the characteristics of defendants' cases. At the same time that they plunge into the court, at the same time that they develop attitudes about the defendant's guilt and the contestability of issues in a case, they are also subject to rewards and sanctions that militate in favor of their adopting a positive attitude toward plea bargaining. It is to a consideration of these rewards and sanctions that we will now turn.

The Rewards of Plea Bargaining

In assessing the effects of the reward/sanction structure on judicial adaptation, three rewards that accrue to the judge who opts for "going along" with the plea bargaining system can be discerned. First, and on the most general level, plea bargaining saves the judge some time and effort, and, overall, serves to make his job easier. There is no need to prepare for a trial, to write instructions for the jury, to rule on legal issues at stake in a case. Accepting a guilty plea and asking the defendant the checklist of questions on the voluntariness of his plea is a much simpler process. And when an agreed recommendation is part of the negotiated disposition, one of the most vexing problems for a judge—sentencing—is also removed.

A second oft-noted, and not unrelated reward that judges reap from plea bargaining is the decreased likelihood that their decisions will be reversed on appeal.[21] Understandably, judges dislike appellate reversal; it is certainly not the most pleasurable of experiences to have a higher body produce a publicly available, written reversal of one's decisions. Plea bargaining offers the reward of substantially lessening the probability of the defendant's taking an appeal; trials are far more likely to yield appealable issues, and thus are far more likely to involve the potential sanction of reversal. The following excerpt from an interview with a judge speaks to both the general judicial sensitivity to reversals and the propensity of some judges to go to great lengths to avoid the possibility of appeals.

> Oh yes, we do worry about reversals on appeal, certainly. Some judges are apprehensive about their reputations, not only among fellow judges and the bar, but also on the Supreme Court. If you make a lot of wrong decisions, the Supreme Court keeps sending down "error, error, error," and, you know, you get very concerned about that. Some judges keep a tally sheet of the cases they've won and the cases they've lost, and they're concerned about what the Supreme Court thinks about them. Judges up there know the good judges and the phony judges, and judges that'll settle a case so that the case won't go up and there won't be any chance of being criticized. [35]

The third reward/sanction consideration of import for understanding judicial adaptation to plea bargaining is related to "moving the business." Judges report that they experience pressure from their peers on the court and from the administrative hierarchy of the court system to dispose of cases quickly. Those judges that succeed in processing a substantial number of cases are contrasted with those who handle only a few cases.

An example of the form this pressure can take is evident in the weekly report prepared by the clerk of each of the superior courts. This report is sent to the chief administrative judge of the Connecticut court system, to his executive assistants, and to each of the judges serving in the particular locale. The purpose of these reports is to summarize the status of the cases on the court's docket.

I was able to obtain copies of these reports for one of the superior courts included in my sample. Reading these weekly summaries gives an insight into how judges feel their work is being evaluated. The theme that seems to run through almost all of the memos is the importance of expeditiously "moving the business." Thus, strategies for increasing the guilty plea rate are praised (for example, judges' making themselves available to state's attorneys and defense attorneys for "discussion of a case"); trials are treated, if not disparagingly, as regrettable obstacles to an increase in the overall disposition rate. Some excerpts from these memos follow.[22]

> Last week Judge —— cleared the backlog of motions. One hundred and seven motions were assigned, most of which were heard and disposed. By keeping the plea motion lists current, Judge —— will now be available for trial. We have discovered in the past that with the availability of a third judge to try cases, the rate of dispositions increases sharply. We are hopeful that this effort will provide the stimulant necessary to maintain a high rate of dispositions.

> Both trial judges were on trial throughout the week. This, of course, eliminates the threat of immediate trial and decreases the disposition rate. In an effort to stimulate dispositions this week, Judge —— will be available to conduct informal pre-trials of all the ready cases.

> There were forty-five cases assigned for trial last week. Attached is a table showing their disposition. Three were disposed by change of plea. In addition, three cases not assigned were disposed by change of plea and nolle. Since a total of six cases were removed from the trial list and three were added, there was a net reduction of three cases for the week. The main reason for the low disposition rate is that both trial judges remained on trial during the entire week. Both trials turned out to be extremely lengthy. Also, Judge —— remained very occupied with motions and lengthy hearings and was unable to pre-try cases last week. For this week, however, a schedule of pre-trial sessions has been set up and will be announced from the bench.

> This week, in an effort to increase the rate of dispositions, Judge —— will encourage counsel to negotiate their cases and be available to conduct informal "pre-trials" in cases not disposed after negotiations. This method was tried during the September session and resulted in our most productive weeks.

> Despite a short week, the steady reduction of cases on the trial list continued last week for the eighth consecutive week. Being the sort of week

> that defense counsel were reluctant to begin trial, Judge —— kept the pressure on by continuing to assign ready cases for immediate trial. The results were as follows: of the thirty-five cases assigned for trial, sixteen (45 percent) were disposed by change of plea, nolle, and bond forfeiture. In addition, three cases which were not assigned were disposed by change of plea and nolle. Since a total of nineteen cases were removed from the trial list and ten were added, there was a net reduction of nine cases. As the number of cases on the trial list continues its descent, reaching the two-hundred mark by the end of this session becomes a realistic probability. What should be pointed out, however, is that the reduction made this session was accomplished despite a barrage of cases which, if they proceeded to trial, would have occupied the trial courts from two to six weeks each. Those cases included eight defendants charged with murder or manslaughter and seven charged with other serious offenses including assault with intent to murder and arson. The value of disposing of these cases without trials is obviously immeasurable and not reflected in the weekly statistics report.

The cumulative effect of these memos—which are supplemented by periodic exhortations from the chief administrative judge to "dispose of business"—is that judges come to feel that their work is evaluated at least in part by the disposition rates of the court in which they are sitting. As the following excerpts make plain, there is little doubt that judges become well aware of the priority accorded to "moving the business."

> *Q*. But who is it that puts this pressure on you to move cases?
> *A*. The chief justice, —— [the administrative assistant to the judicial branch]. They send you stuff all the time. It seems that moving cases is becoming the name of the game—get rid of those cases.
> *Q*. How does this stuff affect you?
> *A*. Let's say there are three hundred cases in ——. Well, I do the same things that I have always done. I do things in the same way as always whether there are five cases or five thousand cases. In that sense, it has no effect on me. So the statistics per se have no effect on me in terms of my method of disposition. But, on the other hand, if I can dispose of cases, I do, and I feel good. But I don't change my way of doing things. It also affects me this way—I concentrate more on encouraging plea bargaining dispositions of cases. I give an impetus to the parties involved. I tell the state's attorney to talk to the defense attorney, the defense attorney to talk to the state's attorney. I tell them to see if they can work something out. [69]

> *Q*. Do you receive pressure to move the business?
> *A*. Lots of pressure. We have a chief administrative judge, and he makes us fill out forms and count what we spend our time on and what cases we got rid of. Now, some judges, they seem oblivious to all this. They'll go out and try a case to the end, which means they'll make it through one

> case every three weeks, and they'll say how busy they are with their jobs. Maybe they are, I don't know. To me, going through fifty cases in about three weeks is doing a better job. [29]

> What they do, they call the judges in and they read the riot act to them: "Geez, you got to move more business, you gotta do this, you gotta do that. You got to move business." [11, prosecutor]

> It's a happy judge who can dispose of a lot of business. [35]

Judges react to the emphasis on "moving the business" in different ways. A handful remain oblivious, content to hear whatever matter crops up, be it a plea or trial. These judges "don't want to know" about plea bargaining; they feel a "judge should be judging," and not involved in helping the opposing parties reach agreements. Nonetheless, even these judges expect guilty defendants to plead guilty.[23] Other judges—and this was the most common position—participate in plea discussions both pretrial and during trial on an ad hoc basis. Their participation may be self-initiated (that is, the judge may feel that in a particular case the parties have not sufficiently explored the possibility of a negotiated disposition), or he may participate at the request of either or both of the opposing parties. Finally, several judges have either moved or are moving in the direction of institutionalizing judicial participation in plea bargaining. They announce from the bench that they will be available during a specific time to "pre-try" cases.[24] These are the judges for whom "efficiency" concerns loom largest, for they have taken it upon themselves to facilitate the processing of cases systematically.[25]

Though judges vary in the degree to which they structure their activities to enhance the speedy processing of cases, I think all judges feel in at least a general way a pressure to be "efficient." After all, it is easy to justify a concern for speedy resolution of a case by reference to the old adage "justice delayed is justice denied." The reports from the clerk's office, the memos from the administrative judge, and peer pressures serve to insure that a concern with speedy disposition remains—at a minimum—a salient concern for judges.

I am not suggesting that because of case pressure judges are forced to urge plea bargaining dispositions on the defendant. It is true that in crowded courts plea bargaining facilitates moving the business. But this does not mean that when judges encourage pleas it is because of case pressure. Judges in both high and low volume courts expressed similar attitudes toward "efficient" resolution of a case. Part of the explanation for their attitudes rests on the fact that judges learn some cases simply are not "worthy" of trial. Also, as I have indicated, judges pursue "efficiency" with or without case-volume pressure because its alternative, "inefficiency" is not among a list of universally laudatory goals.[26] Finally, some respondents suggested that even if the concern for rapidly disposing of cases was a reaction to increased case pressure, it has had a sort of "unthought-through, carry-over effect" on judges. Judges may become enamored with the notion of speeding cases through the court even when no explanation for why they are rushing is evident.[27] One rather introspective judge commented:

> You know, we're all trying to rush the things through the court, and if you think about it, it has become kind of a phobia. We certainly don't have much to gain by it; the only one who might benefit is a part-time prosecutor because he has a private practice also. I don't have any reason to rush. I get paid no matter if I'm here or there, and I've got the time to handle all of the business. I'm perfectly willing to sit here till five o'clock every day, so it's kind of a fantasy, this idea of rushing things through. But I still do it. I guess it's that you get tired of these things after a while. Maybe it's human nature. You know you can do it quicker, so that's how you do it. I'm not sure. [18]

What the argument does suggest is that judges are taught that disposing of cases is a valued practice, that plea bargaining provides a means of efficiently moving the business, while at the same time minimizing judicial expenditures of time and effort and reducing the risks of appeal. The rewards that flow from most cases being plea bargained, and the potential sanctions related to trials, contribute to the favorable posture toward plea bargaining evidenced by most judges. Furthermore, at the margins (for particular cases, for particular judges, and perhaps for especially high case volume jurisdictions), judicial behavior with regard to facilitating (coercing) plea bargains can be accounted for in terms of rewards and sanctions felt by the judge. But even without these sanctions, for the reasons discussed in the preceding sections, judges would come to expect that plea bargaining ought to be employed to resolve most criminal cases. Judges learn and are taught about plea bargaining, and we ought not allow the easily assailable (as improper) reward/sanction explanation to cloud this basic finding.

Some Conclusions about Judicial Adaptation to Plea Bargaining

The new judge and the experienced judge have at least one thing in common: neither is preoccupied with developing justifications for plea bargaining. As we saw, the newcomer is thrust into the court, and he struggles along just to keep his head above water. He reacts to the negotiated dispositions that come before him and, thus, gradually drifts into an acceptance of the plea bargaining system. As he gains experience in the system, he becomes so accustomed to the centrality of the negotiated disposition that he rarely gives much thought to plea bargaining as a "problem." Time and time again experienced judges referred to plea bargaining as "the common-sense way of disposing of cases" (41) or as "the practical solution for cases" (4, 29). It was not uncommon for judges who had assumed office without much criminal experience but with a background in civil law to eventually liken the "reasonableness" of plea bargaining to the "reasonable" approach followed in negotiating civil cases. Thus, when I pursued questions about plea bargaining, they often fell back on this civil analogy.

> It's just like in civil cases. Why are they settled? Because, one, they're exposed to a risk no matter what they do, whether there is a liability or not. It's the jury who finds that, so they're running a risk of exposure. So rather than risk paying out five thousand dollars they may be willing to pay five hundred dollars, rather than take the risk of that exposure. So for practical reasons it's better for them to pay out that five hundred dollars or seven hundred fifty dollars than face the risk of exposure. Now, why does the plaintiff settle? Because to him there's an advantage. He could come out with nothing, no matter how good a case he thinks he has. It is the jury that will decide. He may come out with nothing. So each side gets an advantage. When you finally narrow the difference between the two sides to an area where each one has gained sufficient advantage, you've got a settlement. The same thing happens in a criminal case. No matter what, there's a certain risk of exposure. There's the cost of defense, and so on. And the same holds for the state. So you might say to me—we get right back to your first argument—that innocent people who will, although they're innocent, plead guilty, and I say, yes, there is that risk, and it probably happens. Except, that it happens so little that it's not a factor because from my practical experience in criminal court, 96 to 98 percent of people who come into court are guilty in some degree. [32]

> Well, now, let's take the cases on the civil side, where you're dealing with money instead of putting a guy in jail for a certain period of time. And it's not so different, though when you're dealing with money it's a lot easier, I think, to assess plea bargaining, which is actually what you're doing even if you are talking about something different. There, you know, a fellow's got a broken leg which he sustained in an automobile accident. Well, you know, broken legs are worth roughly X dollars, and the fellow's got a 10 percent disability, so we add a little something for that, and he's had medical bills which amount to so much, so you add something for that. So you figure the case is worth, you know, if it went to a verdict, a jury might bring back ten thousand dollars. Well then, maybe there are things that would detract from that; the fellow might be a very prepossessing individual, and maybe he's got a lousy background and he won't make a good witness on the stand. You discount a little bit; then when you get all through, there's the problem about, well, supposing he went to a verdict and he got so much, the other side might appeal. If he goes up on appeal, it's going to cost you so

> much, and when you get all through, what's the net going to be to this guy? It might be seventy-five hundred dollars; it might only be three thousand dollars, so will he take five thousand dollars right now? I'm just saying that there are a lot of things to be taken into consideration in deciding whether a guy plea bargains for six months, factors just like those in deciding on the five-thousand-dollar offer. [35]

Essentially, the judge believes that it ''makes sense'' to negotiate most criminal cases, in the same manner, and often for the same reasons, that civil cases are negotiated. As has already been noted, he feels that there is simply no point to trying many of the cases that come before him. In a very telling comment, one judge remarked:

> I don't think that a trial necessarily represents a failure in the plea bargaining system. I really believe that the trial is a necessary adjunct of the system. [63]

It is important to consider the import of this judicial attitude toward plea bargaining for the overall plea bargaining system of the local criminal court. A casual observer of the constant negotiations between prosecutor and defense attorney and the ratification of the ''deals'' by the judge might conclude that the judge is pretty much a peripheral figure. This is not quite the case.

First, though judges accept most plea bargaining outcomes and go along with most prosecutors' recommendations, they do so because they are in fundamental agreement with both the process used to obtain these settlements and with the actual outcome of the settlement.[28] Their cooperation with the parties involved in the negotiations is not simply an expedient to lessen their own work loads.

Second, judges do not always go along with plea bargaining outcomes. Though they do so exceptionally, judges do balk at the prosecutor's recommendation.

> *Q*. Do you go along with agreed recommendations?
> *A*. Yes, in most cases. But not always. I had a case in —— this session where I gave a lower sentence than the agreed rec. And I did the same thing up in ——. There a kid was caught with a substantial quantity of marijuana. The recommendation was for thirty days. The state's attorney said thirty days was the office's policy. But the kid's mother had cancer, the kid was in high school; he worked in the evening, and this wasn't any ''eleventh-hour religion''—he'd been working for six months. I gave the kid a suspended sentence. The state's attorney was aghast. He told me that all judges gave thirty days in such cases. I told him: ''What is this, justice by automation?'' In ——, I increased an agreed recommendation. Had they asked, I would have let the defendant withdraw his plea, but they didn't ask . . . As a general rule, the judge has to defer and consider what the prosecutor and the defense attorney tell him with regard to their agreement. But they shouldn't put the judge in the position where he

> always has to agree. Most of the time I'll go with an agreement. It's simply a matter that three reasonable men—the judge, the prosecutor, and the defense attorney—concur. Even when the judge doesn't agree, sometimes he'll go along with the other two, since two men did agree. In the vast, vast majority of cases I do go along. [69]

> Generally, I'll go along with the recommendation, but not always. In ——, these two fellows—good Army backgrounds, both with tremendous records in the service, all kinds of citations and everything else, fully employed, good family backgrounds, no criminal records—but on this one night they took two girls to a dance, dropped the girls off, it was late, and they were driving on Route 44 near —— and ran out of gas at about two thirty in the morning. They coasted till they got into a gas station. They fell asleep there because they'd had quite a bit to drink. They woke up at four o'clock, chilled and everthing else. The guy had worked in the station two years previously, so he goes in there, knocks out the glass, reaches in, opens the door, and activates the pump, goes outside, is pumping the gas into his car when some priest living next to the gas station observes something, calls the police station. They come arrest the guy, naturally, breaking and entering, criminal theft. When I read the records, the background, I said: "These men shouldn't have felony records for the rest of their lives," so I called the prosecutor and said: "Look, we've got to reduce this charge at least to a misdemeanor," and he resisted, so I finally got to the point where I said: "Now look, either you're going to reduce it or I'll go out there and reopen the judgment and dismiss the charges." So then he relented, but then he came in and said, "Your honor, you've got to remember . . . " I said: "For Christ's sake, they would have nolled this in New Haven or Hartford." He says, "You're not in New Haven and you're not in Hartford; people out here are very strict about property laws." I said: "But, felony, how do you know what is going to happen to these young boys?" So from his point of view he thought he was right, and I knew I was right from my point of view. [32]

The significance of such judicial actions transcends the case at hand. It serves notice on all participants that the judge can—and will— exercise his prerogatives. The effect of this message is to set rough guidelines for prosecutor and defense attorney alike to the range of dispositional outcomes that the judge considers appropriate. A number of respondents suggested that in a plea bargaining system this is the major role reserved for the judge. The comments of two defense attorneys are illustrative. "The role of the judge is to keep the system honest, so that prosecutors can't be unrealistic, irrational" (2).

> . . . because that judge sitting up there with the black robe is still, you know, like my cat at home. When we had a female cat who had kittens, she lets them stray so far; she lets them stray, but then if something

happens, she'll gather them up. So the judge, like the cat, is omnipresent. [25]

The judge's significance for the plea bargaining process, then, rests in his potential power to upset negotiated dispositions. Prosecutors and defense attorneys must plea bargain within the bounds set by their perceptions of what the judge will "go along with." Thus, the fact that judges rarely overturn negotiated settlements reflects success on the part of the court "adversaries" in anticipating the judge's own sentencing proclivities.

In a more fundamental sense, the judge's willingness to go along with a plea bargain also reflects his belief that it is proper for these "adversaries" to negotiate dispositions. Indeed, the thrust of this chapter has been to explain why judges are so content to delegate formal judicial powers to prosecutors and defense attorneys.

7 Conclusions and Implications

Thus far, I have considered the adaptation of prosecutors, defense attorneys, and judges in isolation. A more complete understanding of adaptation requires that we integrate these separate inquiries and offer some general conclusions about the adaptation process and the substantive outcomes that result from it. In turn, these conclusions enable us to clarify the actual relationship between case pressure and plea bargaining, and thereby assess the feasibility of proposals to abolish plea bargaining.

As a final note, I explore the implications of my findings for plea bargaining reform policy and for the development of a comparative approach to the study of local courts in the political system.

The Adaptation Process

For the most part, new judges, prosecutors, and defense attorneys are not well prepared for their jobs in the court. Law school—and, for a handful of newcomers, prior civil court experience—simply does not engender a realistic perspective on the operations of the criminal court. What the newcomers bring to the court is a series of vague expectations about the factual and legal culpability of defendants and about the means that ought to be employed to process these defendants' cases. They assume that many cases are factually and/or legally contestable, and that the trial is the proper means to resolve the disputes. Plea bargaining is, if not an unmitigated evil, certainly something only to be used when case pressure renders trial impossible.[1]

Armed with these general expectations (or perhaps more accurately, with these amorphous impressions), the newcomer is thrust into the court. No formal program—with the exception of sitting with an experienced colleague for a brief period of time—is available to guide him. In short order he is handling cases on his own.

The newcomer is set adrift amid a welter of conflicting demands. Defendants expect their attorneys to negotiate cases; prosecutors expect attorneys to negotiate; attorneys expect prosecutors to be willing to work out a "deal"; judges are expected to ratify agreed recs, and so on. The newcomer attempts to muddle through as best he can; and as best he can usually means on a case-by-case basis. Problems are addressed sequentially as they arise in the context of a particular case, and then are set aside in favor of whatever issue crops up in the other cases the individual is handling.

At the same time that the newcomer is involved in this "frenzied drifting" into his role, he also is learning and is being taught about plea bargaining. He learns that the reality of the local criminal court differs from what he expected, and that compelling reasons to negotiate cases are often a product of this "reality"; he also is taught by rewards and sanctions that benefits are attached to plea bargaining and that costs may be levied for a trial. The importance of this dichotomy between learning and teaching cannot be emphasized enough. It suggests that independent of rewards and sanctions newcomers will plea bargain most of their cases. Contrary to the conspiratorial perspective reviewed earlier, newcomer adaptation is not simply a process in which well-motivated idealistic newcomers are coerced to cooperate in a bureaucracy obsessed with moving the business. Without sanctions for trial, without rewards for plea bargaining, the newcomer would still learn that plea bargaining serves his interests in many cases.

I will return to a consideration of these substantive outcomes of the adaptation process shortly. Here, I simply want to stress that the most fruitful way to view the adaptation process is by adopting this learning and teaching perspective. This approach guards against the naive assumption that the "system" singularly shapes newcomers into cooperative participants, and that the "system's" efforts explain the newcomer's adaptation.[2] Juxtaposition of the newcomer's "learning about the system" with the rewards and sanctions employed in the system, yields a more realistic—though more complex—perspective on the adaptation process.

To highlight these dual components of the newcomer's adaptation, I have sorted and discussed separately what newcomers learn and what they are taught. But this artificial neatness does not correspond to how the newcomer actually perceives his own adaptation to the court. He does not go back to his office at day's end and systematically sort and consider what he learned and what he was taught that day. Indeed, it is unlikely that he spends much time at all consciously and systematically considering his experiences in the court. He may be struck by something he learned about a defendant in a case, or by something he was taught in a case. But it is exceptional for the newcomer to then piece these insights into a coherent perspective on the system and his role within it. It was not uncommon for respondents to admit that they had not given much systematic thought to their own behavior.

> *Q*. Let me get this [his style of plea bargaining] straight.
> *A*. It's not all straight in my mind. You don't have time to sit back and philosophize in this job. I did when I went to law school and when I went to college and played all those games, but down here you're working all the time. [51, prosecutor]

> *Q*. Why did you leave L.A.A.? [This attorney had just left his job as a legal assistance attorney for a research job in a university]
> *A*. In three years of hitting my head against the wall, and I don't regret any of it, it was getting to be a little too much routine, and I was still emotionally, mentally, and physically exhausted after being in court every day, and I was looking or hoping for the opportunity to sit back and think about what I was doing, not being so tired at the end of the day that I could not sit back and read a book about criminal law from the theoretical point of view. I wanted to take a step back; I wanted to think about what I was doing. [33]

Changed expectations about how a case ought to be resolved, and corresponding behavioral changes, evolve gradually, and without conscious consideration. The newcomer becomes a seasoned court veteran without articulating—and often without being able to articulate—the reasons for his changed perspective and behavior.[3]

> Well, you see, you're very busy as a judge, so you don't spend any time engaging in philosophical introspection, or I don't, very little. So it's taken me years to formulate and put into words these feelings. I trust I've been operating on them for a long period of time, but now I begin to recognize them as guiding principles that should be in the forefront of a person's mind. [18, judge]

> A lot of these things you don't even do consciously. You don't think . . . it's almost a reflex. [2, defense attorney]

Adaptation within the local criminal court, then, is a complex process in which learning and teaching interact to reshape newcomer behavior and the premises which underlie this behavior.[4] The process is gradual and subtle; newcomers adapt on the basis of experiences in particular cases, and often they are unable to articulate just how and why they have changed. But change they do, and over time they find that they have altered their own premises about how one ought to proceed with a case. In short, they have adapted to the plea bargaining system, and have adopted plea bargaining as the means to resolve most criminal disputes.

Adaptation Outcomes: An Explanation for Plea Bargaining without Case Pressure

The central theme that emerges from our inquiry into adaptation is that prosecutors, defense attorneys, and judges share the basic belief that plea bargaining is the appropriate means of disposing of many, if not most,[5] criminal cases.[6] Considerable time has already been devoted to explaining why court personnel assume this posture toward plea bargaining, and there is little point in reviewing all of the role-specific explanations. But there are several factors that cut across roles, common factors of import for understanding the adaptation of defense attorneys, prosecutors, and judges, factors that I think ought to be distilled from the specific analyses and be considered here. Specifically, court personnel learn and are taught that (1) approximately 90 percent of the defendants in the court are factually guilty; (2) of these, a sizable percentage have no substantial grounds to contest the state's case; that is, they are factually and legally guilty, and their trials would be barren of any contentions likely to produce an acquittal; (3) if a defendant pleads guilty he is likely to be rewarded in terms of a reduction in charge and/or sentence. These perceptions do not necessarily add up to a negation of the legal tenet of the presumption of innocence. Court personnel simply recognize the factual culpability of many defendants, and the fruitlessness, at least in terms of case outcome, of going to trial. From these perceptions flows the notion that if the obviously guilty defendant cops a plea, he will receive some award. Whether the defendant believes this results from his show of contrition, or, more prosaically, from saving the state time and money, is not of concern here; the fact that he perceives that he receives a reward is the key point. Similarly, prosecutors and judges do not believe that they accord this reward simply to "move the business." They feel that by giving consideration to the defendant who pleads guilty, they are furthering their own professional goals (sorting serious from nonserious cases, obtaining certain time in serious cases, and so on). Though defendants may believe that they are being rewarded for not "hassling the system," prosecutors and judges feel that plea bargaining is the best means to realize their own legitimate professional goals, and that it is not at all simply an expedient to dispose of "onerously large case loads."

Learning and being taught these three perceptions seem to be at the heart of the adaptation process of judges, prosecutors, and defense attorneys. Each learns that most defendants are factually and legally guilty, and each finds plea bargaining to be a "realistic" and beneficial way of disposing of these defendants' cases. Defense attorneys feel that their obviously guilty clients receive a better disposition through plea bargaining than they would at trial; prosecutors feel—based on the standards they employ to assess the seriousness of cases—that adequate agreements at a minimal cost are achieved; judges believe that an "efficient" resolution of cases not "worthy" of trial is effectuated. As the actors spend more time in the system, these assumptions become so ingrained that they no longer think in terms of trial. Instead, they presume that a deal will be struck, that the defendant will plead guilty, and that expeditious resolution of the matter will result.

The significance of this perspective on the plea bargaining process—a perspective generated from our inquiry into newcomer adaptation—becomes clear when we reexamine the disposition data presented in chapter 3. Recall that these data demonstrated that historically there has been a low trial rate in high and low volume courts, and that a substantial reduction of cases before the superior court (with personnel remaining constant) did not lead to an increase in the trial rate. These data were presented to cast doubt on the "case pressure leads to plea bargaining" argument; however, no explanation for the absence of variation in trial rates was offered. Instead, I indicated that the explanation had to await the conclusion of the adaptation inquiry.

In both high and low volume jurisdictions, it is reasonable to hypothesize that a substantial percentage of defendants are guilty and that many of these defendants do not have any realistically contestable factual or legal issues to raise at trial.[7] Prosecutors and judges view these defendants' cases as not being "worthy" of trial, and expect a guilty plea; the defendants and their attorneys are likely to act in accordance with this expectation because of their perception that there is a "reward" for the guilty plea. Thus, independent of the court's case volume, the presumption that the guilty defendant ought to plead guilty holds sway.[8]

The low trial rate evident historically can be explained by the same line of reasoning.[9] Assuming that the criminal justice system has always processed a substantial number of defendants who were factually guilty and who did not stand a very good chance of acquittal at trial, we would expect the guilty plea—not the trial—to be the predominant means of case resolution. And this, of course, is precisely what the time series data indicate.[10]

The Inevitability of Plea Bargaining

The preceding discussion implies that plea bargaining is far more central to the local criminal court than has heretofore been recognized. Guilty pleas characterize high and low volume courts, and have done so for at least ninety years. The trial is not—and has not been—the central means of case resolution. In this section I will carry the argument one step further. Specifically, I will argue that plea bargaining is inextricably entwined with local criminal court disposition processes, and that, notwithstanding a very prominent study that concluded to the contrary, its abolition is an impossibility.[11]

Let us begin by assuming that a formal rule proscribing plea bargaining is promulgated. "No more plea bargaining in the court, no more deals, no more prosecutorial negotiations" reads our hypothetical rule. "Plea bargaining from this day forward is not permitted in the local criminal court.'' If I am correct in arguing that plea bargaining is inextricably entwined with the criminal court, such a rule will necessarily falter.

The linchpin of my argument is that, though it might be possible to proscribe ''explicit plea bargaining'' (that is, explicit negotiation between prosecutor, defense attorney, and judge), it would be impossible to proscribe what we might call ''implicit plea bargaining.'' By implicit plea bargaining I mean nothing other than what was a central theme in the adaptation chapters, namely, that there is agreement among all court actors that most guilty defendants should plead guilty and be rewarded for their plea. Thus, even if formal negotiations were verboten, the expectation that guilty defendants should plead would remain. All criminal court actors would recognize ''implicitly'' that the defendant who pleads receives a reward and that the defendant who goes to trial does not. Perhaps those working in the system would have to learn to tolerate a bit more uncertainty because of the proscription against formal agreements, but I would guess that not too much time would elapse before the implicit rewards became well known, and defense attorneys could then make ''good guesses'' as to what sentence the defendant would receive.

Furthermore, I would hypothesize that even with these ''good guesses'' the system would be unstable. Defendants would not be satisfied to place complete faith in their attorneys' guesses and would continue to press for specific agreements regarding charge and sentence reduction.[12] And I think after the initial ballyhoo surrounding the ''abolition of plea bargaining'' abates, the defense attorney's efforts to arrange more explicit deals would meet with success.

I base this conclusion on two related considerations distilled from the interviews. The first we might label the ''everyone wants to negotiate sometimes'' factor; the second is a sort of ''slippery slope'' factor.

Recall that when I discussed prosecutorial adaptation to plea bargaining, I noted that a small minority of veteran prosecutors did not like plea bargaining. The same holds true for defense attorneys. Within each of these roles, one finds individuals who express normative disenchantment with many aspects of the plea bargaining process. Though they plea bargain most of their cases, they are inclined to explain their behavior more in terms of the practical necessity of plea bargaining (case pressure, and so on), than in terms of arriving at just decisions through a plea bargain.[13]

A policy proscribing plea bargaining would probably meet resistance from the majority of court personnel, who do not share the antipathy of these ''philosophical opponents'' to plea bargaining. But, one could argue that if a rule to abolish plea bargaining were imposed, it is precisely these ''philosophical opponents'' who would move to the fore to champion the ruling, and perhaps even to convert some of their brethren. What the ''everyone wants to negotiate sometimes'' factor suggests, however, is that even these philosophical opponents would not hold firm in refusing to make explicit guarantees to defense attorneys.

Specifically, the philosophical opponents to plea bargaining do not oppose—and, indeed, they want—plea bargaining in certain cases. We saw earlier that prosecutors who oppose plea bargaining in general are eager to plea bargain cases in which they think the defendant guilty but have a problem of proof or a technical defect in the case. Similarly, defense attorneys who feel that in general plea bargaining is abhorrent still very much want the plea bargaining option to remain open. They cite, for example, instances where informal discussion with a prosecutor facilitates consideration of mitigating circumstances.

Rather than attempt an exhaustive cataloging of all the exceptions raised by prosecutors and defense attorneys (we will return to their views in the following section), I think it sufficient to present several illustrative excerpts from interviews with these "philosophical opponents." The following excerpts (the first is from an interview with a prosecutor, the following two from defense attorney interviews) convey a sense of the equivocation felt by "opponents" of plea bargaining. Both the "anti–plea bargaining" sentiment, and the qualification placed on this hostile posture later in our interview, are presented.

> I don't like plea bargaining. Right? I mean, you might as well understand my philosophy because a lot of people don't agree with it. I am tired after many years of being a prosecutor of hearing . . . of going to so-called public forums, being invited to speak, and then being attacked. The jails are full of people who were put there by lawyers who plea bargained them in. In the best of all worlds, every case should be tried. Let a jury of twelve acquit him, take the responsibility, or convict him. But once convicted, then, let them go up to the prisons and scream that twelve good people did it to him. Not the system. I think it's a real cop-out to say, "I'm in here because the lawyer said so and so." You know, the experienced criminals that we deal with, felony people, almost to a man know exactly what's going down. They know what plea bargaining is. They know about the system, and they like the system. They benefit. Then they bitch about it. I don't like the bitching. I think we should give them a trial; we're ready, willing, and able to give them trial.

> If we have a weak case, we probably will come down, yeah. If we know that there is some really glaring error, police procedure, or the proof, yes. I mean, in other words, there are times when we know the guy is guilty and we know it beyond a reasonable doubt, because we know that, for instance, maybe the police goofed on the search warrant and we're not going to get it in, and rather than let him go free, we'll come down . . . . I don't want to cut off all plea negotiations, don't misunderstand me. See, that's the problem, that if you lock into a system [of no plea bargaining]

> you . . . there should be an ability to talk to the defense. And I think there are some times when, you know, you want to take something into consideration. Maybe the defendant is cooperative, you know, and I don't want to have to try him. I want to give him a break. Maybe the mother spoke to me and said: "Mr. ——, really he was wrong, but . . ." I want to be able to discuss that. I don't want to be locked out, either. [30]

> I think the client should have his trial, have a chance of beating the case completely, and be assured that he'll get a full defense. I think it's desirable that he gets his trial. And, in fact, the trial often brings out facts that are mitigating; the guy may have been involved but not to the extent. So there may have been circumstances that are involved, or the witness may prove unreliable. That kind of stuff would come out in a trial that might not otherwise, and so if there wasn't the idea of punishing the person for claiming the trial I think it would be in all circumstances beneficial because otherwise you don't have the chance of being found not guilty, if you plead guilty. And you don't have the chance of vindicating certain legal issues which may be meaningful to the client.

> Well, that's [plea bargaining] at least one avenue that should be open to the courts because . . . I think the defendant needs the benefit of the chance of both [the trial and the plea bargain], and, you know, to eliminate the possibility of the informal discussion of the case, that wouldn't be desirable. So sometimes you want to use informal methods of resolving cases with prosecutors. [12]

> I just hate pleading guilty. I feel dirty. It seems to me that plea bargaining is a very corrupt thing . . . And I would rather, frankly, have a good battle. I only feel clean when I win a case, win a case by fighting. Ideally, I think every case should be decided by a jury trial, after completely fair procedures by both sides, and no trickery, in which each side had equally able counsel, equally skilled investigators, a trial presided by a truly detached, neutral, and learned magistrate.

> And I do plea bargain, and it may be that I plea bargain in a slightly different way, in that I don't accept a lot of offers that other lawyers will accept. But in most cases, at some point, I always say: "Hey, listen, what will you give me?" . . . And obviously there are some kinds of cases that are just going to be pled out.[14] [31]

The point to be stressed here is that even those most opposed to plea bargaining would find it uncomfortable to function in a system in which the plea bargaining option was completely closed. They want—and need—for reasons of their own (and these reasons differ across roles), the availability of a negotiated settlement for some of their cases. I think their willingness to negotiate some cases, when coupled with the "slippery slope" factor, lends credence to my argument that, even if plea bargaining were abolished, eventually explicit deals would be consummated.

The "slippery slope" factor suggests that once an exception to a no plea bargaining policy is made, it inevitably leads to claims for exceptions in subsequent cases. Prosecutors cannot have it both ways; they cannot maintain a no plea bargaining policy, and eagerly seek exceptions for particular types of cases (for example, those cases where legal problems exist). The line that justifies making an exception in one case is not so sharply drawn that it readily divides the excepted cases from the run-of-the-mill cases. Attorneys, seeing a chink in the no plea bargaining policy, will quickly attempt to present their own cases in a form that fits the prosecutor's exceptions. Gradually, I would hypothesize, more and more cases will filter through the chink. The following excerpts illustrate this "slippery slope" factor.

> . . . and what I think would happen [if plea bargaining were abolished] is that you would get a sort of snowball effect. Once the state's attorney starts letting the bars down for one guy, they would have to let them down for others. I don't want my guys going for longer than someone else's, and vice versa. [38]

> If I give one suspended sentence in a robbery with violence case, then the next ten guys in here will want it. Then what will you say to them? So we try to avoid stupid recommendations, but we do make mistakes sometimes, and they have these aftereffects. [62]

> Even in superior court [no backlog], if they were to try every case in superior court they'd [the state's attorneys] have a lot of grief. Once you begin talking to people, it's hard to be very selective in that process. Once you say to yourself: "All right, we're going to try every single case. We're not going to talk to you about anything. If you want to plead guilty, okay, that's up to you; we don't give a shit. Plead guilty to what the charges are. We're not going to discuss anything with you." Unless you're going to do that on every case, it's very hard to not talk to people. Look at the mandatory minimums, where people have to do five years no matter how compelling a psychological problem there may be in the case or without regard to past record or anything else. Where would the system be if prosecutors couldn't talk about those cases? . . . Unless they really are gonna try every case and just not do anything for anyone, they've got to talk to everyone because how are they going to draw lines? I can see if some guy has lied to them on a case, and they've been burnt by this, that, and the other thing, then they may say: "We are not going to give him shit." But otherwise, it's pretty hard not to just talk to everybody, and once you start talking to anybody from there it's no stop at all. I mean, what if I say, "What will you do to avoid a trial?" What does he say then? "I don't want to avoid a trial. I want to try your case." [37]

Plea bargaining appears to be as integral and inevitable in the local criminal court (whether high or low volume) as is something like the committee system in the Congress. I suppose it would be possible to proscribe actual plea bargaining negotiations and announce with great flourish the "abolition of plea bargaining." But the guilty plea is legally protected, and concessions to the defendant who pleads guilty may readily be justified in terms other than saving the state time and money. Factually guilty defendants without much hope at trial will probably be disposed to plead guilty and avail themselves of the reward reputedly accorded contrite and cooperative defendants. Defense attorneys will seek assurances from prosecutors that the expected implicit reward will be forthcoming, and gradually explicit deals—at least for some defendants—will be struck. As these explicit discussions multiply, as the slide down the slippery slope progresses, I would hypothesize that a more explicit plea bargaining system would emerge again, albeit in *sub rosa* fashion.

Thus, to speak of a plea bargaining–free criminal justice system is to operate in a land of fantasy. At a minimum, implicit plea bargaining would be the norm in the system that abolished plea bargaining, and I suspect that not too much time would elapse before explicit plea bargaining would again move to the fore. The fancifulness of any proposal to abolish plea bargaining was perhaps best summarized by a rather colorful Ortaville defense attorney:

> *Q*. There is some talk now about outlawing plea bargaining?
> *A*. No, no, no. How can you outlaw plea bargaining? How can you outlaw a screw, and how can you outlaw gambling, and how can you outlaw drinking? There are three or four things that are going to be with us forever. There they are: screwing, drinking, gambling, and plea bargaining. [34]

Alternate Plea Bargaining Styles and an Agenda for Research

This study has been primarily concerned with clarifying the core aspects of newcomer adaptation to the local criminal court and with considering the import of the outcomes of the adaptation process for the development of an explanation of plea bargaining that does not rest on a case-pressure foundation. Thus, I have emphasized the core themes that characterize adaptation to all three roles, and have used these to explain why plea bargaining characterizes high and low volume courts, and why I think it is inevitable in the local criminal court.

But not everyone in the local criminal court is a champion of plea bargaining. The interviews suggested a fair amount of variation in normative preferences regarding plea bargaining, though it is important to stress that this variation was more a matter of degree than of kind. This is to say that, though some actors liked plea bargaining more than others, all were in favor of—at a minimum—the retention of the plea bargaining option in the local criminal court. Differences blossomed above and beyond this common consensus on the desirability of some plea bargaining in the court, but these differences are more a matter of how much plea bargaining and what type of plea bargaining than they are of no plea bargaining versus plea bargaining.

Unfortunately, the research instruments employed in this study were not sensitive enough to generate a parsimonious typology of the various attitudinal postures toward plea bargaining. Several classificatory schemes were essayed, but each of these was found to be wanting. An exhaustive and mutually exclusive typology simply could not be developed with the data at hand.

Since we have already considered most of the arguments advanced in favor of plea bargaining, and since a satisfactory typology is precluded by data constraints, I will limit the discussion to a description of why a minority of prosecutors and defense attorneys dislike plea bargaining.[15] As will become plain below, even this very limited approach suggests several important problems for subsequent research.

Prosecutors who avow a dislike of plea bargaining are particularly exercised about the plea bargaining of "good cases." They have no objections to plea bargaining in cases with factual or legal problems, or cases in which publicity should be kept to a minimum (for example, a case involving the rape of a young girl). But they believe prosecutors ought not plea bargain "good cases," cases in which no problem of proof and no restriction as to publicity exist. In their opinion, the defendants either should plead guilty as charged without any expectation of a reward, or the case should be tried. What really gnaws at these prosecutors is the spillover expectation of defense attorneys that because deals are offered in some cases, prosecutors should be equally forthcoming in "good cases."

A second factor that weighs heavily on their minds is the claim made by imprisoned defendants that they were coerced into accepting a plea bargain, that their defense attorney conspired with the prosecutor to railroad them into a state prison term. These prosecutors resent the defendants' claims, and would rather give the defendant his day in court, convict him, sentence him to "what he really deserves," and foreclose what they see as nonsensical protestations of conspiracy.

Obviously, defense attorneys who dislike plea bargaining found their antipathy on quite different grounds. They plea bargain because the "deals are good," but they are concerned by the low number of trials they actually undertake. The source of their consternation is their sense that there is something wrong with a system that discourages, under risk of penalty, adversary motions and trials. They feel uncomfortable relying on prosecutorial largesse, and would prefer to file motions formally, rather than approach the prosecutor with "hat in hand." In short, a handful of attorneys would prefer a more formal adversary system, with greater emphasis on motions and trials and less informal reliance on pretrial discussions and plea bargaining. They believe that combativeness would be rewarding to their clients and would bring dignity to the system.

These seemed to be the most salient concerns of those prosecutors and defense attorneys fitting within the "dislike plea bargaining" mold. Though I suspect other concerns could be detected upon closer scrutiny of their positions, I think these are sufficient to suggest that there are—among a handful of court personnel—fairly strong objections to current plea bargaining practices. I have concentrated on the more common "positive" attitudinal attachment to plea bargaining in this study. Subsequent research ought to be directed at (1) clarifying why some of those working in the court evidence this antipathy to plea bargaining; (2) assessing the import of these attitudes on behavior.

Assume that the salient concerns described above could be operationalized, and then could be used to sort those less than enthusiastic about plea bargaining from the overwhelming majority of court personnel who, as we have seen, are strong proponents of plea bargaining. With a reasonable *n*[16] for both groups,[17] one could attempt an explanation of why these differences emerge. Is it the adaptation process? Are they taught different lessons? Is it something they "brought to" the court, such as law school attended, personality variables, and so on?

Secondly, one could systematically assess whether their attitudes correlate to behavior. My samples were too small to detect any effect of these attitudes on behavior; however, a number of plausible hypotheses do spring to mind. Prosecutors who dislike plea bargaining might be (1) more inclined than their colleagues to want to go to trial on any given "good case";[18] (2) less inclined to make sentence recommendations; (3) more inclined, when they do make sentence recommendations, to insist that the defense attorney cannot "pitch" for a lower sentence. Similarly, defense attorneys who dislike plea bargaining might (1) file more motions for bills of particulars, discovery, and so on; (2) try a greater percentage of their cases;[19] (3) have a longer average period of confinement per client; (4) have more satisfied clients.[20]

In addition to these rather specific hypotheses, a more general examination of the role served by these "nonconformists" should be undertaken. For example, it may be that it is functional for a prosecutor's office to have an attorney who is reluctant to plea bargain on its staff. The deals offered by the disenchanted plea bargainer would make the offers of the other prosecutors seem all the more appealing.[21] This, of course, presupposes that the chief prosecutor allows "shopping" by defense attorneys. If no shopping is allowed, one would hypothesize that the defense attorney who gets "stuck with" the disenchanted plea bargainer would fare worse. Alternatively, the chief prosecutor could establish a division of labor within his office. Prosecutors who did not want to plea bargain would be assigned to do exclusively trial work; they would try the cases in which other prosecutors could not reach agreement. In this fashion, those who like plea bargaining would plea bargain; those who dislike it would try cases.[22]

Similarly, the defense attorney who does not want to plea bargain may serve several important roles within the court. Several respondents suggested that attorneys who spoke critically of plea bargaining and who appeared to raise more motions and to take more cases to trial were actually ''safety valves'' for the system. These attorneys could—and did—attract the most hostile defendants, and by their actions convinced these defendants that just representation was available. I also noted that the newcomer often pointed to the ''nonconformist'' attorney as a standard of comparison for his own behavior. Early in his career he hoped to emulate this attorney. As he gained experience, however, he began to distinguish the way he handled a case from the way the critic of plea bargaining did. Finally, when he considered himself to have become an experienced attorney, he was likely to have changed his initial assessment and would maintain that the attorney who deviates from the plea bargaining norm does a disservice to the client. Indeed, it is not inconceivable that prosecutors relish having a small number of attorneys who are reluctant to plea bargain in the court. By wisely using rewards and sanctions they can very visibly teach newcomers that the nonconformist route is not the road to success in the local criminal court.

Whether these speculations about the role of the nonconformist attorney in the court are accurate can only be answered after more complete data are collected. What is clear, however, is that there is some ''slack'' in the court, some room for prosecutors and defense attorneys who do not perfectly fit the plea bargaining mold.[23] Not every newcomer's attitudes and behavior are shaped in a fashion that is ideally compatible with the plea bargaining system. A small minority avow a normative dislike of plea bargaining, and maintain that they plea bargain less and enjoy their jobs more. Why these individuals emerge from the adaptation process with attitudes and behavior patterns different from the overwhelming majority of those who experience the teaching and learning that the court arena provides, and what role they play, and serve, in a system in which they are ''outsiders,'' remain important problems to be resolved by future research.

Policy Implications and Notes toward a Comparative Approach: Some Final Conclusions

The research findings bear on a number of policy and theoretical issues that heretofore have not been explicitly considered. Of particular interest are the problems of plea bargaining reform policy, and the development of a comparative approach to the study of local courts. In this final section, I will move a bit beyond the data and advance somewhat speculative propositions concerning the implications of my findings for these areas. Though time and space constraints militate against an exhaustive analysis, I think it important to at least note the prescriptions generated from my research for each of these areas.

Plea Bargaining Reforms

In this study, I have not detailed the potential and actual problems associated with plea bargaining. Instead, I have explained existing plea bargaining dynamics, and as a result I have concluded that plea bargaining is inevitable in the local criminal court. This approach to plea bargaining, and the conclusions reached through it, however, do not mean that I am unaware of, lack sensitivity toward, or am skeptical about, the parade of plea bargaining-related horrors that can be set forth. Innocent defendants can be coerced to plead guilty; seriously guilty defendants can be released without what many would consider appropriate punishment. Defendants may hesitate to exercise legal challenges lest their actions invoke prosecutorial sanctions; prosecutors may feel pressure to forsake the goal of "dispensing justice" and in its stead concern themselves with "disposing of cases."

A number of authors have spent considerable time discussing these (and other) abuses, and I see little point in recapitulating their arguments.[24] Instead, I think it more profitable to consider briefly the way the results of this study structure questions about reforming plea bargaining. This approach will yield a framework within which specific reforms of plea bargaining can be considered.

First, and foremost, reform policy ought not be geared toward the abolition of plea bargaining. The reason: the abolition of plea bargaining is impossible. Perhaps in the best of all worlds, only a criminal justice system without plea bargaining can function with dignity; and perhaps this is something that philosophically inclined observers should continue to speculate about.[25] But, in the real world, the argument that plea bargaining can be eliminated is illusory, and efforts to develop and implement plans to abolish plea bargaining are pointless expenditures of time and money. Instead, the same time and resources should be used to consider how to reduce abuse within the plea bargaining system.

A fruitful first step would be to "open up" the plea bargaining process. When a deal is negotiated, it would be put on the record. Defendants would thus be assured that the prosecutor would fulfill his end of the bargain and, furthermore, they would be spared the demeaning "cop-out ceremony."[26] And if a judge finds that he cannot go along with the prosecutor's recommendation, the defendant would be given the option of withdrawing his plea, and electing a trial.

These are the minimum changes that ought to be instituted in the criminal courts. Other possible reforms (and this list is by no means exhaustive) include (1) requiring prosecutors to present a prima facie case establishing the defendant's guilt and demonstrating why possible legal challenges would not succeed; (2) requiring defense attorneys to state for the record why they negotiated the settlement; (3) requiring defendant participation in the actual plea negotiations; (4) requiring judges to explain the reasons for a sentence in a particular case;[27] (5) allowing defendants to appeal their sentences.[28] By opening up the plea bargaining process, by making it subject to greater scrutiny, by sensitizing participants to due-process concerns, abuse within the plea bargaining system can be reduced. Plea bargaining cannot be eliminated, but it certainly can be made more fair. This list of possible reforms suggests the kinds of things that can be done.[29]

One reform strategy, then, is to work within the criminal justice system to make plea bargaining as palatable as possible. A second avenue for further exploration is the complete removal of some cases from the criminal courts. By this, I do not mean the decriminalization of certain offenses. Instead, I am talking about alternatives to the criminal court itself. If the options within the court are either trial or plea bargain, and if there is—as I believe—good reason to be skeptical about both processes, why not conceive of alternate channels for case disposition? There is nothing holy about the trial, just as there is nothing holy about plea bargaining.

The alternative that I have in mind—and I am sure that there are others—is the use of arbitration to resolve some criminal disputes. Limited experimental projects have been undertaken using this method, and the initial results are promising.[30] Certain crimes (some misdemeanors and minor felonies) are diverted from the court and are sent to an arbitrator. The parties involved in the dispute that resulted in criminal charges being brought (the cases often involve disputes between two citizens) appear before the arbitrator and "tell their stories." The formal rules of evidence are dispensed with, the proceeding is relatively informal, and no criminal records result. A premium is placed on trying to mediate the dispute without issuing a binding arbitration order.

The limited available data suggest that arbitration is a quick, flexible, relatively cheap, and, most importantly, an efficacious means of resolving criminal disputes. Though these data are somewhat suspect, and though arbitration has not yet been tested widely, I think the idea of mediating and arbitrating disputes outside the confines of the criminal justice system merits further attention.[31] It is a refreshingly different way to approach the problems of the plea bargaining/trial system, and it has an intrinsic appeal because of its emphasis on seeking solutions for—and not just disposing of and dispensing with—the problems of a case.[32]

There is little point here in engaging in a lengthy and detailed evaluation of the merits and defects of an arbitration plan, for I have suggested the plan more as an illustration of a way of approaching perceived problems in the criminal justice system than as a concrete policy proposal.[33] I am arguing that, rather than expend limited resources on reforms of plea bargaining, the critic might reap greater returns on his investment of these resources by exploring alternatives to the plea bargain *and* the trial. There are limits beyond which the disposition processes of the local criminal court cannot be changed; core aspects of plea bargaining simply cannot be reformed away. Thus, those most disenchanted with the centrality of plea bargaining in the local criminal court ought to give careful thought to alternatives—such as arbitration—which provide a means for some litigants to circumvent the criminal court. Within the criminal court there is going to be plea bargaining; outside it, the alternatives may or may not be preferable to plea bargaining, but they ought at least to be carefully considered and evaluated.

Notes toward a Comparative Approach to the Study of Plea Bargaining

The hypotheses generated from this inquiry into plea bargaining in Connecticut must be tested in comparative settings. It is possible—though, I think, implausible—that the findings reported herein are unique to Connecticut, that somehow Connecticut's court system, political culture, political structure, and so on differ so greatly from those of other states that its court disposition processes are totally atypical. More likely, I think, is the possibility that a comparative study will suggest marginal differences between states in adaptation processes and plea bargaining dynamics. I suspect that the core explanation of adaptation and of the centrality of plea bargaining will hold across states but that some small—but nonetheless significant—variation exists.[34]

Three sets of variables should be employed to choose comparative settings. First, case-pressure variables should be taken into account. Both high and low volume jurisdictions should be included in the sample. The low volume courts are important because they will allow us to test the generalizability of my contention that plea bargaining rates even in low volume/well-staffed courts are high. The high volume courts, on the other hand, might allow us to sort "pure" plea bargaining from plea bargaining as affected by a very high case volume. This is to say that the explanation of plea bargaining presented in this study accounts for most of the variance in plea bargaining. But when a court's volume becomes very high, and personnel remains constant, case pressure probably has some effect on the plea bargaining of certain cases. Including high volume jurisdictions would allow us to clarify these effects.[35]

The second set of factors that should be considered when choosing research sites is structural in nature and takes into account the formal organizational characteristics of the court and of the offices of the judge, prosecutor, and defense attorney. Does a court have jurisdiction over misdemeanors and felonies? Are motions heard at a separate stage, or are they heard at the same time as the trial? Do judges rotate from one jurisdiction to another, or are they permanently assigned to one court? Does the prosecutor exercise tight or loose control over his subordinates? Do public defenders or assigned private counsel handle indigents' cases? Again, I would hypothesize that variables such as these will affect both the plea bargaining and the adaptation process. Newcomers will learn and be taught slightly different things within systems "shaped" by various constellations of these structural variables. A future research design would optimally include enough settings to isolate each of these structural variables, and thus would allow us to determine the relative significance of each of these factors.[36]

Finally, my findings must be tested in different political settings. The central hypothesis here is that the political culture of a local community or state affects—albeit in indirect fashion—plea bargaining dynamics. In this study, I have given short shrift to the political culture/plea bargaining nexus because the data did not support the development of any theoretically interesting propositions. For the most part, plea bargaining dynamics and adaptation to the plea bargaining system could be most parsimoniously explained by the teaching and learning variables that we examined, and not by political culture variables. But in a more general and indirect fashion, the political variables may be of import.

I suspect that in most communities a "zone of indifference" surrounds court practices.[37] Within this zone, the community is indifferent to how and why cases are plea bargained or tried. Court personnel are accorded substantial leeway to handle cases in whatever way they deem appropriate. Outside the zone, however, be it for a specific case (for example, a particularly notorious local case) or for a specific type of case (for example, sale of narcotics) court personnel feel the eyes of the community upon them and are more hesitant to grant the usual concessions for a guilty plea. These "out of the zone" cases punctuate the points where political factors and, more generally, the community's political culture influence case disposition.

But even within the zone of indifference, the community has left its mark. By recruiting certain individuals for roles in the court and excluding others, the community carves out an area within which it trusts its operatives to perform satisfactorily.[38] Prosecutors, judges, and public defenders can act pretty much as they please within the zone, but these are the prosecutors, judges, and public defenders that the community has selected.

As political cultures of communities vary so, too, will the size and character of the zone of indifference vary.[39] And with these changes will come effects on local court disposition processes. Plea bargaining patterns, sentencing patterns, and so on may be altered either directly through community pressure or indirectly through the extent to which the community influences recruitment. Plea bargaining—for the reasons set forth in this study—will remain the bedrock for case disposition in all communities, but, as with case pressure and structural variables, political culture variables can affect, marginally, the way cases are disposed. Again, the dearth of data presently available precludes any confident observations about these effects. Clearly, the problem of unraveling the effects of political culture on local criminal courts should be high on future research agendas.[40]

The theme that ran throughout this book is the inevitable centrality of plea bargaining in the local criminal court. By using quantitative disposition data, I have called into question the prevailing view that plea bargaining is nothing more than a function of crowded court dockets; and by analyzing the adaptation of newcomers to the court, I have developed an explanation of plea bargaining compatible with the quantitative disposition data, and incompatible with the view that newcomers are coerced to plea bargain by a conspiratorial group of court veterans obsessed with moving the business. Finally, I have argued that these explanations for plea bargaining are so compelling that schemes to abolish plea bargaining will necessarily fail.

Plea bargaining—like the trial—has its problems as well as its advantages. Reforms in plea bargaining processes can be instituted and alternatives to plea bargaining outside of the criminal court can be explored. But within the criminal court, plea bargaining cannot be "wished" or "reformed" away. It will inevitably provide a central means of disposing of cases, be it in high or low volume jurisdictions. If a concern for justice motivates many who do research in the legal arena, one thing is plain. The quest for justice in the "trial courts" necessitates a comparable quest for justice in the "plea bargaining courts." These courts process—and will continue to process—most criminal cases.

Notes

Chapter One

1. For one of the more in-depth studies of plea bargaining, see Abraham Blumberg, *Criminal Justice* (Chicago: Quadrangle Books, 1967).

2. For estimates of the plea bargaining rates in different jurisdictions, see Donald McIntyre and David Lippmann, "Prosecutors and Early Disposition of Felony Cases," *American Bar Association Journal* 56 (1970):1156–57; Walter Hoffman, "Plea Bargaining and the Role of the Judge," *Federal Rules Decisions* 53 (1972):499; American Bar Association, *Project on Minimum Standards for Criminal Justice, Standards Relating to Pleas of Guilty-Tentative Draft* (New York: Institute of Judicial Administration, 1967), pp. 1–2.

3. Private criminal attorneys, public defenders, and legal aid attorneys are included in the defense attorney sample.

4. Joel Grossman's work has been in the forefront of these recruitment studies. See Joel Grossman, "Judicial Selection and the Socialization of Judges," in *The Federal Judicial System*, ed. Thomas Jahnige and Sheldon Goldman (New York: Holt, Rinehart and Winston, 1968), pp. 7–8; Joel Grossman, *The ABA and the Politics of Judicial Selection* (New York: John Wiley and Sons, 1965). Grossman's discussion of the socialization of judges is limited to prerecruitment socialization.

Only two studies systematically address postrecruitment adaptation. The authors of these studies point to the same gap in the literature discussed in the text. See Beverly Blair Cook, "The Socialization of New Federal Judges: Impact on District Court Business," *Washington University Law Quarterly* 1971 (1971):253–54; and Robert Carp and Russell Wheeler, "Sink or Swim: The Socialization of a Federal District Judge," *Journal of Public Law* 21 (1972): 364–65.

5. Blumberg, p. 21.

6. These data will be reviewed in chapter 3.

7. President's Commission on Law Enforcement and Administration of Justice, *The Challenge of Crime in a Free Society* (Washington, D.C.: United States Government Printing Office, 1967), pp. 134–36.

8. National Advisory Commission on Criminal Justice Standards and Goals, *Courts* (Washington, D.C.: United States Government Printing Office, 1973), pp. 41–49.

9. Langton argues that most definitions of socialization include the view that it is "a process in which individuals incorporate into their own attitudinal structure and behavior patterns the ways of their respective social groups and society." Kenneth Langton, *Political Socialization* (New York: Oxford University Press, 1969), p. 4. Frederick Elkin defines socialization as the "process by which someone learns the ways of a given society or social group well enough so that he can function within it." Quoted in the Introduction to *Socialization and Society*, ed. John Clausen (Boston: Little, Brown and Co., 1968), p. 3. Finally, Roberta Sigel defines political socialization as the "gradual learning of the norms, attitudes and behavior accepted and practiced by the ongoing political system. The goal of political socialization is to so train or develop individuals that they become well-functioning members of the political society." Quoted in Carp and Wheeler, p. 363. None of these definitions is inherently incompatible with my definition of adaptation. But, for the reasons indicated in the text, I think *adaptation* better describes the process that I am examining.

10. Most of the socialization literature focuses on the socialization of children, and this literature simply did not yield any nonobvious hypotheses of applicability to my study of adult adaptation.

There is a substantially smaller body of literature on adult socialization. Typically this material deals with "re-socialization" efforts within institutions such as prisons and mental hospitals. Again, this material was not relevant to my research problem.

Brim, in the leading work on adult socialization, was struck by the paucity of research on areas such as occupational adjustment. Such a body of literature would have been of utility for my study, but as Brim notes: "It is surprising, then, to find, that for the occupational world, there is no comparable body of information on the process of socialization which unilaterally takes place between colleagues or between an employee and his boss . . . studies are rare, although the richness of this area of research is evident . . ." (Orville Brim, Jr., "Socialization through the Life Cycle," in *Socialization after Childhood—Two Essays*, ed. Orville Brim and Stanton Wheeler [New York: John Wiley and Sons, 1966], p. 203.)

11. Again, I do not mean to suggest that "socialization" necessarily implies that this inculcation takes place, or that it necessarily excludes "learning." But, as Langton notes, the bulk of socialization research has in fact stressed the "teaching" component. See Langton, p. 163.

12. The newcomers' expectations will be discussed in chapters 4, 5, and 6.

13. Fenno employs a similar approach in his study of adaptation of newcomers to the House Appropriations Committee. (Though Fenno uses the term "socialization," his usage comports with "adaptation," as employed in my study.) Fenno notes that: "[Newcomers] must be taught and they must learn—and the process of teaching and learning Committee perceptions and Committee norms is called the process of socialization" (Richard Fenno, *The Power of the Purse* [Boston: Little, Brown and Co., 1966], p. 209).

It is also instructive to note that Lindblom makes a similar distinction in a somewhat different, but related context. In his discussions of negotiation patterns, Lindblom distinguishes situations in which threats and promises are employed from those in which "mutual persuasion" takes place. "Sometimes the negotiators do no more to influence each other than point out for each other that the facts are different from what they have been thought to be, or that a policy that one negotiator believes he wants does not actually serve his own interests . . . In this kind of interchange . . . neither policy maker threatens the other or promises any benefits to the other except those that emerge from re-analysis of the problem at hand'' (Charles Lindblom, *The Policy-Making Process* [Englewood Cliffs, N.J.: Prentice-Hall, 1968], p. 95).

14. See, for example, Blumberg, pp. 70, 124–25.

15. Stanton Wheeler, ''The Structure of Formally Organized Socialization Settings, '' in *Socialization after Childhood—Two Essays*, ed. Orville Brim, Jr. and Stanton Wheeler (New York: John Wiley and Sons, 1966), p. 54. Other examples of the importance of clarifying the organizational context abound in the literature. Wahlke et al began their study of state legislatures by discussing the ''organizational facts'' which are ''boundary elements that presumably shape the legislator's view of the situation'' (John Wahlke, Heinz Eulau, William Buchanan, and LeRoy Ferguson, *The Legislative System* [New York: John Wiley and Sons, 1962], p. 46). Paul Berman, in a fascinating account of adaptation within the North Vietnamese National Liberation Front, observed that: ''Conformity, and all adaptation, occurred within the parameters set by the organizational structure'' (Paul Berman, *Revolutionary Organization* [Lexington, Mass.: Lexington Books, D. C. Heath and Company, 1974], p. 152). Kaufman, in his famous study of forest rangers, discussed ''the flavor of administrative agencies, the tensions and satisfactions, the atmosphere of life in large scale organizations,'' and suggested that studying compliance-obtaining mechanisms in an organization is really nothing less than trying to come to grips with ''this flavor,'' or ''essentially is an effort to capture the elusive phenomenon of 'what actually happens in an organization' '' (Herbert Kaufman, *The Forest Ranger* [Baltimore: Johns Hopkins Press, 1960], p. 240, and pp. xi–xii, respectively).

16. See note 4.

17. Though most of the biographies have dealt with appellate court judges, there is some material on trial judges. See, for example, Botein's fascinating autobiography: Bernard Botein, *Trial Judge* (New York: Cornerstone Library, 1952).

18. See, for example, Leonard Downie, *Justice Denied* (New York: Praeger Publishers, 1971), pp. 37–38, 161–62, 182–93; Albert Alschuler, ''The Prosecutor's Role in Plea Bargaining,'' *University of Chicago Law Review* 36 (1968):54, 64, 104, 110–11; and Blumberg, pp. 61, 70, 124–25.

19. Cook, pp. 253–79; and Carp and Wheeler, pp. 359–93.

20. Cook's study was both narrow in design and inconclusive as to what factors affect judicial adaptation. She only looked at federal judges, at the effects of a formal series of informational seminars designed for these new judges, and, for most of her analysis, only at adaptation to the processing of civil cases. She concluded that the formal programs did not make much of a difference (at least with regard to disposition rates) and offered her suspicion that the factors that do explain judicial adaptation lie outside these formal programs. She concluded: ''Informal socialization processes on an affective and one-to-one basis might have the most significant effect upon judicial behavior but would also be the most difficult to research'' (Cook, p. 278).

Carp and Wheeler attempted a more comprehensive study of federal district court judicial adaptation. They conducted thirty interviews with federal judges in five states, and found that new judges are faced with legal, psychological, and administrative problems. The newcomers received assistance in resolving these problems from other judges working in the circuit, from attorneys in the area, and from the court staff. Additionally, the new judges read extensively on their own, and Carp and Wheeler argue that these efforts greatly facilitated the judges' adaptation to the federal district court. See Carp and Wheeler, pp. 359–93.

By examining only the adaptation of federal district court judges, Cook, and Carp and Wheeler, exclude the arena wherein most criminal cases are handled (state courts) and exclude the actors (prosecutors and defense attorneys) who are as important as the judges in the resolution of these cases. It would be unfair to take the authors to task for a study they did not undertake. I am simply noting that their research did not bear significantly on the problems that concern us in this study; namely, the adaptation of judges, prosecutors, and defense attorneys to the plea bargaining system of the local criminal court.

21. Lipsky, in studying the behavior of "street-level bureaucrats" (local court judges, among others) called attention to the significance of examining the adaptation process and to the dearth of data about this process. ". . . concentration on the ways in which street-level bureaucrats are socialized [adapt] into roles, a process which often appears to "wash out" the training and preparation provided by superiors in response to reform demands. . . . The analysis in the paper suggests the desirability of research on the specific determinants of street-level bureaucrats role expectations, a neglected topic in empirical studies" (Michael Lipsky, "Toward a Theory of Street-Level Bureaucracy," paper presented at the annual meeting of the American Political Science Association, New York, September 2–6, 1969, pp. 31, 39).

22. See Herbert Asher, "The Learning of Legislative Norms" (August 1971), "Freshman Representatives and the Learning of Voting Cues" (August 1972), "The Changing Status of the Freshman Representative" (February 1973), all available from Professor Asher, Department of Political Science, Ohio State University. An updated version of the first Asher paper can be found in *American Political Science Review* 67 (June 1973): 499–513. Also, see Irwin Gertzog, "Frustration and Adaptation: The Adjustment of Minority Freshmen to the Congressional Experience," paper presented at annual meeting of the American Political Science Association, New York, September 6–10, 1966; and Richard Fenno, Jr., "The Freshman Congressman: His View of the House," in *Congressional Behavior*, ed. Nelson Polsby (New York: Random House, 1971), pp. 129–35.

23. See, in particular, Arthur Niederhoffer, *Behind the Shield: The Police in Urban Society* (Garden City, N.Y.: Doubleday and Co., 1967); and James Q. Wilson, *Varieties of Police Behavior* (New York: Atheneum, 1970), pp. 140–226.

24. Paul Savoy, "Toward a New Politics of Legal Education," *Yale Law Journal* 79 (1970):446. For further examination of the issue of the inadequacy of law school preparation for criminal practice, see Arthur Lewis Wood, *Criminal Lawyer* (New Haven: College and University Press, 1967), pp. 47–48; and Thomas Ehrlich and Herbert Packer, *New Directions in Legal Education*, a report prepared for the Carnegie Commission on Higher Education (New York: McGraw-Hill, 1972), pp. 14, 20, 42.

25. Quoted in *Newsweek*, December 10, 1973, p. 75. A number of other judges were quick to echo Burger's sentiments. See, for example, "Chief Appeals Judge Here Asks Curbs on Inept Trial Lawyers," *New York Times*, December 7, 1973, p. 55.

26. Asher, "The Learning of Legislative Norms," p. 5.

27. Cook also recognized that research on adaptation will increase our understanding of the organization to which the newcomer adjusts. "Since socialization [adaptation] is training in role behavior, pursuit of research in this area may provide explanation as well as description of the court system's definition of judicial roles and of the nature of the federal judiciary as an organization" (Cook, p. 279).

28. For example, Eisenstein employed an exploratory design in his study of the Office of the United States Attorney. His explanation for this approach comports with the argument advanced in the text. "The major hypothesis underlying the study was that the office was important enough to warrant an introductory, broad ranging, exploratory examination. Rather than test hypotheses, it was designed to provide the background knowledge necessary to formulate them" (James Eisenstein, "Counsel for the United States: An Empirical Analysis of the Office of the United States Attorney"

[Ph.D. dissertation, Yale University, 1968], pp. 1–13. See also Wilson, p. 13; and Jerome Skolnick, *Justice without Trial* [New York: John Wiley and Sons, 1966], pp. 15–16).

29. The need for an exploratory approach is also suggested by the nature of the career patterns of those who were included in this research. A newcomer to a particular role in the court might have previously held a different job in the system; if so, he probably learned many of the plea bargaining–related norms in the prior position. Thus, it is necessary to sort out the differences between adaptation to particular roles and adaptation to the criminal justice system in general, conceding that the sample size problem for any particular role shift renders definitive hypothesis disconfirmation impossible. The burden is lightened somewhat by the plea bargaining focus which allows us to exclude some aspects of the role carry-over. For example, the data suggest that time in the system, rather than in any particular role, accounts for adherence to several of the salient plea bargaining norms. But because the data themselves depend on the limited number of role shifts in the sample, this is far from being a firm, tested hypothesis. Thus we again must fall back on the "exploratory study" argument, and emphasize that at best we are generating plausible hypotheses that seem to fit the data at hand more satisfactorily than any rival candidates.

Chapter 2

1. On October 1, 1971, the appellate jurisdiction for circuit court cases was moved to the court of common pleas. Thus, court of common pleas judges now handle criminal and civil appeals from the circuit court. All criminal trials and plea bargains, however, still take place exclusively in the circuit and superior courts.

2. An excellent source for much of this descriptive material is Connecticut Planning Committee on Criminal Administration, *The Criminal Justice System in Connecticut* (n.p.: 1972), pp. 73–145. In addition to consulting this source, I have also relied on some of the descriptive material obtained in the course of my interviews.

3. I am very much indebted to Joe Shortall, Assistant Executive Secretary, State of Connecticut Judicial Department, for his assistance in helping me to obtain data not available in published materials.

4. This increase in the circuit court's jurisdiction was declared unconstitutional by the Connecticut Supreme Court in 1974. See Szarwak v. Warden, 31 Connecticut Superior 30, 320 A.2d 12 (1974). My research was conducted prior to the court's decision.

5. *The Criminal Justice System in Connecticut* (1972), p. 93. I do not mean to imply that a hearing of probable cause is held for all bindovers. Waiving the hearing is one of the defense attorney's resources in plea bargaining.

6. *The Criminal Justice System in Connecticut* (1972), pp. 106–7. The initial determination of locations for the superior courts, and of personnel levels within them, was partially based on estimates of the distance a judge could cover on horseback in one day. Interestingly, the patterns developed in the early 1800s have persisted to this day. See Connecticut Citizens for Judicial Modernization and Connecticut Bar Association, *First Report of the Joint Committee on Judicial Modernization* (1972), p. 5.

7. Though Waterbury is not technically a county, it has its own state's attorney, and thus nine "counties" are listed on table 2.

8. *The Criminal Justice System in Connecticut* (1972), p. 113. Connecticut is the only state in which judges appoint state's attorneys.

9. See the discussion of modernization drives and the correlates of these efforts in

Kenneth Vines and Herbert Jacob, "Courts as Political and Governmental Agencies," in *Politics in the American States*, ed. Herbert Jacob and Kenneth Vines (Boston: Little, Brown and Co., 1965), pp. 244–49. An abridged version of their earlier argument, but one which includes some new material on the ABA Court Modernization Plan, can be found in the second edition of their book. Kenneth Vines and Herbert Jacob, "State Courts," in *Politics in the American States*, 2d ed., ed. Herbert Jacob and Kenneth Vines (Boston: Little, Brown and Co., 1971), pp. 288–91.

10. See, for example, Abraham Blumberg, *Criminal Justice* (Chicago: Quadrangle Books, 1967).

11. The single court focus always raises the question of "representativeness." An interesting comparative study shows that Blumberg, for one, had chosen an extreme or aberrant court, different in many ways from most criminal courts. See Matthew Silberman, "Determinants of Felony Trials and Negotiations" (Ph.D. dissertation, University of Michigan, 1970), pp. 240–41.

12. For example, Alschuler visited ten different cities and spoke to various court officials. He is frank to admit the nonrigorous quality of his work: "My interviews did not follow a set format, and the resulting study is not a scientific survey; it is a kind of legal journalism." Albert Alschuler, "The Prosecutor's Role in Plea Bargaining," *University of Chicago Law Review* 36 (1968):52. Other examples of these impressionistic studies of plea bargaining include Donald J. Newman, *Conviction: The Determination of Guilt or Innocence without Trial* (Boston: Little, Brown and Co., 1966); Leonard Downie, Jr., *Justice Denied* (New York: Praeger Publishers, 1971); Howard James, *Crisis in the Courts*, rev. ed. (New York: David McKay, 1971).

13. The interview schedule will be described later in this chapter.

14. Two exceptions were made for new judges who had not yet handled criminal cases, but who were interviewed nonetheless.

15. OEO Funds could not be used to support *criminal* representation. Originally, the LAA's doing criminal work in this city received state and Ford Foundation money. The state, under pressure from the private bar, subsequently eliminated its contribution. The four LAA's interviewed (three were still practicing, and one had just left for another job) were being supported under a geographically limited Model Cities program.

16. Jerome Skolnick, *Justice Without Trial* (New York: John Wiley and Sons, 1967), p. 41.

17. James Levine, "Methodological Concerns in Studying Supreme Court Efficacy," *Law and Society Review* 4 (May 1970):593.

18. Kenneth Culp Davis, *Discretionary Justice* (Urbana, Ill.: University of Illinois Press, 1971), p. 120.

19. Blumberg, pp. x–xi.

20. The concealment of plea bargaining, the acting out of the charade, has a history extending well beyond this decade. Thurman Arnold, for example, offered a fascinating explanation for this need to obscure the "deal" based on his observations in the 1930s. See Thurman Arnold, "Law Enforcement," in *Criminal Justice*, ed. George Cole (North Scituate, Mass.: Duxbury Press, 1972), pp. 24–34.

21. Mapp v. Ohio, 378 U.S. 1, 84 S.Ct.1489, 12 L.Ed. 2d 653 (1964); Gideon v. Wainwright, 372 U.S. 335, 88 S.Ct.792, 9 L.Ed. 2d 799 (1963); Miranda v. Arizona, 384 U.S. 436, 86 S.Ct.1602, 16 L.Ed. 2d 694 (1966).

22. The failure of the Supreme Court to "come to grips" with the plea bargaining system was not without its costs in terms of effective implementation of its decrees. Some have gone so far as to argue that, rather than making it more of an adversary system, the Supreme Court simply strengthened the plea bargaining process. See, for

example, Abraham Blumberg, "Lawyers with Convictions," in *The Scales of Justice*, ed. Abraham Blumberg (Chicago: Aldine Publishing Co., 1970), p. 67.

23. Brady v. United States, 397 U.S. 742, 90 S.Ct. 1462, 25 L.Ed. 2d 747 (1970).

24. North Carolina v. Alford, 400 U.S. 25, 91 S.Ct. 160, 27 L.Ed. 2d 162 (1970).

25. Santobello v. New York, 404 U.S. 257, 92 S.Ct. 495, 30 L.Ed. 2d 427 (1971).

26. The period of my field research—July 1972 to February 1973—predated most of the Watergate developments. I suspect that anyone presently conducting plea bargaining related research will be inundated with examples of Magruder, Colson et al. Though these cases are significant in and of themselves, they are not typical of the cases that are plea bargained day in, day out, in our criminal courts. I will concentrate on the more typical cases, though an interesting book could no doubt be written on this "political plea bargaining."

27. For simplicity's sake, I will not distinguish among the prosecutor and his assistants, and so forth, unless it is pertinent to the argument. I will call attention to *the* prosecutor only when the fact that he is *the* prosecutor is relevant to his remarks. In these instances, I will specifically call him "chief" or "head" prosecutor, public defender, or state's attorney.

28. In the Ortaville circuit court, this pattern was upset when a secretary directed me to the head prosecutor rather than to the assistant I had asked to speak with. He asked me to return several days later because he wanted to be interviewed first, to insure that the questions were satisfactory. This was precisely what I did not want, and what I had avoided in the other courts. Fortunately, the interview went well, and I had no problem interviewing the rest of his staff.

29. A similar argument has been made about the receptivity accorded to the reform-minded Vera Institute. Contrary to the prevailing wisdom about bureaucratic resistance to innovation, Vera has had more than moderate cooperation from court personnel, and this success is at least partially attributable to the image of Vera as an informed and realistic organization with no particular ax to grind. See Herbert Sturz, "Experiments in the Criminal Justice System," *Legal Aid Briefcase* (February 1967) pp. 1–5.

30. The phrase is from Wahlke et al., who found it equally as valuable to "cultivate" secretaries. See John Wahlke, Heinz Eulau, William Buchanan, and Leroy Ferguson, *The Legislative System* (New York: John Wiley and Sons, 1962), p. 481.

31. In one of the public defender's offices, I noticed a small publication that had some extremely interesting data on case dispositions dating back fifty years. The secretary told me that she herself had brought this to the office when she left her prior job, salvaging it from some cartons destined for points unknown. She told me I could look through it. However, I was called in for an interview, and I had to put it down. Later, when I came back to look at it she inexplicably blew up. I became somewhat fearful that her antagonism—one only had to be within fifty feet of her to be aware of it—would alienate the public defenders. Fortunately, they instead extended their empathy and the data to me; apparently, this woman had a history of similar outbursts. But the incident sensitized me to the importance of maintaining amicable ties with everyone in these offices.

32. I did not include a question on the respondent's own publications because I assumed that few of them had material in print. One superior court judge, though, was quite upset by this omission. When I finished the background questions and was preparing to begin the actual interview, he asked: "Aren't you going to ask me about what I have written?" Displayed prominently on his desk was his collection of publications, and I had failed even to notice it. Only after submitting myself to a lengthy review of his "monumental" works did I manage to get back into his good graces.

33. See, for example, National Advisory Commission on Criminal Justice Standards and Goals, *Courts* (Washington, D.C.: United States Government Printing Office, 1973), pp. 42–64. I will examine this abolition of plea bargaining argument at length in chapter 7.

34. Herbert Asher had to confront a similar problem in his study of the adaptation of freshmen congressmen. On one hand, he wanted to interview them as early as was possible, but on the other, his interviews required that the freshman know something about the House of Representatives. He finally decided that he would interview the freshmen *after* the formal introductory seminar series offered new congressmen. See Herbert Asher, "The Learning of Legislative Norms," unpublished paper (August 1972), p. 4. A case in point from my own research illustrates the "research choice-of-time problem" clearly. Judge —— was a court of common pleas judge at the time of the interview, but already had been appointed to the superior court bench, his transfer to take place several months hence. Unfamiliar with criminal matters, he seemed to find the interview both informative, insofar as I told him about superior court practices, and discomforting, for he did not know much about criminal case processing, and he was not quite sure about how he would learn. Obviously, he could not contribute very pithy responses to the questions on actual adaptation.

35. Fifteen individuals were classified as "newcomers." They all had less than one year's experience in any part of the criminal justice system. The number of "newcomers" increases, however, when we include those new to a *job* (less than one year). These are individuals who had previously held a job in the criminal court, or had handled criminal cases as private attorneys, but who had moved on to another job in the criminal justice system. I will discuss the factors to be considered in defining a "newcomer" more thoroughly in chapter 4.

36. The retrospective inquiry is common in adaptation studies. See, for example, Paul Berman, *Revolutionary Organization* (Lexington, Mass.: Lexington Books, D. C. Heath and Co., 1974), pp. 122–23. The observations of Eulau et al., on the interpretation that can be accorded retrospective questions is also of relevance here. ". . . 'how' they perceive what happened in the course of their political socialization. Recollections of this kind, it seems to us, have a functional reality of their own constituting a part of the situation in which state legislators define their roles." Heinz Eulau, William Buchanan, Leroy Ferguson, and John Wahlke, "The Political Socialization of American State Legislators," *Midwest Journal of Political Science* 3 (1959):190.

37. If there is any drawback to using a tape recorder, it must be that transcribing the recorded material is a massive and difficult job. Fortunately, I had a grant that covered most of the transcribing, but to insure accuracy a laborious check was made of all the transcriptions.

38. For the interviews that I did not record on tape, I took extensive notes during the interview, and transcribed them the same evening. When I quote from one of these interviews, then, it will be a partial reconstruction, though I did try to record responses verbatim.

An interesting pattern emerges when we examine the distribution by role of those who refused to be taped: three private attorneys, one circuit court judge; and three judges, four public defenders and seven state's attorneys—the three latter groups from the superior court. If we except the three private attorneys (who practice in circuit and superior court), we find that only one of the "no tapes" is from the circuit court; all but one of the twenty-eight circuit court officials were receptive to the use of the tape recorder. I think circuit court personnel have a lesser sense of the importance of their jobs than do superior court personnel, and, therefore, they were more inclined to be impressed with the fact that someone wanted to record their comments on tape.

39. Davis found a similar lack of theoretical systematic thought in regulatory agencies. "Regulatory agencies characteristically sit back and wait for questions to arise in particular cases, and the members of the agencies typically do little policy thinking except in the process of adjudicating single cases" (Davis, p. 99). Obviously, the absence of institutionalized means to promote systematic policy thinking has important implications for adaptation. The newcomer may come into the court, get caught up in the flow of case resolution, and not really consider the direction in which he is heading. Again, I will postpone further discussion of this hypothesis until chapter 4.

40. For the years 1880–1900, the superior court disposition data are available in the annual volume of *Connecticut Public Documents*. These reports are entitled: "First Annual [and so on] Report of the Comptroller of Public Accounts of the State of Connecticut in Relation to the Criminal Business of the Courts for the Year Ending —— as Shown by the Returns of the State's Attorneys." After 1900, both the title of the collection, and of the reports themselves, changed. From 1900–1936, they were reported biennially in *Public Documents of the State of Connecticut*, public document no. ——, "Annual Report in Relation to the Criminal Business of the Courts of the State of Connecticut for the Year Ending ——, as Shown by the Returns of the State and Prosecuting Attorneys." In 1926, the Judicial Council of Connecticut was created, and since then, it has reported, biennially, disposition data. See *First [through Twenty-Second] Report of the Judicial Council of Connecticut*. The data "saved" by the secretary in the public defender's office (see note 31) was a review of these reports from 1926–1956. This was quite fortunate, for some of the Judicial Council reports are no longer readily obtainable. The data from the 1960s—including circuit court data—are the most complete and detailed. In many of the earlier years, only summary data were recorded.

41. I was not always so fortunate. The biggest disappointment that I suffered (in terms of obtaining useful material) was with a state's attorney. After explaining my topic, he told me—with great emphasis—that he was extremely interested in my project. We chatted a while, and then he finally revealed that he had been keeping a diary of his experiences, precisely for the purpose of evaluating his own attitudinal and behavior change over time. He was more than reluctant, however, to show it to me, and though I pursued the matter during subsequent visits to the court, my efforts proved to be fruitless.

Chapter 3

1. Albert Alschuler, "The Prosecutor's Role in Plea Bargaining," *University of Chicago Law Review* 26 (1968):51.
2. "Restructuring the Plea Bargain," *Yale Law Journal* 82 (1972):286.
3. "Profile of a Guilty Plea: A Proposed Trial Court Procedure for Accepting Guilty Pleas," *Wayne Law Review* 17 (1971):1239.
4. "The Unconstitutionality of Plea Bargaining," *Harvard Law Review* 83 (1970):1387.
5. "Plea Bargaining: The Judicial Merry-Go-Round," *Duquesne Law Review* 10 (1971):253.
6. Santobello v. New York, 404 U.S. 257, 92 S.Ct. 495, 30 L.Ed. 2d 427 (1971).
7. Ibid., Justice Douglas's concurring opinion.

8. Abraham Blumberg, *Criminal Justice* (Chicago: Quadrangle Books, 1967).
9. Ibid., p. 21.
10. Ibid., p. 61.
11. See Malcolm Feeley, "Two Models of the Criminal Justice System: An Organizational Perspective," *Law and Society Review* 7 (Spring 1973):415–21; and Jerome Skolnick, "Social Control in the Adversary System," *Journal of Conflict Resolution* 11 (1967):52–67.
12. Feeley, pp. 418–19.
13. Trial rates vary across jurisdictions, and a precise figure remains elusive. McIntyre and Lippman reported that the average trials to total dispositions ratio for felony cases from 1965–69 in Kings County, Brooklyn, was 300/3000, or 10 percent; in Detroit, 900/9200, or 9.8 percent; in Harris County, Houston, 360/6260, or 5.8 percent; in Cook County, Chicago, 900/4500, or 20 percent. Donald McIntyre and David Lippman, "Prosecutors and Early Disposition of Felony Cases," *American Bar Association Journal* 56 (1970):1156–57. Hoffman observed that "the negotiated guilty plea is an acknowledged procedure made primarily necessary by the fact that approximately 90 percent of all defendants enter guilty pleas," thus establishing 10 percent as an "upper limit" on the trial rate. Walter Hoffman, "Plea Bargaining and the Role of the Judge," *Federal Rules Decisions* 53 (1972):499. The American Bar Association noted that in some localities more than 95 percent of all criminal cases are disposed of without a trial. American Bar Association, *Project on Minimum Standards for Criminal Justice, Standards Relating to Pleas of Guilty, Tentative Draft* (New York: Institute of Judicial Administration, 1967), pp. 1–2.

McIntyre and Lippman also estimated that 10,400/21,300, or 49 percent, of Los Angeles felony cases were adjudicated by trial; in Baltimore, the figure was 5125/7325, or 70 percent (McIntyre and Lippman, pp. 1156–57). Both the Los Angeles and Baltimore systems frequently resort to the submission-on-transcript (SOT) trial, whereby the case is adjudicated on the basis of the transcript of the preliminary hearing.

This variant of trial more closely resembles a guilty plea. Mather, for example, labels these submission-on-transcript trials "slow plea[s] of guilty." See Lynn Mather, "Some Determinants of the Method of Case Disposition: Decision-Making by Public Defenders in Los Angeles," *Law and Society Review* 8 (Winter 1973):189.

14. The trials to total dispositions ratio is employed because (1) it highlights the fact that processes other than trial account for most criminal court dispositions; (2) discussions about the prevalence of plea bargaining are often couched in terms of the relatively low number of trials relative to other dispositional processes. The data presented in table 4 afford the reader the opportunity to calculate any of the other ratios that could have been employed (for example, the ratio of trials to guilty pleas).
15. The complete term is *nolle prosequi* (unwilling to prosecute). The prosecutor can decide not to pursue any or all charges against the defendant (that is, "nolle" the charges). He can reconsider at any time within a year of this decision; after a year has elapsed, however, the case can no longer be reopened, and the defendant can petition to have the "nolle" ("nolle" is used as both a verb and noun in the court) removed from his record. In practice, it is rare for the prosecutor to reopen the case, and rare for the defendant to bother to have it erased.

With one exception, the Connecticut nolle statistics do not reflect this dismissal of charges. The Connecticut statistics are compiled by defendant, regardless of the number of charges against him, with the proviso that some defendants may have more than one "file" of charges against them. If a defendant has one file, and he pleads guilty to a charge in the file in exchange for the nolle of the rest of the charges in the file, only one guilty plea is tabulated. If, however, he has two files and he pleads guilty to a charge in one file in exchange for a nolle of the charges in the other file, one guilty plea and one nolle are counted.

16. See note 40, p. 179.

17. The unstated assumption here is that guilty pleas are indicative of plea bargaining. Corroborative evidence supporting this assumption will be presented later in this chapter. Additionally, in chapter 7, I will argue that the guilty plea itself is a form of "implicit plea bargaining."

18. This test is indirect because the data were compiled in aggregate, and it is possible that the small, low volume courts provided most of the cases tried. It does, however, cast doubt on the notion that trials were historically a popular source of case disposition. Even Jerome Frank, credited with debunking the "upper court myth" was swayed by belief in the centrality of the trial court. He wrote in his classic *Courts on Trial*: "The fighting method of judicially administering justice has been carried too far, and needs very substantial modification if justice is to be well administered by the courts." ([Princeton: Princeton University Press, 1949; reprint edition, New York: Atheneum, 1969], p. 37.) Perhaps in those cases actually tried, the fighting method did inhibit the quest for the truth; but, as we have seen, the number of trials was low. Justice was administered through means other than adversary combat even during those years when Frank focused so exclusively on trials.

19. The absolute number of cases processed annually in the low volume courts is so low that I think using volume as a surrogate for case pressure is a justifiable approach even if staffing data are unavailable, and even if part-time prosecutors account for most of the case dispositions.

20. For 1970–71, the Connecticut Planning Committee on Criminal Administration reported that there were thirty-five judges and thirty-one state's attorneys in superior court. See their *The Criminal Justice System in Connecticut* (Hartford, 1972), pp. 107, 114. In a personal communication with the Connecticut Planning Committee on Criminal Administration I learned that there were thirty-five judges and thirty-one state's attorneys in 1972–73 as well.

21. One problem with this test is that the increased jurisdiction of the circuit court altered the distribution of types of offenses coming to the superior court. If, for example, the superior court's trials prior to 1972 were largely for offenses now adjudicated in the circuit court, then the 1972–73 statistics would underestimate the impact of the changed jurisdiction. In other words, the superior courts in 1972–73 would be trying cases that in 1971–72 they had plea bargained, and though trial rates remain constant, trial rates for the comparable cases increased. The available data do not allow a check on this hypothesis; a priori, however, there is no plausible substantive argument that would lead one to believe that the distribution of trials was as hypothesized above.

22. The "old-timer's" contention is supported by Raymond Moley's and Justin Miller's studies, which were conducted in the 1920s. These authors discussed the importance of negotiated dispositions in the criminal courts. Moley, for example, found that "[plea bargaining] has in the practice of American criminal courts become a definite type of defense strategy. It usually follows discussion between counsel for the defense and the prosecuting attorney in which either implied or expressed conditions are imposed by the defense in return for a willingness to plead guilty." Raymond Moley, "The Vanishing Jury," *Southern California Law Review* 2 (1928):103. See also Justin Miller, "The Compromise of Criminal Cases," *Southern California Law Review* 1 (1927):1–31.

23. See note 4, p. 175.

24. Joseph Shortall, Assistant Executive Secretary of the Judicial Department of the State of Connecticut, has been extremely helpful in providing data on these questions, and I am very much indebted to him. In a personal communication (February 15, 1973) Mr. Shortall noted the limited impact of the changed jurisdictions on circuit court business. Prior to the change, approximately 8000 offenses were bound over annually to the superior court; with the increased circuit court jurisdiction, around 4000 of these were no longer bound over. But 4000 is a relatively small portion of total circuit court volume (over 100,000 non-motor vehicle criminal cases, and another 100,000 or so motor vehicle cases). Thus, the impact of the change was far more evident in the superior court, with its relatively small case load, than it was in the circuit court.

25. For a frequency distribution by year of these circuit court offenses see Connecticut Planning Committee on Criminal Administration, *The Criminal Justice System in Connecticut* (1972), p. 96.

26. I think it reasonable to conclude that most of the 45,449 guilty convictions resulted from a plea and not a trial. My interviews and observations suggest this very strongly. Also, we can venture a very rough approximation of the number of trials included in the guilty convictions statistic. In the superior court, for July 1971 through June 1972, the ratio of court trial acquitted offenses to convicted offenses (the circuit court data are by offense) was 27/20; by defendants the ratio was 16/16. The superior court relies more heavily on the jury trial, and it is instructive to examine the comparable ratios as well: offense, 57 acquitted/163 convicted; and defendants, 33 acquitted/91 convicted. The larger role of the court trial in the circuit court suggests that the relevant ratios are probably closer to the superior court trial figures (the predominant mode of trial) than to the court trial figures. But even without proof of this hypothesis, I think we can conservatively estimate that the number of circuit court convictions by court trial did not exceed the number of acquittals. Thus, of the 45,449 guilty determinations, probably not more than 3200 were the result of court trial. The superior court trial data can be found in *Twenty-third Report of the Judicial Council of Connecticut* (December 1972), p. 41.

27. Nolle statistics have to be interpreted carefully. The data in table 8 are for charge and not defendant; we do not know the extent to which the nolle was used to "throw out" the case against the defendant (one or more charges) as compared to its use in plea bargaining, wherein a few counts or charges are nolled for a plea to the remaining charge. I was given access to the summary disposition sheets of the public defenders in one of the circuit courts. Seven hundred and forty-five defendants were included in these records, and they had 1215 charges outstanding. A total of 517 nolles were given (42.5 percent), but 321 of these were in cases where the defendant still pled guilty to one or more other charges; 196 of the 744 defendants (26.3 percent) had their cases completely nolled. The nolle rate, then, varies for the same court, depending on whether one includes all charges nolled or only those nolles that result in no plea to any charge by the defendant. Though both these measures are useful indicators of plea bargaining (and perhaps police) practices, one should be particularly suspicious of the "charges nolled" measure. I was told several times in the course of my research that this figure could be easily altered by a prosecutor concerned about nolleing too many cases and appearing "soft." He could simply redraw the "information"—the indictment specifying charges against the defendant—and omit those charges that he agreed to nolle. In this fashion, the number of nolles obviously decreases, the prosecutor appears less lenient, and the defendant gets the same deal (actually the deal is slightly better, since the nolle, in theory, can be reopened).

28. Circuit court plea bargaining takes place in other locations as well. The courtroom, the court corridor, the prosecutor's office in the afternoon, the restaurant at

lunch time—are all possible arenas in which cases can be negotiated. Additionally, cases are sometimes "disposed of" over the telephone.

29. These circuit court recommendations do not always include incarceration. The prosecutor may recommend a fine (and specify the amount), probation, or a particular treatment program.

30. Mileski found that circuit court judges were more likely to issue the warnings when serious charges were involved. See Maureen Mileski, "Courtroom Encounters: An Observation Study of a Lower Criminal Court," *Law and Society Review* 5 (May 1971):485.

31. In one of the circuit courts the prosecutor designed a color-coded chart—reminiscent of everyone's kindergarten days—on which defendants were assigned specific colors corresponding to the painted cardboard sign affixed atop each of the courtroom entrances. Groups of defendants and attorneys gathered around this chart, and then went off to look for the "green courtroom," the "red courtroom," and so on.

32. Journalists in particular, have tended to stress the relationship between poor facilities and plea bargaining. See Leonard Downie, *Justice Denied* (Baltimore: Penguin Books, 1971); and Howard James, *Crisis in the Courts* (New York: David McKay Co., 1971).

33. Fifty-six percent of the convicted defendants (1927 of 3439) in Superior Court in 1971–72 received "time" of one sort or another (jail, prison, reformatory, and so on). See *Twenty-Third Report of the Judicial Council of Connecticut* (December 1972), p. 42.

34. The difference in negotiating strategies when "time" is involved will be discussed in the following chapter.

35. Defendants with multiple charges or counts against them benefit more from this policy than do defendants charged with a single offense. The extra crimes are not assessed at the same "price" as is the first; indeed, past a certain point (which, no doubt, varies depending on the nature of the offense) the additional crimes probably "don't count."

36. The determination of the effects of personal ties between state's attorneys and defense attorneys on case outcome is a very sticky matter. I think it fair to state that for most serious cases personal ties had no direct bearing on case outcome. "Favors" simply were not the norm, and, most certainly, I did not observe, nor did any respondent report, corruption in Connecticut's courts.

Good personal relations can, however, have an indirect bearing on final outcome. For one, the state's attorney might be more willing to share his files with the cooperative attorney, and the information gleaned from these files can strengthen the defendant's case. Secondly, the state's attorney may be more inclined to nolle a marginal case (marginal in the sense that the state's attorney is unsure about whether he has the evidence to win a conviction) for a defense attorney with whom he has an amicable relationship. Again, this is not a favor per se; more likely it reflects the state's attorney's willingness to give greater credence to the defense attorney's claim that there is not really a case for the state. We will have more to say about these matters when we explore the reward/sanction system of the local criminal court.

37. I think it likely that it was the use of this variant of the "agreed rec" in particular that led the defendants Casper interviewed to perceive the judge as an "irrelevant man." See Jonathan Casper, *American Criminal Justice* (Englewood Cliffs, N. J.: Prentice-Hall, 1972), pp. 136–44.

It is also important to note that a failure to consider the underlying sentence recommendation policies can seriously jeopardize the validity of judicial sentencing studies. The greater the reliance on agreed recs, the less the input from the judge. Though sentencing is formally the judge's responsibility, it might well have been the state's attorney, not the judge, who actually decided the sentence.

38. Some state's attorneys are also opposed to the frequent use of sentence recommendations. They, however, view the judges as being responsible for these recommendations. Witness, for example, the views of an Arborville state's attorney:

> When I was in the circuit court I found that judges were more inclined to accept their responsibility in sentencing, and you did not find yourself so much involved in agreed rec situations. You just didn't find it. Oh, sure, you found it occasionally; generally you found it, I think more often than not, when an individual has been given a suspended sentence and you could concur with the defense attorney and say: "Yes, I think under the circumstances I am aware that this individual is definitely guilty, but there are circumstances here which warrant a suspended sentence . . . Now, in the superior court, perhaps because of the overwhelming power of the judge here, they are less inclined to want to make a decision because it has more far-reaching effects on the individual that's affected. So, as a result, you find more often in superior court, at least this has been my experience, where you are placed in a position where they [the judges] are looking for an agreed rec. [16]

39. "Sausage factories" is Downie's phrase. See Downie, pp. 18–51.

40. Other factors that can affect the defense attorney's pitch include the fee he is receiving, the presence in court of family and friends of the defendant, the availability of others who can testify to the defendant's good character, and the particular state's attorney handling the case.

41. There are a number of very serious problems associated with the preparation of these presentence reports. For a summary of these criticisms see Marvin Frankel, *Criminal Sentences* (New York: Hill and Wang, 1972), pp. 26–38.

42. I am simplifying matters a bit here. If the defendant pleads guilty and the presentence report is already prepared (as is typical if the defendant has a prior felony conviction) the judge will usually accept the guilty plea and sentence the defendant on the same day. In this situation, all of the questions discussed in the text are asked. If, on the other hand, the defendant pleads guilty at one point and there is a delay before he is sentenced, the judge may ask the questions about the voluntariness of the plea at the time of the defendant's plea, and the questions concerning sentence promises on sentencing day. However, I found that most superior court judges ask most of the questions on sentencing day, even if some of these questions had already been asked at the time the defendant pled guilty.

43. As already noted, one of the warnings includes a caution to the defendant to the effect that the judge is not bound by any sentence recommendation. However, in "agreed rec" situations it is unusual for the judge to deviate from the state's attorney's suggestion. The judge can exercise greater discretion if there was no "agreed rec" or if the negotiations included a proviso permitting the defense attorney to "pitch" for a lesser sentence.

44. The fact that the judge has often prepared his sentence prior to hearing the final arguments supports the idea that sentencing day is nothing other than charade. The sentence was determined before the final arguments were heard; of what use, then, are these oral arguments?

45. Frankel levels a scathing attack on the failure of judges to explain their sentences. He calls for a rule that would require judges to provide written explanations of their sentences. See Frankel, pp. 39–49.

Chapter 4

1. For a discussion of the considerations that enter into selecting cutoff points in adaptation studies, see Robert Carp and Russell Wheeler, "Sink or Swim: The Socialization of a Federal District Judge," *Journal of Public Law* 21 (1972):391; Beverly Blair Cook, "The Socialization of New Federal Judges: Impact on District Court Business," *Washington University Law Quarterly* 1971 (1971):265; Herbert Asher, "The Learning of Legislative Norms," Department of Political Science, Ohio State University (August 1971), p. 4; and Richard Fenno, *The Power of the Purse* (Boston: Little, Brown and Co., 1966), p. 129.

2. Superior court public defenders and state's attorneys usually had some prior civil court experience; their circuit court counterparts generally had no such prior experience. Judges in both the circuit and superior courts had civil court experience (either as attorneys or as judges in the court of common pleas) prior to appointment to the criminal bench.

3. Herbert Packer and Thomas Ehrlich, *New Directions in Legal Education: A Report Prepared for the Carnegie Commission on Higher Education* (New York: McGraw-Hill, 1972), p. 14.

4. Ibid., p. 20.

5. Quoted in Arthur Lewis Wood, *Criminal Lawyer* (New Haven, Conn.: College and University Press Services, 1967), p. 132.

6. A very prominent Ortaville attorney also spoke rather caustically about his experience in law school with a somewhat empirical criminal law course.

> *Q*. When you were in law school, you had no idea you would be working in the criminal field?
> *A*. No, I'll tell you. I had the worst course in law school in criminal law that I think was ever taught. I had ——, and it was all statistics. Do you realize that 19 percent of divorced Irish-Catholic parents who have children are juvenile delinquents; and that 22 percent of Russians who have a wooden leg wind up as third-degree sexual molesters; and the flag wavers, you know, the indecent exposure cases, 29 percent come from a home dominated by the mother . . . the goddamned course didn't teach me any criminal law. [34]

7. Several of the respondents had clerked for judges after graduation from law school. Their experiences reinforced the perspective fostered by law school; that is, they worked primarily on briefs for appellate cases. Clerking did not in any consequential way facilitate their adaptation to the plea bargaining system.

8. Among the motions the attorneys expected to file, the most common one was a Motion to Suppress (Evidence). This motion is employed to challenge the propriety of the search or interrogation of the defendant.

9. These observations apply to many new judges as well as to prosecutors and defense attorneys. Most of the judges interviewed did not have substantial prior experience in the criminal courts; they knew little about the operations of the plea bargaining system.

Their surprising lack of sophistication was evidenced in two interviews conducted with judges who had not yet received their first court assignment. I found that these newcomers knew so little about the way plea bargaining worked that they were unable to answer many of the basic questions included in the interview schedule. Indeed, a large portion of our time together was spent with their asking me about how the system operated! I will discuss judicial adaptation in greater length in chapter 6.

10. Jerome Skolnick, ''Social Control in the Adversary System,'' *Journal of Conflict Resolution* 11 (March 1967):60.

11. This first excerpt is from an experienced attorney's interview; the second excerpt is from a newcomer's interview.

12. These files may be a bit biased, in that they may overrepresent the percentage of hopeless cases. Public defenders maintain that they receive more difficult cases than do their counterparts in the private sector. As one public defender observed:

> What should be taken into account is who has the toughest cases, private counsel or public defenders. By the very nature of the beast, we have all the incorrigibles and all the repeaters to start with. There is nothing worse to deal with than the incorrigibles and the persistent offenders, so right off the bat you are handicapped. The best way to get the feel of this is to talk with some of these fellows we get over here as special public defenders. They take one look at some of these files and some of these defendants and they're ready to leave. They'll say: ''I can't do them. What can you do with them, for them, in spite of them. Nothing.'' It's an exasperating confrontation. [23]

Nonetheless, the interviews with private attorneys support the general argument that a sizable percentage of all cases lack substantial grounds for factual or legal challenge.

13. An offshoot of this argument that is also used to explain harsher sentences after trial is the contention that the case looks worse after trial. All the facts of the crime have been paraded in vivid detail before the judge, and though sometimes the presentation of witnesses and evidence can have a mitigative effect, more generally they result in a harsher sentence after trial.

14. Casper, for example, found that most of the defendants he interviewed were either currently guilty of the charge against them, or had in the past committed this crime, and thus were ''categorically''guilty. See Jonathan Casper, *American Criminal Justice: The Defendant's Perspective* (Englewood Cliffs, N.J.: Prentice-Hall, 1972), pp. 33–34.

15. In minor cases, ''getting it over with'' is, of course, implicitly associated with the nature of the disposition. The defendant is willing to accept the conviction record because he assumes this will be the major cost he bears. He does not expect to receive a jail or prison sentence.

For more serious cases, the defendant's interest is less likely to be summed up in terms of simply ''getting it over with.'' He faces substantial prison time, and quick disposition becomes less important than negotiating a satisfactory disposition. Again, the defendant pressures the attorney, but in these serious cases, his pressure focuses on avoiding ''time'' whenever possible, and if impossible, on certainty about the amount of ''time'' he will have to serve. When ''time'' can be avoided, the defendant generally will gladly forsake the opportunity for exoneration at trial and accept a suspended sentence and probation. When he realizes that some time is inevitable, given the offense, his record, and so on, he obviously wants the amount of time to be as minimal as possible; but he also wants a guarantee in advance of sentencing as to the amount of time he will receive.

Plea bargaining provides the means to meet the defendant's desires. Prosecutors and state's attorneys are willing to negotiate time as well as charge. Though their recommendations to the judge are not binding, we saw in chapter 3 that almost invariably they are accepted.

In both minor and serious cases, then, the newcomer is surprised by the defendant's preoccupation with dispositions rather than vindication. He feels pressured by the defendant to negotiate charges and sentences; he receives little support for his inclination to contest the defendant's guilt in an adversary hearing. In short, the defendants pressure the newcomer to explore the plea bargaining option.

16. The prosecutor's offer does not always improve as the trial approaches. Indeed, the opposite may be the case; the offer may "disappear," and the prosecutor may insist upon trial. Prosecutors may evidence this firmness when they want to teach an attorney that if he does not accept the original deal, he will have to be prepared to face the consequences.

There are, however, several reasons why prosecutors do "sweeten their offers"when trial approaches. The reliability of their witnesses may have decreased with the passage of time between the offense and the trial date; also some witnesses may no longer be available. The defense attorney may have raised serious doubts about the state's case. Finally, the prosecutor may feel upon closer inspection of the issues raised in the case that it simply is not worth his time to hold firm. If the case can be resolved by a better offer, disposing of it may be preferable to spending time and energy on a matter of minimal import.

17. I can offer some quantitative support for a number of the contentions concerning charge and sentence reduction raised in this section. I had access to the files of one circuit court public defender's office and one superior court public defender's office, and I used this access to collect quantitative case disposition data. Since there are obvious biases in these data (for example, public defenders handle somewhat different cases than private attorneys), I offer these only to suggest the pattern of charge and sentence recommendation.

In the circuit court, the summary disposition sheets of 744 defendants were examined and coded. These sheets are maintained by the public defender responsible for a case, and as one might suspect, some were more careful than others in keeping accurate records. The most common error was a failure to note the original charge(s), and to indicate only the charge(s) the defendant pled out to. Thus, the data underestimate the number of original multiple-charge defendants.

Notwithstanding this problem, the data are instructive. The 744 defendants had a reported total of 1215 charges against them. Five hundred and seventeen of these charges (42.6 percent) were eventually nolled, indicating that prosecutors were willing to forego prosecution of many offenses in return for a plea on a single charge. Furthermore, for 213 of the defendants (28.6 percent), the charge or charges were completely nolled or dismissed. This figure supports the newcomer's view that prosecutors are not particularly vindictive; if there is a problem of proof in the case, or an outstanding legal question, or if the prosecutor does not believe the case to be serious enough to warrant full-fledged prosecution, he can simply nolle the case. Thus, if the defense attorney thought he could extract a victory during a preliminary hearing or at trial, and the prosecutor agreed that this was likely, the case could be nolled, and the need for an adversary hearing would be eliminated. Finally, the data show that only 74 of the 744 defendants (10 percent) received a jail sentence. As indicated in this section, most of the prosecutor's and defense attorney's time in the circuit court is spent on disposing of cases with penalties that include fines and suspended sentences. With these "nontime" penalties in the offing, defendants generally pressure their attorneys to "get it over with."

A different pattern emerges from the more serious cases reflected by the superior court data. As discussed in chapter 3, the 88 defendants had a total of 300 charges. One hundred and two of these charges (34 percent) were eventually nolled, suggesting again that state's attorneys will trade off charges for convictions and, as we will see, for "time." In contrast to the situation in the circuit court, only 12.5 percent of the defendants had their cases completely nolled (28.6 percent in the circuit court). The likelihood of the state's attorney nolleing the case simply to be rid of it is far lower in the superior court than in the circuit court. He may offer the defendant a "good deal," but he wants some kind of plea in return.

A marked difference between these sets of disposition data can be seen in the number of defendants sent to jail or prison. In contrast to the 10 percent incarceration rate of the circuit court, 43 of the 88 defendants (48.8 percent) were sentenced to jail or prison. "Time" is much more of a factor in these serious cases.

Forty-five defendants managed to obtain a no-time disposition: eleven, as indicated, had their cases nolled; three were sent for some form of treatment in a clinic or hospital; and thirty-five received a combination suspended sentence and probation. These no-time dispositions were the primary goals of the defendants, and the data suggest they are possible in about one-half of the cases.

The other pressure brought to bear by the defendant on his attorney is for assurance in advance as to the amount of time he will have to serve (in those cases where he concedes time is inevitable). Of the 43 defendants who received time, 25 (58.1 percent) had worked out an agreed recommendation prior to sentencing day. This is to say, their attorneys could assure them in advance about the sentence they would receive. The likelihood of the judge not concurring was close to nil. It is impossible to estimate from the information in the files how many of the remaining 18 defendants had worked out an agreement whereby the prosecutor would not make any "pitch," a form of sentence agreement discussed earlier. In other words, it is quite likely that some deal satisfactory to the defendants—and preferable to the time the prosecutor was offering—was worked out for some cases in which no explicit agreed rec was offered. Of course, there also were cases in which the state's attorney refused to budge, and thus the defendant faced an uncertain future when he appeared before the judge. But these cases are the exception, not the rule. In a large majority of cases, plea bargaining led to some form of advance agreement about sentence.

The circuit and superior court data support the qualitative assertions made in the text. Plea bargaining yields results that comport with the defendant's interests. Thus, the newcomer is again forced to consider plea bargaining.

18. Sometimes the issue may be seen as frivolous but not worth the prosecutor's time to contest. In these instances the defense attorney's strategy of raising motions and setting the case down for trial succeeds. The prosecutor sweetens the deal (rather than bringing sanctions to bear) not because the issue is serious, but because he views the case as a whole as being of minor import; instead of expending the effort to fight the case, he "caves in" on what he feels is not a very important matter.

19. Prosecutors concur with these defense attorneys' contention that a "feel for a case" develops with greater experience in the system. In the following comments by prosecutors we see that the defense attorney's "feel" is often not very different from that of the experienced prosecutor. Each seems to know what the likely outcome of a given case will be.

> —— [a public defender] has been here for twenty years, and we can talk for two minutes about a case, and arrive at what will happen. Two minutes. If we haven't settled, we are never far apart. That is because he is experienced, and I am experienced, and he knows that it takes us a few minutes and we won't be far apart. [62]

> An experienced lawyer, or a public defender, who has been around a while, can also feel what a case is worth. They won't waste our time with needless haggling.

> But the inexperienced attorney has no sense of what a case is worth, so, for example, if you offer two to five [years] they feel that you are taking advantage of them. [21]

20. Even the same attorney may vary his style for particular cases.

> *Q*. Well, let's say you are negotiating with —— [a state's attorney]. Do you go in and say: "Look, I want a suspended sentence," when really what you're looking for is six months or something?
> *A*. That varies. I guess there is more strategy to it than I thought. I guess there is a strategy to it, but it's really a play-by-ear strategy. Sometimes I'll go in there and ask for something much lower than I expect. Sometimes I'll go in there and ask for exactly what I want, if it's suspended sentence, or a reduction in charge or whatever. [33]

Prosecutors are well aware of these various negotiating strategies. A prosecutor recounted the following anecdote as illustrative of the types of bargaining postures available.

> *Q*. What does the plea bargaining process look like? Do you haggle or automatically reach agreement?
> *A*. Very often you do have to haggle. I am always willing to negotiate, but you have to know the attorney you are dealing with. Some of them haggle, while with others you can just give them the "price of the case" and they know you are doing the best you can, and that is what the case is worth. Others want the feeling that they are haggling or "handling" with you. There is this old story about two rivals, Epstein and Alioto. One day Epstein came to Alioto's store and asked the price for a particular piece of material. Alioto said that it was $3.95. Epstein said "fine," paid, and left. Epstein's friend asked him why he didn't bargain with Alioto. "I'm sure you could have gotten it for less." "Well, I'll tell you," Epstein replied, "this way he'll go crazy. He'll keep asking himself why he didn't ask for $5.00." This is the way we have to haggle with some lawyers. If you give them the best offer right away they are apt to think that if they pursued it they could have done even better. [21]

21. In the discussion of each of the three stages, I will include one lengthy interview excerpt. Obviously, no one respondent can be assumed "typical" and thus it is reasonable to assume that responses from other attorneys during the same stage vary somewhat. I think, however, that the thoughts and feelings of most of the attorneys interviewed are captured in these selections.

An additional consideration led to the singling out of these three attorneys. In the course of my interviews, I was struck by a number of shared traits among the three. They were all young, liberal, introspective, committed to their jobs, and sincerely concerned about the quality of the defendant's representation. They seemed in many ways to be carbon copies, except that their time in the criminal justice system differed. Though, of course, a panel study of the same attorneys over time would be preferable, I felt that given research constraints, these attorneys could serve as indicators of the changes many attorneys experience.

To the extent that these attorneys are atypical (sincerely concerned, liberal, and so on), they provide support for the analysis. This is to say that it is most difficult to understand why this type of attorney moves in the plea bargaining direction. It would come as no surprise to learn that a newcomer eager only to befriend prosecutors (perhaps to increase his earnings by "turning over" a lot of cases) plea bargains. The more complex and important problem is to understand why the attorney who begins with the highest and sincerest commitment to the due process model ends up plea bargaining many of his cases. I will have more to say about this issue after completing the discussion of adaptation to all three roles in the local court.

22. In chapter 7, I will discuss these normative orientations toward plea bargaining. Suffice it to say here that though normative preferences vary substantially, neither defense attorneys nor prosecutors nor judges desire the abolition of plea bargaining. Each—at a minimum—wants plea bargaining to remain as an option for case disposition.

23. The attorney's sense of "what he can do with a case" is not always immediately communicated to the defendant. I spent several hours in the office of a private attorney, listening to his conversations with his clients. (I was introduced as an associate.) Among other things, I was struck by the attorney's unwillingness to give the defendant a realistic appraisal of what he thought would happen. The attorney tended to overestimate the gravity of the charges and to stress the maximum exposure the defendant faced. After the client departed, and we discussed the case, it became apparent that the attorney knew what the likely outcome would be, and knew that it would not be nearly as severe as he had suggested.

I suppose the attorney could explain his comments by claiming that he did not want to raise the defendant's expectations, only to find later that his appraisal was overly optimistic. I think a more honest explanation, though, is that the attorney needed to justify his fee. By stressing the maximum and then obtaining a plea bargain that was substantially below the maximum, the attorney could claim that the disposition was a product of his arduous labors.

24. Experienced attorneys held similar views toward newcomers. As with "outsiders," they felt the newcomer simply did not understand the reality of the local criminal court. With more experience in the system, they expect the newcomer to change his views. The following comments by the chief public defender of one of the superior courts is illustrative.

> Yeah, well, I think that —— [a new public defender] learned stuff as a student, and he came in here with the same sort of impressions that I came in with and the same tendency to be ready to criticize or find fault, and then found out that by and large things weren't as horrible as they may have appeared at first blush, and a lot of things that he was prepared to criticize or pick apart really shaped up better as you get used to the idea. Now this is because, well, you understand a little better. [23]

25. I do not mean to imply that there is no room for an "outsider" in the court. A defense attorney can continue to file motions in every case and opt for trial in many of these. Court personnel argue that in the long run the client suffers as a result of these actions, but this may not necessarily be correct. Once an attorney has a reputation for being a complete adversary, he may attract clients who are willing to run the risks attached to motions and trials. In other words, the outsider's clients may not be a random selection of all defendants, and thus they might have opted for trial in any event.

Also, as court personnel come to expect the outsider's actions—that is, they take for granted that he will file motions, and so on—the penalties he incurs may decrease; they get "used to him," and are willing to tolerate what they see as his eccentricity. Some even feel that it is healthy for the system to have such an outsider; he serves as a sort of safety valve for the most discontented defendants.

The outsider—and one very notable outsider is included in my sample—believes that his adversary posture benefits even those defendants not really interested in trial.

He feels that court personnel know his threats are credible, and therefore they often capitulate and offer excellent plea bargains. Yes, even the outsider "takes offers he can't refuse."

Elite practitioners—but not outsiders—disagree. They think that on balance the outsider's clients suffer. A credible threat of trial can be established in ways other than harassing the prosecutor by filing motions in every case, and by trying "frivolous" cases. Furthermore, they feel the outsider suffers one great disadvantage. He cannot count on the prosecutor to "give him a break" in the borderline case. There are some cases which can go either way in terms of disposition, and the elite practitioner feels that if his own word is good, and if he has amicable relations with the prosecutors, the probability is high that the defendant will receive a break. They argue that it is for these types of cases, in particular, that the prosecutor's resolve to see it through stiffens when dealing with the outsider. It ought to be plain that these divergent views cannot be reconciled without obtaining more reliable quantitative evidence.

26. There are exceptions to this generalization. In some cases, everyone realizes early that a trial will probably be necessary. For example, take the case of a prominent banker charged with embezzlement. It is likely that any conviction will so damage his reputation and future that he must contest the charges at trial.

27. Some differences may characterize the cases in low and high volume jurisdictions, but I think it plausible to hypothesize that these differences cancel each other out, resulting in fairly comparable proportions of defendants fitting within the categories discussed in the text. For example, one might argue that in low volume, unhurried jurisdictions less technical errors are made, and that therefore a greater percentage of cases in these courts fit the "nothing to contest" mold. But it is also quite possible that personnel (police, prosecutors) working within these jurisdictions are less professional than their counterparts in high volume jurisdictions, and thus make more technical errors (in Centerville, lack of professionalism—and indeed, unfamiliarity with portions of the penal code—was commonplace).

28. It is also important to recall some of the newcomers' responses presented in the text. When I pressed them (the newcomers working in high volume courts) about the effects of case pressure, they conceded that they might be using it as an "excuse" for their participation in the plea bargaining system. If asked what, if anything, they would do differently if given unlimited time, again they admitted that essentially they would end up plea bargaining most of their cases. They might research their cases more carefully, or spend more time on investigation, but they expected that the end-product would still be a negotiated settlement.

Chapter 5

1. Only when the adaptation of prosecutors differs from that of state's attorneys will I distinguish between these roles. For the most part, adaptation to these two roles entails essentially the same considerations.

2. See pp. 7–9 for a discussion of the organization of the prosecutor's office.

3. It is important to emphasize at the outset that the role played by prosecutors in negotiating sentences varies across states. In Connecticut, prosecutors negotiate sentence as well as charge; in other states they may only negotiate charge. The discussion of prosecutorial adaptation that follows is predicated on the notion that prosecutors learn that they can—and ought to—negotiate sentences, and thus the discussion is only apposite to states in which prosecutors can make sentence recommendations.

4. In a handful of jurisdictions, the chief state's attorney requires that all dispositions negotiated by his assistants be sent to his office for approval. It is difficult to

estimate the amount of scrutiny accorded these dispositions; suffice it to say that it is most unusual for a disposition to be rejected.

5. It seems puzzling that so much leeway would be given the inexperienced prosecutor or state's attorney. After all, as noted earlier, the newcomer's actions reflect on the office as a whole. Though the interviews did not yield any completely satisfactory explanations, two factors seem partially to explain the latitude accorded the newcomer. The first is the court's case volume, or perhaps, the pressures of some other business on the chief prosecutor. He simply does not have the time and/or inclination to exercise tight control over his subordinates. Second, the chief prosecutor and state's attorney believe it necessary for the newcomer to "get knocked around" on his own. Only by experiencing the system on his own, or so the argument runs, will he learn the realities of the prosecutor's job.

6. Failure by the prosecutor to follow through on a plea agreement would also violate the dictates of the United States Supreme Court's decision in Santobello v. New York, 404 U.S. 257, 92 S.Ct. 495, 30 L.Ed. 2d 427 (1971).

7. Over 80 percent of the circuit and superior court offenders (an estimate based on my examination of the defendants' files) had prior records.

8. Experienced defense attorneys are well aware of the newcomer's tendency "to take crime more seriously." The following comments by a superior court public defender are illustrative.

> *Q*. You mean new state's attorneys tend to be harder or . . .
> *A*. Well, they don't know what's an appropriate penalty, and they're very prone to be outraged that anybody broke the law. You know, they've got to get used to the idea that there are lawbreakers over here. [23]

9. In this instance, the "boss" was not completely honest when he reported these encounters to his young assistant prosecutor. Though he did sometimes send the defense attorney off with a disclaimer that "there was nothing he could do," he also was known to undercut his own assistants if he himself had a good rapport with the defense attorney and if he felt the assistant was being unnecessarily severe.

Indeed, I uncovered some evidence suggesting that a number of prosecution offices informally institutionalized a sort of "Mutt and Jeff" routine. One prosecutor [not necessarily a newcomer] plays the hard-bargainer, the "tough guy," the reluctant compromiser. After attorneys have heard the meager deal offered by this prosecutor, they appreciate all the more the "reasonable" offer made by the second prosecutor they had searched out. For a comparable "Mutt and Jeff" practice in police interrogation procedure, see *Miranda v. Arizona*, 384 U.S. 436, 86 S. Ct. 1602, 16 L.Ed. 2d 694 (1966).

10. The defense may concede the defendant's guilt explicitly ("you've got my guy, but he's not so bad") or implicitly (by not contesting the question of guilt and discussing sentence exclusively). As the prosecutor gains experience in the system, he assumes that the defense attorney will not contest the defendant's guilt; that is, he becomes so accustomed to the attorney's explicit or implicit concession of guilt that he no longer thinks in terms of innocent defendants.

11. The following excerpt illustrates the "obligation" state's attorneys feel toward at least listening to defense attorneys' requests.

> If someone came to me and wanted to talk in terms of disposition, I felt I should listen and hear what the person had to say, and, in turn, if I had a counter offer to make, make it. I never solicit. People would come to me and say: "We want to plea bargain." I'd say "fine." I looked upon that as part of my job. [15]

12. The explanations of "why" these standards are adopted by the prosecutor will be presented at the end of this section (for the serious/nonserious standard), and in the following section (for the time/no-time standard).

13. Since what is viewed as serious in the circuit court may be seen as nonserious in the superior court, defense attorneys occasionally opt to have a case bound over to the superior court even if a fairly satisfactory plea arrangement could have been worked out in the circuit court. They hope that the comparative nonseriousness of the offense will yield an even better deal in the superior court.

14. The fact that the prosecutor did not view the nine-months settlement as indicative of "giving an inch" is an excellent illustration of the "certain time" standard employed by prosecutors. This standard will be discussed later in this section.

15. I suppose it is arguable whether this is properly viewed as nonserious. Though the offenses themselves were not serious, one could maintain that, based on the defendant's record, he is a "serious offender." I think, though, that court personnel would still sort the defendant into the nonserious cell.

16. Obviously, this generalization does not hold across all cases. One could refine the argument by introducing concepts such as "minimal time" (a brief period of incarceration to teach the defendant a lesson) and "substantial time" (a lengthy period of incarceration for particularly serious cases). But, I think for most cases this refinement is unnecessary because prosecutors really do think in terms of the time/no-time dichotomy discussed in the text.

17. For a discussion of the various sentence bargains, see pp. 43–44.

18. A question that remains unanswered in the text is why the new prosecutor comes to expect the defendant to plead guilty in a case with a *contestable* legal issue. Recall that the newcomer is eager to litigate cases, and that it is only after he discovers that most cases are barren of any contestable issues that he develops standards for processing the cases of guilty defendants. Seriously guilty defendants are accorded one treatment; nonserious defendants are accorded another. But I imply in the text that this sorting operation applies to all cases the prosecutor handles. The question is: What happened to his eagerness to litigate?

I will address this question in part in the following section. One possible explanation not explored there is worthy of note here. It might be that the prosecutor develops his perspective on plea bargaining from processing the sorts of nondisputable cases discussed in the text, and that he then applies this perspective to all cases he handles. Over time, he comes to expect a guilty plea in cases regardless of their disputable characteristics.

19. The prosecutor asserted that new juries (this was the first case heard by these jurors) are disinclined to convict. Also, he observed that more than a year had elapsed since the defendant's arrest and that this might have cast some doubt over the witnesses' testimony. Finally, he suggested that racial factors might have played a role in the acquittal. The defendant in the case was Jamaican, and one of the prosecutor's witnesses said something from the stand to the effect that "all Jamaicans are alike." The proscutor felt that this remark cast further doubt on the witness's credibility.

20. The "unpredictability of juries" theme is widely shared by court veterans. Witness, for example, the prosecutor's observation in the following excerpt.

> You knock your brains out before a jury on a drunk driving case, let's say, and you think you have a hell of a case, but there is something about the accused that excites some sympathy, and one or more of the jurors . . . Jurors are not rational basically. They react based on their prejudices, their innate prejudices . . . [42]

We need not attempt an assessment of the accuracy of the argument; for our purposes it is sufficient to note that prosecutors believe jury decision making to be "irrational."

21. The new prosecutor's need for trial experience cannot be questioned. A number of defense attorneys gleefully recounted the ways in which they had bamboozled novice prosecutors. Two examples should suffice.

> Let me tell you about new prosecutors. You know ——. Well, he thought he was hot stuff when he was new. He had won a couple of trials in a row over in the circuit court; he thought he was a great trial attorney, and he said he was going to take me on. They had my guy cold; he was stiff when they got him, there's no question in my mind. It was a drunken driver case, and they had him. Anyway, while I'm trying this case against —— [the new prosecutor], I always, in all these drunk driving cases, drop coins on the floor, the California test, and I show how hard it is to pick up the coins even if you're sober. So in his case I said to ——, and this is inexperience again on his part, I said: "——, I got a wife and four kids at home," and meanwhile I'm looking in my pocket, "I never have any money. I'm always broke, and you're in the lap of luxury with the state of Connecticut. Give me some coins." Se he gave me some coins, all this out in front of the jury, right. I drop the coins, and I make out how hard it is to pick them up. When I get done I put the coins back in my pocket, and —— says to me: "Well, you didn't return my coins." I said: "Mr. ——, I need them more than you do, with all my kids." And things like that in front of the jury are really important. And I beat —— in that case. The first one he ever lost. [36]

> *Q*. Have you noticed any differences between new prosecutors and . . .
> *A*. I love to see them. I eat them up.
> *Q*. I thought you said they were more hard-assed?
> *A*. Shit, they're hard-assed, so you get them to try a case with you, and you show how inept they are, and you make a goddamn fool out of them. I've had cases with these hard-nosed new guys. I said, "Fine, we're ready for trial." Now, I'm probably the most objectionable lawyer around in that I object to every question. I don't know what the law is today, it may change tomorrow, but I know how to object. Every question they ask I object to. I sit in the trial and object, and after you bust their ass a little bit they've been embarrassed in front of the jury, they haven't got a question out that's meaningful, and they're realizing what it's like to go against an experienced attorney. I didn't want to say good lawyer, just experienced lawyer who can hold out evidence. In other words I think I'm a champion at that, that's really my strength. I can make it very difficult to get in evidence against me. I make it difficult for the state, and if a guy is not experienced, forget it. He couldn't get his own name in the record. That's what I do well. And I can take his witnesses,·witnesses who are absolutely telling the truth, and make them appear to be dishonest. You know, take them down the path each way and get them on subjects that are not really part of the case, that they are not familiar with, that they haven't been briefed by the prosecutor on, and make them look stupid. And the more positive they are in their answers, the easier it is to destroy them. [65]

22. Though the modal pattern appears to be—or is perceived to be—a penalty after conviction at trial, respondents indicated that occasionally defendants fared no worse (and sometimes did better) after trial.

23. Again, even if it is only the exceptional case in which the prosecutor does not "profit" by trial, this is sufficient to cause him to think twice or thrice before rejecting a negotiated time disposition in subsequent cases.

24. The assistant prosecutors are, of course, all professionals and thus, it would be unseemly for the chief prosecutor to urge settlements upon them just to move the business. Furthermore, though the chief prosecutor is concerned about case backlog, he need not assume responsibility for court congestion. He can—and does—attack defense attorneys in this regard, arguing that it is their propensity to ask for frequent continuances that account for the court's backlog.

25. The fundamental reasons for prosecutors' moving in the plea bargaining direction have already been discussed. In the final section, I will explore the consequences of their change in attitude and behavior.

26. Several respondents suggested that defendants would still plead guilty, notwithstanding the strictures against plea bargaining. Thus, the backlog might not result. In the final chapter of this study, I will consider this argument in greater detail.

27. I asked all respondents to assess a policy proposal calling for the abolition of plea bargaining.

28. To appreciate just how farfetched the prosecutors thought the notion of abolishing plea bargaining, it should be emphasized that "realistic increases" was used quite loosely in the text. Prosecutors indicated that not even a ten-fold increase in personnel and courts would be sufficient to manage the increased workload resulting from plea bargaining's abolition. Thus, if a ten-fold increase is "realistic," it would still fall short. When prosecutors began speaking of a hundred times the number of prosecutors, judges, courtrooms, and so on as being necessary to handle the workload, I labeled such estimates as falling outside the "realistic" range.

29. This view of the prosecutor as the central figure in the court, and of the judge as irrelevant, comports with the defendant's perceptions of these actors. See Jonathan Casper, *American Criminal Justice* (Englewood Cliffs, N.J.: Prentice-Hall, 1972), pp. 126–44.

30. See, for example, Arthur Lewis Wood, *Criminal Lawyer* (New Haven, Conn.: College and University Press, 1967), p. 207.

31. See pp. 97–99, 101–14.

32. The private bar can be further divided into a relatively large group of solo practitioners, each handling a "volume business," and a few "elite practitioners" (often members of a law firm) retained by wealthier defendants who can meet their fees.

33. This is an estimate provided by a number of the respondents. My observations—and a check of the court docket—support this characterization of the defense bar.

34. Defense attorneys do, though, attempt to negotiate cases with particular prosecutors. For example, some attorneys attempt to "shop around" and to avoid the prosecutor who "has a thing for" certain crimes. Alternatively, other defense attorneys feel most comfortable—perhaps because of personality compatibility—maneuvering all their cases before the same prosecutor. Thus, one finds "pairing-up" taking place; that is, a defense attorney has a prosecutor with whom he most frequently negotiates regardless of the issue at stake in a case.

35. See, for example, Abraham Blumberg, *Criminal Justice* (Chicago: Quadrangle Books, 1967), pp. 108–15.

36. I was witness to—or informed about—a number of these "breaks" given because of friendship. For example, a defense attorney told about a case involving marijuana, in which his cousin was the defendant. After the attorney spoke to the prosecutor and discussed (honestly) the defendant's unblemished past history, the prosecutor agreed to a disposition that was probably somewhat milder than would have been the case were the defendant not the attorney's cousin.

37. The notion of past plea bargaining dispositions serving as "precedents" for subsequent cases suggests that law school training has some import after all. If a goal of the law school is to develop "legal minds" capable of utilizing precedent cases in novel situations, it is, no doubt, comforting to those advancing this goal to find that their efforts are not for naught. Rather than using appellate cases as precedents, criminal court actors use case dispositions; but at least the approach to the problem at hand is the same. The "legal mind"—albeit in altered form—is alive and well in the trial court.

38. See, for example, Marvin Frankel, *Criminal Sentences* (New York: Hill and Wang, 1972), pp. 17–25.

39. See, for example, Blumberg, p. 105.

40. The scope of this study precludes a systematic examination of why prosecutors develop "things" for particular types of crimes. I suspect, however, that personality variables would loom large in any inquiry into this issue.

Chapter 6

1. Jobs in the city court were all part-time in nature. Typically, they were political rewards for loyal party workers, and the expectation of those "working" in the city court was that not very much time had to be expended in performance of one's duties.

2. Robert Carp and Russell Wheeler, "Sink or Swim: The Socialization of a Federal District Judge," *Journal of Public Law* 21 (1972):368.

3. Beverly Blair Cook, "The Socialization of New Federal Judges: Impact on District Court Business," *Washington University Law Quarterly* 1971 (1971):254.

4. "Thus, whereas much of the maneuvering and negotiation elsewhere in government are overtly and explicitly oriented toward shaping the substance of decisions, the visible foci of judicial politics are selection of personnel and design of organization and procedures ... In appearance, at least, judicial politics is politics of personnel and procedure rather than of program." Wallace Sayre and Herbert Kaufman, *Governing New York City* (New York: W. W. Norton and Co., 1960), p. 554.

5. No identifying number follows this quote because the speaker was not included in my sample. He was simply an attorney with whom I spoke while observing plea negotiations in a circuit court.

6. For a good summary of these arguments, and further references to research in this area, see Richard Watson and Rondal Downing, *The Politics of the Bench and the Bar* (New York: John Wiley and Sons, 1969), pp. 1–14.

7. Occasionally, a prosecutor is elevated to the bench; but, at least in Connecticut, this is not the typical route to advancement. Prosecutors indicated that state law proscribed political involvement by prosecutors, and that this restriction reduced their chances for a judgeship.

The effects of the ban on party activity can be partially offset by the prosecutor. For one, his wife can contribute to party coffers, and I was told that this was not an uncommon practice. Second, the prosecutor's job facilitates interaction with powerful party members (committees, planning sessions, and so on), and thus serves as a vehicle for keeping his name in the minds of local influentials. Notwithstanding these two considerations, however, prosecutors still are not the primary candidates for judgeships in Connecticut.

8. A longer period may elapse if the nominee is currently on the bench (for example, as a court of common pleas judge), and his elevation to the superior court takes effect at the end of the common pleas sessions.

9. Though Cook found that the program is only of minimal import in predicting

subsequent judicial behavior, it still functions in an informational capacity. Basic descriptive material is made available to the newcomer. See Cook, pp. 263–66. Even this seemingly obvious step has not been taken in Connecticut.

10. If the newcomer is assigned to a jurisdiction in which he is the only judge (and this occasionally is the case), obviously he will not be able to sit with a veteran colleague for a week. Even in multijudge jurisdictions, newcomer courtwatching is sometimes precluded by the assignment patterns of judges (for example, if one judge is presiding over a trial, and the other is hearing civil cases).

11. The newcomers also regretted the absence of "sentencing councils." These are experimental sentencing arrangements currently in use in several federal district courts. Under this innovative plan, judges formally confer with two of their colleagues before sentencing. For a more complete discussion, see Marvin Frankel, *Criminal Sentences* (New York: Hill and Wang, 1972), pp. 69–74.

12. A veteran state's attorney concurred in this assessment. When asked about how judges adapt to the local criminal court, he responded: "Trial and error. It's our trial and his error." [30]

13. The adaptation of federal district court judges seems to follow the same "muddle through" process. A federal judge interviewed by Carp and Wheeler observed that: "The new judge sort of hits the ground running." Similarly, another judge included in their sample noted that "becoming a Federal judge is like being thrown into the water and being told to swim." Quoted in Carp and Wheeler, p. 374.

14. The importance of these informal exchanges ought not be underestimated. As Cook noted: "Informal socialization processes on an affective and one-to-one basis might have the most significant effect upon judicial behavior . . ." Cook, p. 278.

15. Sentencing is also one of the most troublesome problems for new federal district court judges. See Carp and Wheeler, p. 373.

16. In many of these assignments the newcomer represents an unwelcome element of uncertainty for prosecutors and defense attorneys. Indeed, attorneys may attempt to maneuver their cases to avoid the newcomer. Witness, for example, the remarks of a state's attorney in the following excerpt.

> With new judges, defense attorneys worry about what will happen. They may try to duck getting cases before him, fancy-foot around getting things postponed. They'll try to wait until they get a new judge. And this happens a lot when we get new judges here. You find that more motions are suddenly filed, that additional investigations are undertaken, that all kinds of requests are made to delay. There are 401 things you can do to postpone a case, and when they see a novice judge up there, that's what they do. [62]

17. Judges with an extensive prior background as a defense attorney or prosecutor bring this assumption to the bench. In the text, I am considering those judges who did not have such a background, and thus learn of the defendants' culpability while on the bench.

18. A few judges feel that factually guilty defendants ought to plead even if they have a credible legal argument. But most judges "understand" the motions and the trials of factually guilty defendants as long as the contested legal issue does not appear to be "frivolous."

19. See pp. 122–26.

20. This "pleading guilty is the first step toward rehabilitation" argument is fairly common among judges, though I think it is of less import than the assessment as to whether there were realistically contestable issues at stake in the case. Several additional examples of the penitent/rehabilitation position follow.

> If a man is truly repentant and wishes to throw himself on the mercy of the court and shows that he's on the way toward rehabilitation, then he should get a discount from the usual sentence. We don't feel that a man should be penalized for having his trial, but we feel he should get a discount if he shows he's on the way toward rehabilitation by repentance and by coming clean and by helping the police and saying he's sorry enough to want to make amends. So a man who is truculent and wants his trial—which he's entitled to—that's all right, but if he is found guilty by a jury and the jury thereby proves that he has committed perjury, he gets more than a fellow who's repentant, and should get more because he's not only been found guilty by the jury and cost the state a lot of money, which is only incidental, of course, but he has committed perjury in addition. [29]

> One of the things you run into and one of the things that you judge a guy on is the fact that he's repentant. He did something, he's sorry he did it, and basically he says: "I'm not going to do it again." If the fellow goes to trial and insists upon his rights, goes all the way through and is found guilty and is sentenced you haven't got that element in there, you don't have him admitting his guilt. And I've never seen a fellow who had been found guilty after a trial come in and say to me: "I insisted on my rights because I kind of hoped that I'd get away, but I really am sorry, I realize that I did it, and I was wrong, and therefore take that into consideration." None of them have done it. But you see how you're going to feel a little different toward the guy who pleads guilty, who admits that he did it. You're going to have a different attitude toward this guy regardless of whether he should be treated exactly the same. Don't you think so? [25]

21. In addition to the anxiety factor, appeals require a substantial expenditure of judicial time and effort. During trial, for example, the judge is constantly asked to rule on disagreements over legal issues. Knowing that an appeal is likely to be taken if the defendant is convicted, the judge must insure that his rulings comport with current case law. This, of course, necessitates time-consuming research as well as extensive consideration of the appropriateness of the precedents for the issue at hand.

22. In order to preserve the anonymity of the individual who provided these memos, I will only identify them as memos written during 1972 and 1973 by a clerk in a superior court of Connecticut.

23. It is important to emphasize that these judges still encourage guilty pleas by rewarding those defendants who plead and/or penalizing those who go to trial. Notwithstanding their unwillingness to take overt steps to facilitate the plea bargaining process (they feel it improper for a judge to become involved), these judges share with their colleagues the belief that guilty defendants ought to plead guilty. Thus, these "don't want to know about plea bargaining" judges encourage guilty pleas by the sentences they mete out.

24. *Pretrial* denotes a formal procedure in civil cases, wherein the opposing parties meet prior to trial and discuss the evidence to be presented at trial. Formally, the term has no meaning in criminal proceedings, but, as suggested in the text, several judges are now labeling their efforts to resolve the cases by negotiations "pretrials."

Generally, the judge who pretries cases will not be the same judge who hears the case if no agreement is reached. It would be improper for a judge who hears the defendant's offer to plead guilty, to preside over the defendant's subsequent trial. Note, though, that this is what may happen when judges make ad hoc efforts to induce pleas in cases before them.

25. The judges who have chosen to institutionalize some variant of the pretrial have done so on their own. There are no administrative rules or directives about this process;

it is simply something instituted by individual judges concerned about facilitating negotiations.

Judges differ in their assessments of the propriety of judicial participation in pretrials. The following excerpts illustrate these conflicting assessments:

> Some of my colleagues, yes, they are starting to talk about pretrying criminal cases. They want—this is my opinion—to make a name for themselves and . . . Look, I like to move business also. I'm not running off to the golf course. But some of these fellows they have a way of jumping in before they know what they are doing. They're eager beavers who want to show someone that they can get rid of the business . . . but there are a lot of problems with judges becoming this involved in plea bargaining. [8]

> *Q*. What about pretrying cases? I know Judge —— was doing it here in the last session?
> *A*. I won't do it. You open yourself up to becoming the defendant. And I think the ABA standards oppose it. Sure, I get involved in plea discussions sometimes. But I don't like it when I have to hear the case later. But even if the judge isn't going to hear the case, I frown on it. It can lead to stuff like people saying that "—— [this judge] thinks that such and such a disposition would be good." The other judge then hears this, and he might get annoyed and increase the sentence, or he might feel bound by it, even if he does not agree. [69]

> I intend to pretry every case that comes in on the list. I've done it for the cases this term. —— [a public defender] was in two weeks ago and he says: "What about talking about these cases?" And —— [another public defender] had a big bunch of files, so they brought them in also, and —— [an assistant state's attorney] would say, "Now this is what I got, I've got these statements, and these pictures, and so on." And I would think about it and say to —— [public defender]: "——, what have you got?" And then he'll tell me, and then I'd say to —— [assistant state's attorney]: "I think you got a lousy case here. I don't think that you got a very good case. What do you want in this case?" And he'd say, "Two to four." And I'd say: "No, it isn't worth that at all. At best it's worth one to three, maybe it's worth only six months. Would your guy take six months, ——?" And he might say: "I'll recommend it to the guy." Now, I think we should do this not to just move the business, because we're current. But this fellow, for example, if I gave him six months and he started doing his time, he'd be out quickly. And if he couldn't make bail, then he'd get credit for that time also. He might want to get the thing over with, clear his record. That's just one example. I just think that it's very important that judges hold these pretrials. I told —— [the clerk] that I was going to bring these guys together and sit them down and get them to negotiate. One of the problems that you might have noticed in court was an attorney will get up and say, "We haven't got the transcript from the circuit court yet," or "We haven't got this information or that information." I get these guys in here and say to the defense attorney: "Now, what do you want?" And I'll say to —— [state's attorney] "Give it to him." So this way I can eliminate all this crap that I get out in the courtroom. All of this "We haven't got this and we're not prepared to try." I can insist right away: "Go out and make a record of it, copy this thing, and give it to him right away so we can get this junk out of the way." Then we get around to the honest-to-God bargaining. "Now what do you want? What have you got?" So I serve two purposes. I can eliminate this problem out there that they're not ready for trial because the state's attorney

hasn't given them something, smooth out all the procedural problems about going forward, and then we can get to the real issue, can we settle this case? [35]

26. Obviously, dichotomizing the variable is somewhat of a simplification. Judges, though, do tend to view it as a matter of efficiency versus inefficiency.

27. I suppose non-job–related factors could explain why judges rush to complete the business. One rather embittered judge called my attention to some such factors.

> We had a judge here the other day, who just can't get home quick enough. He has a sheep farm; he raises sheep. We have another judge who just wants to get back to his home; in the winter he plays indoor tennis, or outside tennis, and wants to go to his summer home in ——. We have another judge who just can't get out fast enough—he wants to go to his club. The way the court has shaped up is that it is kind of a coasting, semi-retiring thing for judges. Come in, do the minimum, and out. One judge, he's now retired because of disability, he used to divide his cases into three parts—those that he would hear, those that he would declare a mistrial, and those in which he would disqualify himself. So he only decided one-third of the cases that came before him. Every case was, "I am disqualified." Or "mistrial." Or he would hear a few. [4]

Based on my own observations, and on the comments of most of the respondents included in this study, I am reluctant to subscribe to this sort of "rushing to the golf course" explanation. It is certainly true for some judges, but most of the judges I observed, interviewed, or heard about seemed conscientious about their role obligations. This does not mean they were "good" judges; all it suggests is that it is inaccurate to maintain that judges rush through the docket because the time to tee off at the course is approaching.

28. Judges, like prosecutors, sort cases by the serious/nonserious, and time/no-time standards.

Chapter 7

1. For the exceptions to this generalization see figure 3.

2. Langton argues that this simplified approach too often characterizes socialization studies. See Kenneth Langton, *Political Socialization* (New York: Oxford University Press, 1969), pp. 162–63.

3. Herbert Kaufman makes a similar point in his conclusions about the adaptation of forest rangers to the Forest Service. "Without realizing it, members of the Forest Service . . . 'internalize' the perceptions, values and premises of action that prevail in the bureau; unconsciously, very often, they tend to act in the agency-prescribed fashion because that is the way that has become natural to them" (Herbert Kaufman, *The Forest Ranger* [Baltimore, Md.: Johns Hopkins Press, 1960], p. 176). See also Kenneth Culp Davis, *Discretionary Justice* (Urbana, Ill.: University of Illinois Press, 1971), p. 189. Davis, in discussing the prosecutor's decision as to whether or not a case ought to be prosecuted, observes that: "Why these various assumptions [about prosecuting] are made is not easy to discover; the best short answer seems to be that no one has done any systematic thinking to produce the assumptions, but that the customs about prosecution, like most customs, are the product of unplanned evolution. Whatever caused the assumptions to grow as they did, prosecutors usually assert that everybody knows that they are necessary."

4. A number of respondents resisted generalizing about their own patterns of plea

bargaining behavior. They claimed that it was easier for them to discuss specific cases than to articulate the general premises upon which their behavior was based.

> Plea bargaining strategies are difficult to talk about. I have trouble talking about systems. It's much easier for me to talk about cases, as to how happy I am about a particular result . . . [37]

> I don't think you work out a theory of how you're going to handle your cases in general. You have to take each case on its own merits. Each case is different; even if the charge in two cases is the same, the cases still differ vastly because the facts are always different. So you can't approach it from an ideological viewpoint or with a preconceived notion. You've just got to read each case and see how you feel about it. [54]

Notwithstanding these protestations, confident generalizations about these respondents' plea bargaining styles could be drawn by observations of their behavior and by asking pointed questions in the interview. They had a style and philosophy of plea bargaining; it was just that they could not—or would not—systematically discuss them.

5. The "many" versus "most" cases description reflects the fact that "most" criminal court actors believe most cases should be plea bargained; a minority believe that only some cases should be plea bargained. Thus, if we speak of all criminal court actors, "many" cases seems to be an appropriate compromise. I will address these differences later in this chapter.

6. Several respondents preferred to emphasize their antipathy toward trial, rather than their strong preference for negotiating dispositions per se.

> No one really wants to try a case; that's what it all boils down to. [3]

> It's like Norm Van Brocklin says. Quarterbacks run only out of terror. In our system people litigate only because they have no choice. If they've got reasonable people on both sides, they should be able to work it out. Sure, there are some cases that there is just no way it can work out; right from the beginning the lines are clearly drawn. But in most cases, you can work things out. [37]

Whether respondents emphasize their normative preference for plea bargaining or their antipathy toward trial does not affect their perceptions of the outcomes that result from negotiating cases. Both sets of respondents feel that "substantial" justice, "practical" solutions, and so on are realized through plea bargaining, and they view these as the best that one can expect in an imperfect system. The following excerpts are illustrative.

> Justice is pretty rough at times, but essentially a rough justice is reached in most cases. We are in an adversary system but we are not enemies. We are here to achieve a just result on both sides. And I think that most of the time substantial justice is achieved. [6]

> It's a funny situation in our system. I think that substantial justice is worked out a good percentage of the time; you kind of reach the right results, but in a very strange way. The right result seems to come out of plea bargaining, though the illusion of justice, the trial and what not, aren't present. [33]

> But practicing the law is first and foremost doing the possible. Not what should

> be, but what is. And to practice law this is what you've got to understand. And that's why we plea bargain. We get practical results. [24]

> After all, what we can accomplish is a rough approximation of substantial justice. Rough. Nothing refined, but a kind of rough approximation of substantial justice to the state, to the accused, to the courts, to society. That's all that we can do. As far as perfect justice, that's out; you know it's out. So the best that we can do is to do the best that we can under the circumstances. It's a rough approximation of justice, that's about all that can be expected. [4]

7. See note 28, p. 191.

8. This is not to say that case volume never affects plea bargaining. If volume in a court increases dramatically and personnel levels remain constant, changes in the plea bargaining process may become manifest. The prosecutor may nolle the marginal case which he might have pursued for a plea earlier. He may offer to reduce more charges and recommend lighter sentences, or he may simply demand more severe sentences after trial. Unraveling these case-pressure effects will require more precise and accurate data than now available. But, it also should be emphasized that these case volume effects operate on the margins; most cases are plea bargained for the reasons discussed in the text, and these do not rest on case volume considerations.

9. See fig. 1.

10. The guilty plea data, of course, do not prove that defendants plea bargained. However, as discussed earlier (see pp. 31–32), "oldtimers" included in my sample reacted scornfully to the notion that plea bargaining was something new to the criminal court. They maintained that the explicit give and take of plea bargaining characterized local criminal court proceedings for at least as long as their memories served them, and that guilty pleas were indeed products of these negotiations.

> That's [plea bargaining] a new expression, see, within the last two or three years, and I resent it. I don't like the sound of it. They make it sound as though it's reprehensible in some way, and it's not, of course, by any means. Anybody with any sense of history who will look back beyond today will understand the system, and understand why they have always settled their differences somehow. Call it a settlement, I think, or something like that. [18]

> Now they call it plea bargaining, or a legitimate compromise of a criminal charge. In the old days, we called it a deal. But plea bargaining is not a new thing; as long as I've been in the courts it has been there. It probably has always been in the courts. [70]

Furthermore, I will argue in the next section that the guilty plea itself is—and was—a form of "implicit plea bargaining." Thus, even if the oldtimers' recollections are incorrect, the guilty plea data are indicative of at least "implicit plea bargaining."

Finally, there is some independently collected empirical evidence supporting my arguments that explicit and implicit plea bargaining explain the high guilty plea rate historically. See Raymond Moley, "The Vanishing Jury," *Southern California Law Review* 97 (1928): 97–127; Justin Miller, "The Compromise of Criminal Cases," *Southern California Law Review* 1 (1927):1–31; and Jay Wishingrad, "The Plea Bargain in Historical Perspective." *Buffalo Law Review* 23 (1974):499–552.

11. National Advisory Commission on Criminal Justice Standards and Goals, *Courts* (Washington, D.C.: United States Government Printing Office, 1973), pp. 41–49. The NACCJSG concluded that plea bargaining could—and should—be "abolished" by 1978.

12. Casper observed that the desire for certainty weighs heavily in the decision of many defendants to cop a plea. I assume that this desire for certainty would be transmitted to defense counsel, who would then pressure for an explicit guarantee. See Jonathan Casper, *American Criminal Justice: The Defendant's Perspective* (Englewood Cliffs, N.J.: Prentice-Hall, 1972), pp. 67, 87.

13. The views of these "philosophical opponents" of plea bargaining will be further discussed in the following section.

14. In addition to cases that are "sure losers," this respondent is referring to certain types of crimes such as incest, wife swapping, child molesting, and so on. In these cases the defendant is particularly eager to avoid the glare of publicity, and hopes that by copping a plea the resultant publicity can be kept to a minimum. The attorney understands his client's concern, and thus, from the start, he is looking for a plea bargain.

15. Judges are excluded because my sample was too small to advance any confident generalizations about differences among experienced judges.

16. A large sample size is needed to insure that enough "dislike plea bargaining" respondents are included.

17. Actually, more than two general categories of attitudes toward plea bargaining may emerge once the data are analyzed. For example, in one of the typologies that I fiddled with—and subsequently rejected—I included a sort of "indifferent to plea bargaining" group. A group such as this would occupy a middle ground between the proponents and opponents of plea bargaining discussed in the text. I was forced to discard this typology because I could not satisfactorily sort respondents into this category (for example, I lumped together individuals who took jobs in the court because the "benefits" were good, with respondents who simply "had not made up their minds" about plea bargaining). Once I attempted to refine the category I found that the cells were beginning to exceed the *n*.

18. This hypothesis would have to be tested in a decentralized prosecutor's office in which some form of "prosecutor shopping" is allowed. In some offices a case is permanently assigned a prosecutor, and the defense attorney cannot "shop around." In others, prosecutors indicate on the case file the offer they make and here, too, it would be unusual for another prosecutor to undercut his colleague. Thus, in a comparison of plea bargaining offers, jurisdictions in which cases are not assigned to particular prosecutors, and those in which prosecutors do not note their offers on the file, would have to be considered.

19. The difficulty in testing this hypothesis is that the cases handled by these "opponents" of plea bargaining may differ from those of other attorneys. For example, the "opponents" of plea bargaining may attract a clientele whose cases "need" to be tried; that is, if other attorneys had the same cases, they, too, would try them. Thus, a higher rate of trial by "opponents" of plea bargaining does not necessarily indicate that these attorneys choose to plea bargain less; it may simply be a reflection of the different types of cases they handle.

Though this problem is severe, it is not insoluble, Occasionally, quasi-experimental situations afford an opportunity to compare defense attorneys' behavior for randomly assigned cases. If, for example, wide disparities in attitude toward plea bargaining are held by public defenders within a jurisdiction, and if cases are assigned randomly, we could compare disposition patterns. Or if assigned private counsel and public defenders are used for indigent cases, and if a random procedure is followed in distributing cases, a comparison both among public defenders and between private attorneys and public defenders could be undertaken. These, of course, are not optimal situations, since a "different" kind of attorney becomes a public defender, and/or agrees to handle indigents' cases. Nonetheless, I think these would be fertile locations to begin to test the hypothesis.

20. Hypotheses 3 and 4 are somewhat contradictory. If longer sentences result, why would defendants be more satisfied? The point is that any given defendant may feel more satisfiied because his attorney "fought more for him," and may not believe that he suffered in sentence because of his attorney's stance. On the question of how defendants perceive their attorneys, and their attorneys' actions, see Casper, pp. 100–125.

21. See p. 192, note 9 for a discussion of this "Mutt and Jeff" phenomenon in the prosecutor's office.

22. The resemblance to the British system (a division of labor between solicitors and barristers) is not unintentional. A number of respondents suggested that both the office of the prosecutor and the office of the public defender should establish separate departments for plea bargaining and trial work. Attorneys could then develop expertise in either plea bargaining or trial skills. This proposal ought to be considered further, though I foresee at least one major problem with such an arrangement. Defendants would be denied continuity of representation. If a deal could not be arranged, another attorney would try the case. I suspect that defendants would feel disconcerted by the shift in their counsel.

23. The amount of slack may be at least partially a function of organization size. Kaufman observed that:

> In smaller organizations, for example, the fortitude and determination to stand up against the consensus of a face-to-face group are exceptional; the hostility of close comrades is usually much harder to endure than the disapprobation of the majority in large, impersonal surroundings. Moreover, the deviant is more visible in the smaller setting; social pressures on him to conform are more continuous and intense. What is more, a single nonconformist might upset the whole routine of a small system, while a large system may be less concerned about his oddities because it is not similarly threatened; the importance of conformity in the former leads to greater efforts to keep people in line or weed them out (Herbert Kaufman, *The Limits of Organizational Change* [University, Ala.: University of Alabama Press, 1971], p. 106).

24. See Albert Alschuler, "The Prosecutor's Role in Plea Bargaining," *University of Chicago Law Review* 36 (1968):50–112; Albert Alschuler, "The Defense Attorney's Role in Plea Bargaining," *Yale Law Journal* 84 (1975):1179–1314; Abraham Blumberg, *Criminal Justice* (Chicago: Quadrangle Press, 1967); Jonathan Casper, *American Criminal Justice* (Englewood Cliffs, N.J.: Prentice-Hall, 1972).

25. On the other hand, these observers might conclude that a "plea bargaining free" system is less just. They might argue that justice by mutual consultation better comports with our notions of fair play than does justice by battle. Plea bargaining affords the defendant an opportunity to participate in the decision-making process; perhaps this is "fairer" than a system in which decisions emerge from adversary combat and judicial decrees.

26. For a discussion of the cop-out ceremony see pp. 44–46. Interestingly, some assistant prosecutors are now putting the agreement on the record. They are acting largely on their own; that is, there are no formal office policies on how to handle agreements. Thus, a gradual evolution toward the more open plea bargaining system is already underway. Again, the fact that some prosecutors do it and some do not presents an opportunity for a quasi-experimental design to assess the impact of publicly announcing plea bargaining agreements.

27. Judges are under no formal obligation to explain their sentences in criminal cases. See Marvin Frankel, *Criminal Sentençes* (New York: Hill and Wang, 1972), pp. 39–49.

28. This is one of Frankel's major reform proposals. See Frankel, pp. 75–85.

29. For further discussion of possible plea bargaining reforms see "Restructuring the Plea Bargain," *Yale Law Journal* 82 (1972):286–312; Welsh S. White, "A Proposal for Reform of the Plea Bargaining Process," *University of Pennsylvania Law Review* 119 (1971):439–65; Gregory Hobbs, "Judicial Supervision over California Plea Bargaining: Regulating the Trade," *California Law Review* 59 (1971):962–96; Paul Borman, "The Chilled Right to Appeal from a Plea Bargaining Conviction: A Due Process Cure," *Northwestern University Law Review* 69 (1974):663–715; and Richard Kopek, "Standards for Accepting Guilty Pleas to Misdemeanor Charges," *University of Michigan Journal of Law Reform* 8 (1974–75):568–93.

30. See National Institute of Law Enforcement and Criminal Justice, *Citizens Dispute Settlement* (Washington, D.C.: United States Government Printing Office, 1974); National Center for Dispute Settlement, "The 4-A Program (Arbitration as an Alternative to the Private Criminal Warrant and Other Criminal Processes)," n.d., paper on file at National Center for Dispute Settlement, Washington, D.C.; "IMCR Dispute Center to Serve 30th and 34th Police Precincts: Will Provide Community-based Mediation as Alternative to Arrest and Courts," *Conflict* 2 (March 1975):1–3. The discussion that follows is based on material in these sources.

31. No attempt to randomize assignments to arbitration has been made. At present, defendants must volunteer for the arbitration alternative, and thus there is an obvious sample bias.

32. In the course of conducting my interviews, I detected a strong streak of frustration/resignation among court personnel. They were well aware of problems in the way cases were processed, but were at a loss to suggest meaningful alternatives. I suspect that they might be quite receptive to a "different" approach to some of their problems.

33. A major problem is, of course, the elimination of many due-process protections. Thus, a strength of the arbitration process (its informality) is also a potential threat to the very protections that the Warren Court accorded criminal defendants.

34. Impressionistically, I have found that the explanations of newcomer adaptation and of plea bargaining dynamics developed from the Connecticut data apply—with some minor exceptions—to the Michigan courts. In addition to testing these impressions of similarities across states more systematically, thought ought also be given to conducting cross-national comparisons. I would hypothesize that some functional equivalent of plea bargaining is employed in most criminal courts. For example, a friend recently traveled to Great Britain, and after observing criminal court case dispositions there, he reported that if a defendant faces a multiple count indictment, and if he pleads guilty to one count, the prosecutor frequently "does not enter evidence" on the other counts.

35. See p. 202, note 8.

36. With enough jurisdictions, we could hold all but one structural variable constant, and thus test its effects.

37. The argument that follows in the text parallels Wilson's discussion of political culture and the zone of indifference for police behavior.

> The community is a source of cues and signals—some tacit, some explicit—about how various police situations should be handled, what level of public disorder is deemed appropriate, and what distinctions among persons ought to be made . . . Police work is carried out under the influence of a *political culture* though not

> necessarily under day-to-day political direction. By political culture is meant those widely shared expectations as to how issues will be raised, governmental objectives determined, and power for their attainment assembled; it is an understanding of what makes a government legitimate . . . With respect to police work—or at least its patrol functions—the prevailing political culture creates a "zone of indifference" within which the police are free to act as they see fit . . . The most important way in which political culture affects police behavior is through the choice of police administrator and the molding of the expectations that govern his role [Wilson's italics] (James Q. Wilson, *Varieties of Police Behavior* [New York: Atheneum, 1970], p. 233).

38. Circuit court jobs as assistant prosecutors or assistant public defenders are neither particularly well paying not prestigious (one respondent labeled these jobs "political prunes"). However, before one can be appointed to these jobs, the applicant must appear before the local political powers that be. Generally, the local "boss" is accommodating, and the applicant is appointed. But several respondents indicated that what the "boss" is really interested in is keeping certain individuals out of the jobs. Thus, the application of a very experienced legal aid attorney for a job as a circuit court public defender was rejected, and in his stead a completely inexperienced law school graduate from a none too distinguished law school was hired.

39. By "character" I mean the role played in recruitment. The size of the zone can be the same in two communities, but control over recruitment may vary, and with a greater role in recruitment the community will have a greater indirect effect on court operations.

40. For an excellent discussion of the importance of clarifying the political culture/local court nexus, and of the difficulties inherent in such an undertaking, see James Klonoski and Robert Mendelsohn, "The Allocation of Justice: A Political Approach," in *The Politics of Local Justice*, ed. James Klonoski and Robert Mendelsohn (Boston: Little, Brown and Co., 1970), pp. 3–19.

Selected Bibliography

Alschuler, Albert. "The Defense Attorney's Role in Plea Bargaining." *Yale Law Journal 84 (1975): 1179*–1314.

———. "The Prosecutor's Role in Plea Bargaining." *University of Chicago Law Review* 36 (1968):50–112.

American Bar Association. *Project on Minimum Standards for Criminal Justice, Standards Relating to Pleas of Guilty, Tentative Draft*. New York: Institute of Judicial Administration, 1967.

"Annual Report in Relation to the Criminal Business of the Courts of the State of Connecticut." *Public Documents of the State of Connecticut* (1900–1936).

"Annual Report of the Comptroller of Public Accounts of the State of Connecticut in Relation to the Criminal Business of the Courts as Shown by the Returns of the State's Attorneys." *Connecticut Public Documents* (1880–1900).

Arnold, Thurman. "Law Enforcement." In *Criminal Justice*, edited by George Cole. North Scituate, Mass.: Duxbury Press, 1972.

Asher, Herbert. "Freshman Representatives and the Learning of Voting Cues." Mimeographed. 1972.

———. "The Learning of Legislative Norms." *American Political Science Review* 67 (June 1973):499–513.

Berman, Paul. *Revolutionary Organization*. Lexington, Mass.: Lexington Books, D. C. Heath and Co., 1974.

Blumberg, Abraham. *Criminal Justice*. Chicago: Quadrangle Books, 1967.

———. "Lawyers with Convictions." In *The Scales of Justice*, edited by Abraham Blumberg. Chicago: Aldine Publishing Co., 1970.

Borman, Paul. "The Chilled Right to Appeal From a Plea Bargaining Conviction: A Due Process Cure." *Northwestern University Law Review* 69 (1974): 663–715.

Botein, Bernard. *Trial Judge*. New York: Cornerstone Library, 1952.

Brady v. U.S., 397 U.S. 742, 90 S.Ct. 1463, 25 L.Ed. 2d 747 (1970).

Brim, Orville, Jr. "Socialization through the Life Cycle." In *Socialization after Childhood–Two Essays*, edited by Orville Brim, Jr. and Stanton Wheeler. New York: John Wiley and Sons, 1966.

Carp, Robert, and Wheeler, Russell. "Sink or Swim: The Socialization of a Federal District Judge." *Journal of Public Law* 21 (1972): 359–93.

Casper, Jonathan D. *American Criminal Justice: The Defendant's Perspective*. Englewood Cliffs, N.J.: Prentice-Hall, 1972.

"Chief Appeals Judge Here Asks Curbs on Inept Trial Lawyers." *New York Times*, December 7, 1973.

Clausen, John. Introduction to *Socialization and Society*, edited by John Clausen. Boston: Little, Brown and Co., 1968.

Connecticut Planning Committee on Criminal Administration. *The Criminal Justice System in Connecticut* (1972).

Cook, Beverly Blair. "The Socialization of New Federal Judges: Impact on District Court Business." *Washington University Law Quarterly* 1971 (1971):253–79.

Davis, Kenneth Culp. *Discretionary Justice*. Urbana, Ill.: University of Illinois Press, 1971.

Downie, Leonard, Jr. *Justice Denied*. New York: Praeger Publishers, 1971.

Eisenstein, James. "Counsel for the United States: An Empirical Analysis of the Office of the United States Attorney." Ph.D. dissertation, Yale University, 1968.

Eulau, Heinz; Buchanan, William; Ferguson, Leroy; and Wahlke, John. "The Political Socialization of American State Legislators." *Midwest Journal of Political Science* 3 (1959):190.

Feeley, Malcolm. "Two Models of the Criminal Justice System: An Organizational Perspective." *Law and Society Review* 7 (Spring 1973):407–25.

Fenno, Richard, Jr. "The Freshman Congressman: His View of the House." In *Congressional Behavior*, edited by Nelson Polsby. New York: Random House, 1971.

———. *The Power of the Purse*. Boston: Little, Brown and Co., 1966.

Frank, Jerome. *Courts on Trial*. Princeton, N.J.: Princeton University Press, 1949; reprint ed., New York: Atheneum, 1969.

Frankel, Marvin. *Criminal Sentences*. New York: Hill and Wang, 1972.

Gertzog, Irwin. "Frustration and Adaptation: The Adjustment of Minority Freshmen to the Congressional Experience." Paper presented at the 1966 annual meeting of the American Political Science Association.

Gideon v. Wainwright, 372 U.S. 335, 88 S.Ct. 792, 9 L.Ed. 2d 799 (1963).

Griffiths, John. "Ideology in Criminal Procedure, or a Third 'Model' of the Criminal Process." *Yale Law Journal* 79 (1970):359–417.

———. "The Limits of Criminal Law Scholarship." *Yale Law Journal* 79 (1970):1388–1474.

Grossman, Joel. *The ABA and the Politics of Judicial Selection*. New York: John Wiley and Sons, 1965.

———. "Judicial Selection and the Socialization of Judges." In *The Federal Judicial System*, edited by Thomas Jahnige and Sheldon Goldman. New York: Rinehart and Winston, 1968.

Hobbs, Gregory. "Judicial Supervision over California Plea Bargaining: Regulating the Trade." *California Law Review* 59 (1971):962–96.

Hoffman, Walter. "Plea Bargaining and the Role of the Judge." *Federal Rules Decisions* 53 (1972):499–507.

"IMCR Dispute Center to Serve 30th and 34th Police Precincts: Will Provide Community-based Mediation as Alternative to Arrest and Courts." *Conflict* 2 (March 1975):1–3.

James, Howard. *Crisis in the Courts*. Rev. ed. New York: David McKay Co., 1971.

Judicial Council of Connecticut. *Biennial Report of the Judicial Council of Connecticut* (1926–1974).

Kaufman, Herbert. *The Forest Ranger*. Baltimore, Md.: Johns Hopkins Press, 1960.

———. *The Limits of Organizational Change*. University, Ala.: University of Alabama Press, 1971.

Klonoski, James, and Mendelsohn, Robert. "The Allocation of Justice: A Political Approach." In *The Politics of Local Justice*, edited by James Klonoski and Robert Mendelsohn. Boston: Little, Brown and Co., 1970.

Kopek, Richard. "Standards for Accepting Guilty Pleas to Misdemeanor Charges." *University of Michigan Journal of Law Reform* 8 (1974–75):568–93.

Langton, Kenneth. *Political Socialization*. New York: Oxford University Press, 1969.

Levin, Martin. "Urban Politics and Judicial Behavior." *Journal of Legal Studies* 1 (January 1972):193–221.

Levine, James. "Methodological Concerns in Studying Supreme Court Efficacy." *Law and Society Review* 4 (May 1970):583–611.

Lindblom, Charles E. *The Policy-Making Process*. Englewood Cliffs, N.J.: Prentice-Hall, 1968.

Lipsky, Michael. "Toward a Theory of Street-Level Bureaucracy." Paper presented at the 1969 annual meeting of the American Political Science Association.

Mapp v. Ohio, 378 U.S. 1, 84 S.Ct. 1489, 12 L.Ed. 2d 653 (1964).

Mather, Lynn. "Some Determinants of the Method of Case Disposition: Decision-Making by Public Defenders in Los Angeles." *Law and Society Review* 8 (Winter 1973):187–211.

McIntyre, Donald, and Lippman, David. "Prosecutors and Early Disposition of Felony Cases." *American Bar Association Journal* 56 (1970):1154–59.

Mileski, Maureen. "Courtroom Encounters: An Observation Study of a Lower Criminal Court." *Law and Society Review* 5 (May 1971): 473–538.

Miller, Justin. "The Compromise of Criminal Cases." *Southern California Law Review* 1 (1927):1–31.

Miranda v. Arizona, 384 U.S. 436, 86 S.Ct. 1602, 16 L.Ed. 2d 694 (1966).

Moley, Raymond. "The Vanishing Jury." *Southern California Law Review* 2 (1927):97–127.
National Advisory Commission on Criminal Justice Standards and Goals. *Courts*. Washington, D.C.: United States Government Printing Office, 1973.
National Center for Dispute Settlement. "The 4-A Program (Arbitration as an Alternative to the Private Criminal Warrant and Other Criminal Processes)." Paper on file at the National Center for Dispute Settlement, Washington, D.C. N.d.
National Institute of Law Enforcement and Criminal Justice. *Citizens Dispute Settlement*. Washington, D.C.: United States Government Printing Office, 1974.
Newman, Donald J. *Conviction: The Determination of Guilt or Innocence Without Trial*. Boston: Little, Brown and Co., 1966.
Niederhoffer, Arthur. *Behind the Shield: The Police in Urban Society*. Garden City, N.J.: Doubleday and Co., 1967.
North Carolina v. Alford, 400 U.S. 25, 91 S.Ct. 160, 26 L.Ed. 2d 162 (1970).
Oaks, Dallin H., and Lehman, Warren. *A Criminal Justice System and the Indigent*. Chicago: University of Chicago Press, 1968.
Packer, Herbert. *The Limits of the Criminal Sanction*. Stanford: Stanford University Press, 1968.
Packer, Herbert, and Ehrlich, Thomas. *New Directions in Legal Education: A Report Prepared for the Carnegie Commission on Higher Education*. New York: McGraw-Hill, 1972.
"Plea Bargaining: The Judicial Merry-Go-Round."*Duquesne Law Review* 10 (1971):253–69.
President's Commission on Law Enforcement and Administration of Justice. *The Challenge of Crime in a Free Society*. Washington, D.C.: United States Government Printing Office, 1967.
"Profile of a Guilty Plea: A Proposed Trial Court Procedure for Accepting Guilty Pleas." *Wayne Law Review* 17 (1971):1195–1239.
"Restructuring the Plea Bargain." *Yale Law Journal* 82 (1972):286–312.
Santobello v. New York, 404 U.S. 257, 92 S.Ct. 495, 30 L.Ed. 2d 427 (1971).
Savoy, Paul. "Toward a New Politics of Legal Education." *Yale Law Journal* 79 (1970):444–504.
Sayre, Wallace, and Kaufman, Herbert. *Governing New York City*. New York: W. W. Norton and Co., 1960.
Silberman, Matthew. "Determinants of Felony Trials and Negotiations." Ph.D. dissertation, University of Michigan, 1970.
Skolnick, Jerome. *Justice Without Trial*. New York: John Wiley and Sons, 1967.
———. "Social Control in the Adversary System."*Journal of Conflict Resolution* 11 (1967):52–70.

Sturz, Herbert. "Experiments in the Criminal Justice System." *Legal Aid Briefcase* (February 1967):1–5.
Szarwak v. Warden, 31 Connecticut Superior 30, 320 A. 2d 12 (1974).
"The Unconstitutionality of Plea Bargaining." *Harvard Law Review* 83 (1970):1387–1411.
Vines, Kenneth, and Jacob, Herbert. "Courts as Political and Governmental Agencies." In *Politics in the American States*, edited by Herbert Jacob and Kenneth Vines. Boston: Little, Brown and Co., 1965.
———. "State Courts." In *Politics in the American States*. 2d ed. Edited by Herbert Jacob and Kenneth Vines. Boston: Little, Brown and Co., 1971.
Wahlke, John; Eulau, Heinz; Buchanan, William; and Ferguson, Leroy. *The Legislative System*. New York: John Wiley and Sons, 1962.
Watson, Richard, and Downing, Rondal. *The Politics of the Bench and the Bar*. New York: John Wiley and Sons, 1969.
Wheeler, Stanton. "The Structure of Formally Organized Socialization Settings." In *Socialization after Childhood–Two Essays*, edited by Orville Brim, Jr. and Stanton Wheeler. New York: John Wiley and Sons, 1966.
White, Welsh S. "A Proposal for Reform of the Plea Bargaining Process." *University of Pennsylvania Law Review* 119 (1971):439–65.
Wilson, James Q. *Varieties of Police Behavior*. New York: Atheneum, 1970.
Wishingrad, Jay. "The Plea Bargain in Historical Perspective." *Buffalo Law Review* 23 (1974):499–552.
Wood, Arthur L. *Criminal Lawyer*. New Haven, Conn.: College and University Press, 1967.

Index

Index

Index